EATINGENGLAND

EATINGENGLAND

WHY WE EAT WHAT WE EAT
WITH MORE THAN 500 SPECIAL PLACES TO SHOP AND EAT

PHOTOGRAPHS BY JILL MEAD

HATTIE ELLIS

MITCHELL BEAZLEY

To Gordon, with love

Acknowledgements

All the people mentioned in this book, both in the chapters and the guide section, have generously given me their time and experience. Thank-you – and also to those I talked to, but unfortunately could not mention.

For the production of Eating England, the commissioning editor Rebecca Spry and the photographer Jill Mead are the biggest 'without whoms...' not just for getting the show on the road but for making the whole process fun. I'd also like to thank Faith Mowbray for a broad edit, Susan Low for a close one and Jamie Grafton for the fiddly bits; Miranda Harvey and Phil Ormerod for the design; and Paul Adams @ The Dark Room for printing the photographs so beautifully. The hot cross buns on the cover were made by Paul Merry at Long Crichel Bakery.

This book has come about after eight years of research and travelling, and partly talking to people about food for newspapers and tv programmes. For getting me around the country, I would particularly like to thank Hugh Fearnley-Whittingstall, Andrew Palmer and all at Keo; Nick Powell at Ricochet Films; Tim Hincks and Peter Bazalgette at Bazal Productions; David Presswell; Cassie Farrell; Tim Rice, Guy Walters and Gill Morgan at The Times; Judith Parsons; and especially Jeremy Atiyah for commissioning a series on Eating England in the Independent on Sunday travel section.

Emily Hare, the late Peter Carter, Alice Thomson, my parents and, most of all, Gordon Smith provided inspiration and encouragement in various invaluable ways.

Hattie Ellis

Commissioning Editor:
Rebecca Spry

Executive Art Editor:
Phil Ormerod

Design:
Miranda Harvey

Photography:
Jill Mead

Managing Editor:
Jamie Grafton

Production:
Julie Young

Index:
Laura Hicks

Printed and bound by
Toppan Printing
Company in China

Eating England
by Hattie Ellis

First published in Great Britain in 2001 by Mitchell Beazley, an imprint of
Octopus Publishing Group Limited,
2–4 Heron Quays, London E14 4JP.
Copyright © Octopus Publishing Group Limited 2001
Text © Hattie Ellis 2001

ISBN 1 84000 351 0

contents

introduction

ONE MORNING, IN THE SLEEP-WALK ROUTINE of getting breakfast
together, I half-heard the radio muttering about some survey on
cultural identity. High on the list of 'what it means to be English'
came, of all things, Marmite. It just so happened that my knife
was hovering, butter and crumbs attached, between Marmite or
marmalade for my toast that day. To the manna born, I plunged into
the black stuff to take exactly the right amount, sat down with a
plateful and chewed over the thought that part of me was bound
up with this strange, salty paste. It came from, well, who knew what?
The taste hovers between the deeply savoury and the truly disgusting,
yet its insistent flavour had crept into my life and, apparently, my
country. Patriotism, they say, is what you ate as a child.

My mind moved on to marmalade. Each year, in the dark days
of January, cooks all over the country laboriously cut up peel and
fill their kitchens with sweet boilings of fruity steam. The main
ingredient? A bitter fruit that is grown in Spain for export for this
odd jam. And then toast, or 'hot buttered toast', one of the most
alluring and evocative phrases in the English language and "so
peculiarly English a delicacy" as the food writer Elizabeth David
wrote . I'm more than glad that we eat it – but why? I drank my
tea: a national brew which, in this case, came from India.

Breakfast is the most habitual of meals, the one that most disturbs
us by its absence when abroad. It is one step from the pillow, when

our instincts are still only half-roused from the unconscious, a meal so much part of our collective tastes that caffs serve breakfast fry-ups all day. Even if we hardly ever eat breakfast these days – in the morning, at least – it still forms part of our gut instincts of what it is to be English.

The survey featured on the *Today* programme was part of much general discussion about Englishness that arose as Scotland and Wales got their own governments and Northern Ireland went through wary ventures into peace. Britain was shifting about, wondering whether to edge closer to Continental Euro-land and debating the issues of global markets. "The world is getting smaller," we said often.

Amongst much abstracted debate about nationality and identity, about who we were, my instinct was to latch on to the concrete, to the tangible talismans of culture that gave me a sense of a grounded continuity. Like the people in the survey who voted for Marmite, I turned to the earthy particulars of food.

Of course we know all about English food. It's fish and chips, crumpets, jam sponges and Christmas pudding. It's bacon sarnies and roast potatoes, pork pies and piccalilli. Mum's fruit cake – or Mr Kipling's. Strawberries and asparagus. Beef and beer. But the more I thought, the less I knew. Food surrounds us, inside and out. It is our very means of life, our energy, our personal petrol. In every culture, food has always been one of the most necessary of all needs. No surprise, then, that food connects history, culture and physical surroundings; no surprise that it can tell us about ourselves. The surprise, given the intimate connections between what we eat and who we are, is that I knew so *little* about it.

I became curiouser and curiouser about national tastes. Why do we eat roast beef and Yorkshire pudding? What dark arts produced Marmite? How did we get to the point where the dismal summation of English cooking was a plateful of meat and two veg? How did we gain a reputation as gastronomic illiterates? Under close scrutiny, some of our food habits started to look a bit... *odd*. Instinctual, enjoyable, but not easy to explain. Nobody else does toast the way we do, or eats and drinks with such gusto in pubs. We are world leaders in crisp flavourings and we lag behind other European countries in organic produce. Why? And what on earth is marmalade all about?

To understand English food I started to examine my own cupboards and, bit by bit, to travel around England, talking to people and seeing for myself the lie of the land. The countryside, filtered through my hungry eyes, turned into a vast, outdoor larder. I took up the dangerous sport of identifying sheep breeds while negotiating my car through country lanes; I looked deeper into the detail of a view whilst pausing on the top of a hill during a walk. How do landscapes – round downs, patchwork fields – relate to particular foods? And how do the nuts and bolts of farming affect the animals and plants that are part of what I love about England? Around 80 per cent of the countryside is dedicated to food production. Whenever I looked out of a car or train window at munching cows or black, Fenland soil, I saw places developed to fill bellies. Eating and drinking are two of the most important ways that we interact with our environment through what we choose from shop shelves and menus.

Yet food is so everyday as to be almost invisible. Like inquisitive Alice and her edible inquiries, I had to telescope out to see the wider perspective and shrink to the size of a pea to see small details at close quarters. I rummaged through books and travelled around talking to food producers and historians, cooks and farmers, eaters and shopkeepers, walking up hill and downtown to follow good food back to its roots. At every opportunity, I ate. Surprises blossomed with the unassuming glamour and aplomb of flowers. Eating England was not always a picnic, but sometimes it was a feast.

I pursued pleasure and taste, but my journey to better understand English food began, as for so many people, with bovine spongiform encephalopathy (BSE). The sight of a cow staggering into a drunken slither, intercut with a little girl being fed a hamburger by her father, the agriculture minister, was a short, iconic, televisual sequence that connected food and farm, unhappily, again and again.

Post-Mad Cow, society got a wake-up call. Food comes from somewhere, and we were best off considering what we put into our mouths and take into our bodies. The leap was to make the connection between farm and food, or from 'gate to plate', as it came to be known. From here on, for each news story about food safety – the incipient uncertainties of genetic modification, foot and mouth disease, animal transportation, live exports, outbreaks of food poisoning – anyone alert to the past wanted to know more about the details of food production, wanted to follow the stages several steps back from the plate.

If BSE at least partly came from herbivorous cows being fed on infected animals, then we had to think about not just what we ate, but what they ate, too. And BSE seemed to become part of a more general questioning of authority that grew with a more general unease about the environment. The English patient-queuing, mustn't-grumble mentality was waking up.

Post-Mad Cow, books were bought on green living and organic foods; organic vegetable boxes were ordered. A major shake-up in the farming industry led to more consumers buying directly from food producers and to the rise of farmers' markets. We had lost touch with our food producers; now, both sides wanted to talk. Concerns about intensive systems of meat production and other issues that had simmered for years among food campaigners came to a spluttering boil in the mainstream media, not least after the outbreak of foot and mouth disease in 2001.

One of the problems of the consumer age is that, as income and leisure time go up, we know less and less about the reality of the objects we consume: where they come from – literally and historically – who produced them, what they mean to the environment. We live in a virtual world experienced through TV and computer screens, yet we ignore what is in our hands.

Food and drink – the ultimate consumer goods – are so ordinary, so everyday, that to think about them is a self-conscious obstacle to convenience and pleasure; or so it seems. The risk of understanding so little about the food we eat is that it leaves a vacuum that is easily filled with confusion and anxiety, as BSE proved. Or, more often, dullness: it leads to boring, lifeless food designed to maximize profit for the seller, rather than pleasure and nourishment for the consumer. Perhaps we were being cheated, I thought. Convenience had become a sort of god for the cash-rich, time-poor; it was just so easy not to bother even to peel a potato. Perhaps we were cheating ourselves. I began to realise that some of the foods I had enjoyed as a child were quietly disappearing.

But where does all this lead? To nostalgia, fear and suspicion? To feeding our children one kind of food and ourselves another? Or could thinking about English food lead, gradually, empirically, eventually, to a deeper understanding of what we eat, to richer pleasures and an unfussed care that comes from the assumption that good food matters?

Early on in the writing of *Eating England*, I sat with Denis Watkins, the owner of a successful Yorkshire gastropub called the Angel at Hetton. He looked around his room of customers, full and happy by the fire after roast beef and Yorkshire pudding, and said, "There's going to be a mass reaction to mass production." I wish, beyond anything, that this were true. Much goes against it. But there are signs that we are at a crossroads.

Alongside fears about the environment (which are likely to grow), we are starting to resent the encroachment of anonymity, the blandness of global brands and the homogenization of the high street that have crept into daily life. Food and drink, put at the centre of the plate rather than treated as a tedious adjunct to the day, offer a chance to resist this seemingly unstoppable process. Every high street may appear the same, but go beyond the blue of the Foster's lager signs and the blocks of mass-produced goods on the supermarket shelves and, just around the corner, if you want to find it, an alternative still exists: the independents. To survive, these individuals — be they shopkeepers, food producers or restaurant chefs — must offer something extra. And so there emerges a diverse, collective 'brand' whose survival is crucial to anyone interested in choice and good food. They may provide a weekend indulgence, a holiday treat or everyday nourishment, but if we know that they are there, and relish the difference, they will continue to grow and strengthen.

This book is about the people, places and pies that inspired me to gain a richer understanding of food in England. I spent time in Norfolk, Sussex, London, Northumbria, Cornwall, Devon, Lancashire, Dorset, Suffolk, Wiltshire, the Lake District and Yorkshire – and all the other places detailed in the directory at the back of the book (page 222). It is not comprehensive, but the sorts of issues, ideas and individuals I unearthed can be found, in a rich variety of forms, all over the country.

Standardization and mass-production bring dullness. I write for the opposite. I write for the sweet, awkward carrot that won't go straight and the handmade biscuit with its glacé cherry off-centre and stray drips of jam. For the crafted cheese that took an artisan's endeavour and the wine that carries a flirty breeze of its landscape. For the lacquered kipper from the local smokehouse and for the chefs who dig deep into their part of the world to unearth delicious ingredients from a dozen different producers and let their flavours speak out. For food and drink with provenance and personality, that will not sit bored on a shelf, wrapped in plastic, to be cooked without care and swallowed without interest. Food you know has been in your mouth, not merely passing through, giving no reward. Pleasure.

*Herdwick sheep from Yew
Tree Farm, Borrowdale, in
the Lake District*

1 history and tradition

ROOTS ARE DIFFICULT.
HALF THE TIME, YOU
PULL AGAINST THEM
AND THEY MAKE YOU
FEEL STUCK; AT OTHER
TIMES, THEY ARE THE
SOURCE OF GREAT
NOURISHMENT. DURING
A WEEKEND SPENT IN
FRONT OF A BLAZING
FIRE, I DISCOVERED
WHY THE ENGLISH
BECAME SO FAMOUS
FOR ROAST MEATS.

ROOTS ARE DIFFICULT. Half the time, you pull against them and they make you feel stuck; at other times, they are the source of great nourishment. During a weekend spent in front of a blazing fire, I discovered why the English became so renowned for roast meats, and began to understand why it was worth following a dish back to its roots.

It was a course run by Ivan Day, a food historian who believes in conducting practical experiments with historical recipes. For example, there is an often-repeated story about syllabubs, that they acquired their frothy consistency from milking a cow directly into a bowl of booze. Ivan tried it. The result was an unappetising concoction (as he put it, like baby sick garnished with cow hairs and "the odd speck of bovine dandruff"). During our weekend course on roasting, we rootled through 17th-century cookbooks and played with spits and jacks that Ivan had pieced together from junkyards and antique dealers, studying woodcut illustrations of billowing fires to see how they worked. We fussed over the efforts it took to blanket-stitch the stuffed belly of a suckling pig and ran to lance the spit into the animal with great drama. Luckily there was a surgeon in the group. Sitting red-faced next to the fire, taking turns to keep the meat rotating, it was easy to see why Hell was portrayed as a kitchen.

At the table, it was Heaven. During that night's dinner, the suckling pig fell into my mouth in soft layers, with rich, melting fat. This was the real roast meat of England, cooked in front of the fierce, dry heat of an open fire. The water had steamed off the flesh, concentrating the flavours and the skin crisped up as it was basted with the juicy fat that dripped down into the pan below. Roasting was a prodigal, luxurious way of cooking, wasteful of fuel and heavy on labour. Roasts showed off the wealth of the flesh raised in the country and gave meat pride of place on the plate. Even though we no longer cook in front of a fire and the Sunday joint is, strictly speaking, baked in a closed oven, the flames, the turning spit, the unforgettable flavours and the succulence of that weekend fixed in my mind the soul of the dish. From then on, whenever I ate roast meat I felt a greater respect for it.

Ivan's courses are extraordinary. On another weekend, we made 17th- and 18th-century confectionery, delighting in the wit of quince paste love-knots and the delicacy of bergamot wafers cooked in a cooling bread oven. Perhaps the past really is "a place where they do things differently": Ivan's dishes seemed like the cooking of another country. And yet it was exciting to realise that such good food had been eaten here for so long, to taste a past that was worth discovering. The Parmesan ice-cream we made sounded like a nouvelle cuisine fancy; in fact, it came from an 18th-century recipe. Parmesan is not new to England: when the Great Fire of London threatened in 1666, Samuel Pepys took the trouble to bury his hunk before he fled. In this ice, the cheese came through with the ripe richness of a full-flavoured cream. The dish deserved to survive.

As I sat in front of the fire, half-mesmerised by the flames and the rhythmic turns of the spit, I thought about puddings of the past. Until the second half of the 20th century, meat was more of a luxury; puddings were filling and made the most of the heat from the fire. Some, such as rice pudding, would be baked slowly in the side oven of the fireplace, or next to the bread oven. Within living memory, Yorkshire pudding was cooked in a tray underneath the roasting meat, where the dripping fat and juices added to its flavour, and was served at the start of the meal to fill you up and make the meat go further. It is still served this way in Yorkshire, with gravy, though from tradition rather than necessity. The origins of many puddings lie in the same basic ingredients put together in different ways: flour, eggs, fruit, milk. Batter puddings like pancakes were popular in spring when the chickens started laying more eggs again. Variations were made by adding currants or fresh fruit, such as apple or rhubarb. The simplest steamed suet puddings were wrapped in a cloth and boiled for hours, then cut into slices and spread with jam or treacle. Spotted Dick was made with the addition of currants, but there were other more luxurious versions, eaten by the better-off. Sussex Pond pudding was made in a pudding basin with a whole lemon, butter and sugar in the centre of the suet so that when the pudding was cut open, the inside was flooded with a sweet, lemony, butter sauce. Sponge puddings were more luxurious because they contained butter and sugar, and jam or syrup poured into the bottom of the basin. Other puddings used up bread, such as bread-and-butter pudding, queen of puddings and summer pudding. (Toast also performed this function).

Puddings originated as savoury dishes cooked in part of an animal's intestines or the bladder. These boil-in-a-bag devices were put in a pot above the fire. We know this sort of dish today in the form of haggis, Burns' "great chieftain o' the pudding race", or black pudding. Sweet puddings proliferated after we began to use a piece of cloth, or pudding cloth, from the early 17th century onwards. Our national sweet tooth developed as sugar went, with imports from the West Indies, the invention of beet sugar, other technological advances and the relaxing of duties, from being a luxury to the cheap and cheering form of calories it still is today. To become a national taste food must be widely known. If puddings had been just a luxury for the rich, they would never have become so embedded in English culture.

I had eaten almost all these puddings as a child, whether for school dinners or as home treats. I thought of my grandmother and how we looked forward to her famous 'steamies', which came to the table in a waft of anticipation and a crown of golden syrup. Such puddings remain as comfort foods partly due to their sugar and stodge, but also because they come on a cushion of familiarity which is generations deep.

I wanted to find places that had held on to the thread of the past, that would enable me to trace connections with the eating habits of today. On a May morning, I walked to the top of Nidderdale, in North Yorkshire, and looked down at the village of Middlesmoor. From this distance, it seemed to have sprung out of the landscape. The cushions of protective trees and the houses, close against the wind, were like some complicated slow growth on the grand mass of the dale. At one edge was the church, a stubbly outcrop of gravestones trailing away from it.

That morning, I went to the church, St Barnabas', to a service for the Blessing of the Lambs. The children of the dale brought their lambs into the church and, at the end of the service, we went outside and stood at the end of the churchyard while Father Peter blessed the harvest of the land spread below as the sound of the sheep drifted up to us.

Afterwards, Dinah, one of the vergers, and two local farmers, Alan and Robert, sat with me on a bench in the village and talked of the past. It used to take a month to get sheep down from the hills and the weather was sometimes so cold the sheeps' horns were frozen to their backs and the ice had to be smashed so the animals could bend

their necks to eat. Robert thought his quad bike saved him two days'
work a week, but he could not always find a lamb that had got its leg
caught in a rabbit hole, as the engine drowned out its bleats. There
were far fewer farms these days; Robert was the only farmer left in
his local brass band. At one point, the conversation turned to the pork
scratchings, the crispy remnants of the rendered pig fat that were
a perk of home pig killings. As so often in conversations about food
of the past, or of childhood, their voices filled with a deep pleasure.
And then they had a good scoff at pub pork scratchings.

Dinah took me to meet her Aunt Lucy, an 88-year-old with the
sort of beautiful old-lady skin that is smooth with age. Aunt Lucy
described the food of her youth, when everything was homemade
and often home-grown, too. They baked on Thursdays, making the
best use of the peat which heated up the fireside oven. She
remembered how her mother was done in at the end of the day after
all the kneading and bending and carrying. There might be bread, jam
tarts, mince pies, currant buns and a fruit cake. Dinah mentioned an
iced sandwich-biscuit called daddy-kiss-mummy-with-jam-in-the-
middle. Aunt Lucy talked of the bread rising in front of the fire in
bowls and her father distracting her mother with a different task,
so when she came back the dough would be hanging over the
edge, over-risen. On baking day, her mother might send them off to
school without bread because they had run out, and then meet them
halfway across the moor after lessons with bread, butter and jam, all
homemade. Churning the butter was hard work, and a slow job in
hot weather. I noticed a packet of spreadable Lurpack on Aunt Lucy's
kitchen table.

For Aunt Lucy, the past was full of hard work and frugality; they
ate a lot of rabbit pie, and chicken was a rare feast, for Christmas Day.

But I also got a sense of the freshness and flavours that came from producing their own food and eating food in season. Everyone had a vegetable garden for potatoes, carrots and cabbages, and everyone knew that the best veg were dug from the garden to go straight into the kitchen. Both Lucy and Dinah collected fruit from the hedgerows, including wild damsons and blackberries. Every year Dinah's mother made elderflower 'champagne'. They grew gooseberries and blackcurrants, and blackcurrant jam was kept for winter to be added to hot water and sugar for colds. (For a sore throat, they wrapped a man's heavy, sweaty sock around the neck).

Later, I spoke to the owner of a pick-your-own fruit farm who said that only the older people bothered with blackcurrants and gooseberries. I thought of the gooseberry pies of childhood with their sugary crusts and the verdant, enticing smell of the leaves when you picked blackcurrants, and how these tastes and smells, part of our idiom, could so easily dwindle in a generation or two.

The North provided other places, often in beautiful stretches of countryside, where traditions had taken root and survived. At Ampleforth Abbey, a Benedictine monastery across the Vale of York from Middlesmoor, they started growing apples in 1900 for the simple reason that a monk was told by his doctor to take more exercise to relieve his asthma. The Benedictine Rule encourages monks to do several hours of outdoor work a day. Some of the food instructions in the Rule continue at Ampleforth today. They still take turns to serve at the table and, following a more general Christian tradition from the Middle Ages, eat a meatless meal once a week.

On the day I visited, the orchard looked a little forlorn because so many apples had fallen in recent rainstorms. The remaining fruit hung on the stark branches like Christmas decorations brightening the November gloom. I could imagine the magnificence of the view, down the Vale of Pickering towards Scarborough, and how it would look in the last week of May and beginning of June with all the different shades of blossom. During the season, from September to Christmas, the monks sell from a shed by the orchard. They have begun to link up with restaurants, starting with The Star at Harome, an exceptional dining pub nearby which had Ampleforth apples on its menu.

Bella de Boskoop, Ingrid Marie, Beauty of Bath, Keswick Codling: the Ampleforth apples had racehorse names and flavours you could roll around your mouth like wine. The monks store the fruit in sheds that smell like old cellars, so that apples hard as stones mature throughout autumn and winter. Each variety has its annual peak; they were bred in the first place to ensure that supplies continued throughout the season. Reading *The Anatomy of Dessert* (1929), the classic book by the great fruit connoisseur Edward Bunyard, you get a sense of the progression of time and fruits and varieties that echo the anticipation, fulfilment and change of the English year. This seasonality is at the heart of traditional English food. The fresh, green tastes of early summer, like watercress, elderflowers and asparagus, through to the game, roots and apples of autumn and winter follow their course alongside the farming and Christian calendars. That natural rhythm may get obscured by non-stop supermarket supplies and modern life, but it continues beneath like a deep, tidal tug. Tapping into these rhythms, catching produce at the right time in the right place, was to be a rich part of eating England.

As well as the eating apples, Ampleforth has around 15 varieties of cookers. Father Anthony, one of the two monks who run the orchard, picked me a Howgate Wonder, four times the size of a standard apple and a beautiful object, which I had to hold in two hands. Tart cooking apples are an English speciality and their propensity to collapse to a soft fluffiness gave rise to puddings such as apple snow. The way the English developed a large number of apple varieties over the centuries is covered entertainingly and comprehensively in *The Book of Apples,* by Joan Morgan and Alison Richards. There was, for example, an intriguing burst of horticultural creativity after the Civil War, when Oliver Cromwell's 'Agent for the Advancement of Universal Learning', Samuel Hartlib, set about to promote orchards and market gardens. At the same time, there were royalists who spent the 11 years of Puritan rule in their estates, using their spare energy to play with their land and create collections of fruit trees.

Ampleforth's orchard has continued because, without labour, land or livestock costs, it is inexpensive to run. Behind it I sensed the tradition of stewardship of the land, that the skills they were using were important at several levels. Monks like to do things that enable them to stay in one place, explained Father Anthony, and agriculture in various forms allows them to stay rooted. Some of the dry-stone walls which etch the contours of the Dales are medieval, dating from time the land was divided into great grazing areas for sheep owned by the monasteries. The monks brought skills of brewing and cheesemaking to the area, and tithes were paid in cheese, a transportable form of produce, embedding a tradition of storing milk which continued after the dissolution of the monasteries. Ever since the Reformation, monasticism in England has been more apostolic, concerned with teaching and spreading the gospel, compared to the more settled habits of the Continent, where you get such strands of monastic food and drink as the Trappist beers of Belgium.

Of the ruined monasteries in Yorkshire, Bolton is fine and formal, Fountains is eerie, majestic and more complete than the others, and Jervaulx the most tumbledown and intriguing as you walk through the walls like a ghost, imagining the life in its rooms. Nearest to Ampleforth is Rievaulx, its setting both magnificent and intimate, tucked as it is into a valley.

Wandering around here, I could spot the former hearths by their brickwork, and thought of how fires and kitchens would have provided heating and crucial cheer, as well as food, during a starker, less cushioned time. Food habits followed nature then. Lenten fasting came at a time when there was not much to eat anyway, before the lengthening days brought the first foods of late spring and early summer. Some of our older food traditions have come down to us through the continuities of Christian culture, even in a secular age. Hot cross buns, for example, continue to be eaten because of their connection to Good Friday.

The origins of Christmas pudding lie in a medieval thick, spiced meat soup, or pottage, which in Tudor times gained dried plums (prunes). This even thicker mix evolved and was later boiled in a pudding cloth to be eaten at festive occasions, becoming associated with Christmas in the 19th century. A curious food to eat, really, but we accept what has come to us down the centuries.

After melancholic thoughts over monastic ruins – an English habit almost as long-standing as the crumbling walls – I went to the pub.

Many pubs. Country pubs on blasted heaths with just a couple of tables, where I sat with the landlady talking about local farming; pubs that brewed a fug of city stories, beery laughter and sudden testiness; pubs where I tuned into voices and discerned a demeanour that could not be anywhere else but, say, Leeds; a pub where I wanted to examine some gem of Victorian etched glass and faced five drug dealers on mobile phones at the door. The proudly plain Butt and Oyster on the River Orwell near Ipswich, where men in overalls timed their pints with the tides. Pubs that gathered in the freshness of the land around – plump mussels, fellside lamb – and pubs selling crazy-paving salads of 20 ill-matched components, with cold baked beans next to watery strawberries. A pub on the Isle of Purbeck in Dorset, the Square and Compass, which had great beer, basic food and a museum of dinosaur bones in a side room. (The landlord, Charlie Newman, closes up after a stormy night so he can hunt for fossils that have been washed down from the cliffs.) A pub on the Yorkshire Moors, the Sun Inn, with a cricket pitch on the sloping field outside and the original beer house across the farmyard, little changed from when it was last used in 1910.

Pubs are fascinating because they gather in and continue so many strands of a place, past and present. They are a deep English idiom in a country where so often you have to search quite hard to find rooted food and drink. With the best pubs, you can go round any corner and sit, booze and gossip in the same old way in the same old place where people have done so for perhaps hundreds of years. And yet they are completely normal, workaday places which you enter without a thought or a ticket to visit a 'heritage' site. Public houses, open to all – though, speaking as a woman, it must be said they have become more accessible in my lifetime. The fact that I love

Cheers, Sam Smith!
A drinker in The Princess
Louise in Holborn, London,
which has an interior dating
back to 1891.

English bitter is no small part of my good times in pubs, as well as the fact that they pitch you, as a stranger, into the heart of a place as well as into its past. There are so many of them, too. So many, in fact, that they are easy to take for granted; it's easy to ignore the fact that we are a beer-drinking nation.

After reading the historian Mark Girouard's book on Victorian pubs, I began to sit on the top deck of buses spotting the architecture of more outré former pubs, tarted up in their time, like bricked and scrolled Bet Lynches, to pull in the customers. A burst of refits in the 1880s and 1890s, stimulated by property speculation and competition, spread etched windows that glittered like magical lanterns and decoratively moulded, wipe-down wall coverings and elaborate tiles. Some of the detail is magnificent. I sometimes meet friends in the Princess Louise near Holborn in London, with its colourful tiling of oranges and grapes. "It's like being in a Spanish bar," said one companion, looking around in awe. But skips have claimed the interiors of many a gem that is then refitted, ironically, with ersatz Victoriana or a hotchpotch taken from some theme park of the invented past. There are companies that make a tidy profit out of fake olde worlde lights and memorabilia kits, such as golf club heads in framed cabinets, clay pipes and new corn dollies. The charm of many real pubs comes from all the objects and stories that get washed up over time and stay put: the higgledy-piggledy, incidental history that gives you a genuine sense of walking through a neighbourhood, past and present. Most important of all, genuine pubs have a mix of people, which is not the case in places designed on paper by business people after 'target markets'.

Take, for example, the Red Lion at Snargate, one of those Romney Marsh villages that consists of a couple of houses, a pub and a church. On a weekday lunchtime, the Red Lion had that dead look that pubs often have from the outside. Inside was a fire surrounded by old tiles and the tick-tock of a clock with a blurred face. Behind the bar stood a woman with mid-length white hair. This was Doris Jemison, the landlady who has been here for 50 years, ever since she arrived as a land-girl in the Second World War and married Little Alf, the son of the publican, Big Alf. There were war-time posters hung near the piano in the back room telling you what to do "If the INVASION comes": to think of your country before yourself and disable cars to stall the advance of the enemy.

In another room were photos of Doris' land-girl reunions, and on a shelf, packets people had brought in from all over the world with the word "Doris" on them: biscuits from Finland, tuna from France, rice from Germany. On one wall was the millennium blanket made of knitted squares, each embroidered with a name and personal emblem, like homespun heraldry. Doris had knitting needles made out of cocktail sticks with little red tops and some mini-knitting; Amanda her granddaughter had a motorbike. The plumber had a dripping tap and another regular had peanuts from a habit of insisting that the pub served some food. You can take a picnic into the garden of the Red Lion, with its corner of white honeysuckle, white jasmine, white lilac and white roses, and chickens pecking about.

One time the local authority wanted the Red Lion to remove the marble top of the bar. Little Alf refused. We should not be complacent about the survival of such pubs. You might think that the pub is an English institution; the pubs themselves might even feel as though they are in the ownership of the regulars. But, like so many places in England, they are increasingly units in bigger businesses, susceptible to calculations made on paper. The biggest owner of pubs in England is, at present, a Japanese investment bank, Nomura. The Campaign for Real Ale (Camra), which has done so much to keep good beer going in this country, has a inventory of pub interiors of outstanding heritage interest. Anyone with a curious eye should get Camra's list or spot them in the *Good Beer Guide*, where they are marked with a white star, and seize the excuse to go for a pint. If we appreciate pubs like these, they have a better chance of survival.

Even in the gems that remain, you have to play detective to trace back the past. I sat with Geoff Brandwood, who helped compile the Camra list, in another Red Lion, this one in St James's in London, a busy urban pub with exceptional glass. He showed me how to find the clues to the past in discontinuities in the pub's interior. You could see that it had been shifted about over the years, because the doors didn't quite make sense with the interior, and the structure above the bar did not have the warm wear of other wooden parts of the pub. In fact, it had been added as new drinks required different glasses and somewhere to put them.

There is no point being too precious about pub interiors; they evolve over time. Just so long as they evolve carefully rather than suffer a Disney-fied 'heritage' refit at vast expense. "Conservation costs less" is one of the dictums of the architectural historian Dr Steve Parisienne, who helps judge Camra's annual pub design awards. What he detests are the ignorant redesigns that obliterate special features and so often ignore the needs and desires of the locals. "The pub is surely about character. We like it to be different from the one down the road," he says. Re-fits can be short-sighted in other respects, too. As he points out, if non-smoking areas become obligatory, the old-style compartments would have been an ideal solution. But such compartments have usually been torn down.

I took a gulp of my beer and looked around the pub Steve and I were in. Nice pint, but the pub itself was fussily bland, with its new interior, fake drawers, incongruous candelabra, blackboards with permanent markings and no sense of the different spaces that were built into urban pubs with partitions – spaces that help different groups co-exist in one place. Later in my travels I spent an hour in a pub in Liverpool where there was an calm, esoteric conversation between academics in one bar, a scene lurching towards mayhem in another and me, in a third, writing my diary.

Why erase when you can evolve? Pubs have happily grown to suit their customers while keeping the layers of what has gone before. I would not have strolled so happily into pubs on my own even a decade ago, and certainly would not have eaten so well in them. The Angel in Hetton serves a great slab of rosy-centred roast beef by a big fire. The pub came about because it sat on a drovers' road down which Scottish cattle were taken to the markets in Grassington and Keighley; one of the nearest available foods would have been a bit of beef. When Denis Watkins, the chef-owner of the Angel, saw that the 1980s and 1990s were going to be years of themed restaurants, he thought that the best theme of all was the authentic English pub. "If we put good food in, it could work," he said. Dining pubs work because we feel comfortable in them; they are part of our idiom. (I write more on this in Chapter 9, Eating Out).

For traditions to remain alive they must bear change and avoid becoming the edible equivalent of morris dancing. 'Tradition' was a word I was to hear often on the day I became a judge of the

Mytholmroyd World Dock Pudding Competition in West Yorkshire. This vegetable and oat purée, known as Easterledge pudding in the Lake District, is made using the leaves of the common bistort plant and nettles, both gathered wild in springtime fields or odd spots such as railway embankments and churchyards. In the past, it provided a much-needed shot of greens after the winter; the habit has continued beyond necessity, like picking blackberries in the autumn. "It wouldn't be spring without dock pudding," one maker told me.

In the competition hall, I asked a spectator what to expect. "It looks like a green, wet cowpat," he replied.

The Hebden Bridge Junior Brass Band struck up with a bright vigour as I settled down with my fellow judges in a room behind the stage and asked about the judging criteria. Texture, taste and appearance were mentioned; but top of the pile came 'traditional'. Some years there had been a bit of jiggery-cheffery, with garlic and the like. "We don't like stuff like that in," I was told. "No spices." The dock puddings had been made at home and were cooked live on stage as part of a breakfast fry-up while we sat backstage in our judgely huddle. The first entry arrived on a round piece of toast, looking mercifully unlike a cowpat. "It's nouvelle, but it's not dock pudding," was the judgement. Between tastings, the conversation was full of food know-how, about how it was worth growing your own vegetables for the difference freshness made to taste and how a cold plate spoiled a hot dish. One judge was busy giving soundbites to the attending media. "If Viagra were green, they would have called it dock pudding," he said. Another dish arrived. There was a short, menacing silence. "I think this one's got a bit of garlic," someone said: the kiss of death. The breakfasts arrived on trays. On some, the dock pudding was slimy; others were drier, with the iron tang of the nettles more pronounced. Some trays came with linen and vases of pansies. A helper confided that she thought it would be nice to stuff a trout with dock pudding but that people wanted to keep the competition, which began 27 years ago, on traditional lines with the breakfast theme. The winner was a glamorous old lady with star quality who smiled around the room as beautifully as if she were playing the Palladium, gracefully refusing to divulge her secret ingredient. I wonder what it was? In any case, it was something good enough to count as 'traditional'.

Both the Blessing of the Lambs and the dock pudding competition, like modern dining pubs, were relatively new but grafted onto deep roots. I began to realise that there were fruitful ways of using the past. Traditional farming, organic growing and craft-made foods are often portrayed as old-fashioned, but a large number of the people I met could more accurately be described as progressive.

While writing this book, I met many people, not just from the older generations, who really understood techniques and ingredients and who were able to innovate without losing the thread of the past. These were the people producing enjoyable food. I think of Stuart Oetzmann of the Handmade Food Company, a chef who's returned to his native Norfolk after cooking in London. He is continuing a tradition by making pork pies and breads in Norwich, using pork from Gloucester Old Spot pigs in the pies because they have more flavour than more modern breeds; he sells his wares in delis and pubs in the area, and his pies and breads have the sort of look that you might find in the trendiest restaurant, should they care about food as much as décor. One of Stuart's pork pies is pictured at the front of this chapter.

Tastes run deep. We have all eaten dishes that were a hotchpotch of fashionable ingredients, stacked high on the plate, that ultimately failed to hang together and engage the appetite. One of the themes of my travels emerged: to unearth the roots of native foods and follow them through to their living green shoots.

2 cultures

SO WHAT WENT WRONG
WITH ENGLISH FOOD?
WHAT LED US TO 'MEAT
AND TWO VEG'; TO THE
SOUP AN AMERICAN
VISITOR IN THE 1930S
SAID "TASTED AS IF
IT HAD BEEN DRAINED
OUT OF THE UMBRELLA
STAND."; TO TODAY'S
ENDLESS SHELVES
OF READY-MEALS?

So what went wrong with English food? What led us to 'meat and two veg', to the soup an American visitor in the 1930s said "tasted as if it had been drained out of the umbrella stand", to today's endless shelves of ready-meals?

It is still very English to treat food as an awkward appendage rather than something at the heart of daily life. I went to a lunch given for some visiting French by an English farmer, renowned for his well-bred cattle. The beasts were beautiful, the beef utterly over-cooked. I looked at the French struggling to cut their tough meat with plastic forks. The meal was served with hospitality and generosity; the lack of care was clearly cultural rather than intentional. Here was a national legacy of skill in breeding and stockmanship that was squandered somewhere between the field and the plate. Perhaps it was to do with cooking for a crowd, and the beef on the farmer's own Sunday table would have been perfect.

Even though I ate very well as a child, when I went to live in France for six months, I was surprised to discover that people discussed food at the table. In England there might be a polite "how delicious" and perhaps a request for a recipe. In Paris, they tucked into the subject and dedicated a good five or ten minutes to the cut of meat, the butcher, other memories of the dish. Discussing food in England is no longer regarded as indecent – as something of an eating disorder – but an interest in food is still seen by many as a hobby rather than a delightful fact of life. Why should this be?

I looked for theories and found blame apportioned to various parts of our history. A cartoon flashed before my eyes of how English food had been kicked in the guts over the centuries – POW! BAM! KER-UNCH! – the Norman Conquest – EUGH! – when a French elite looked down on native foods; the Reformation – SLAP! – when

Protestant guilt began to win over Catholic tastes; the Cromwellian Protectorate – SHAME! – when Puritanical fervour deepened the blow. In the Victorian era, the emergence of an urban middle class with servants meant cooking suffered from an upstairs/downstairs stratification, with the kitchen very much downstairs – SNIFF! – and we took a significant step further down the road to sog and stodge. When the Second World War hit – BANG! – food became institutionalised; many traditions, such as the making of farmhouse cheeses, were damaged irrevocably and 14 years of rationing instilled meanness into our tastes. The aftermath of war brought austerity, and then post-austerity, with the showbiz hysteria – YUK! – of Fanny Cradock's piped mashed-potato swan garnishes.

But the major reason for our poor sense of food has been, broadly, industrialization. England industrialized faster and earlier than any other European country; the impact on our diet has been enormous. People left the countryside after the land enclosures and went to the burgeoning cities, where they were no longer able to produce their own food. At this point, we lost much of the 'peasant' base that usually underpins a strong food culture, rooted as it is in people who understand the products of the land. As Stephen Mennell points out in his fascinating comparison between French and English food cultures, *All Manners of Food*, it was the sheer speed of the change, as well as the extent, which made such a difference. In 1811, 35 per cent of Englishmen worked in agriculture; a century later it was just 12 per cent. (In France, 53 per cent still worked in farming in 1856 and 43 per cent in 1901.)

Industrialized food – mass-produced, designed to travel long distances and to fit into large-scale supply chains – developed until livestock came pre-packaged like packets of biscuits, as factory farming gathered momentum after the Second World War. We also have a tradition of taking up new technologies, from the gas and electric ovens that took over from hearthside cooking through to the toaster and microwave. There is a sense that England is a scientific culture which pays as much attention to nutrients as to taste, to mechanical innovations rather than to peasant knowledge.

What strikes me most, looking through books about what people ate in the 20th century, was how long so many of the industrialized, packaged brands we eat have been around. Digestives were launched by McVities in 1892; shredded wheat arrived from the United States in 1908. A chocolate-cream sandwich biscuit was launched by Peek Frean in 1910 and named Bourbon to give it royal kudos. In the thirties, the company started to make Twiglets and Cheeselets after an employee tried their Vitawheat biscuits with Marmite.

Marmite is a by-product of the brewing industry, using a method invented by a German scientist, Justus Liebig, in the second half of the 19th century. Liebig, who was working in Germany, was fascinated by the practical application of chemistry and was already well known for his preparation of a meat extract as a food for infants. The fermentation process of brewing produces four or five times the amount of yeast needed to make the next brew. Could this by-product be put to use? He worked out how to turn the left-over yeast into a dark, salty paste that was similar in appearance, smell and flavour to an extract of meat. The Marmite Food Company was set up in 1902 in the beer centre of Burton-on-Trent, and the paste's reputation was boosted by the discovery of vitamins, as it contains a healthy whack of Bs.

Go into any corner shop and the ascendancy of industrialized food is obvious. Between 1929 and 1933, in a famously creative burst of

Sweets such as these, in a Whitby sweet shop, are classic industrialized foods, ever-more popular as sugar became cheaper.

competition between chocolate makers, Rolos, Mars Bars, Aeros, Kit Kats, Maltesers (or 'energy balls' as they were first named), Milky Ways and Smarties were launched. As a young schoolboy, Roald Dahl took part in trials for Cadbury's in Birmingham, and later used the experience as part of the inspiration for *Charlie and the Chocolate Factory*. When you learn all this, it no longer feels like an anachronism to read that soldiers chewed gum (from American ration packs) in the trenches of the First World War.

No wonder packaged food has such a hold on us. The brands and the habit of buying them have been with us for generations. Some, like Maltesers and Twiglets, taste good. Others less so. Bird's custard, made by a Birmingham chemist whose wife was allergic to eggs, was sold in 14 flavours by the end of the 19th century. "Custard powder," wrote Jane Grigson, "...has been one of our minor national tragedies." We eat custard made from powder because it is there, it saves time and we do not value food enough to care that it does not taste as good as the real thing.

Inventions affect our national tastes. Ready-meals came about because of the sophistication of our supermarket culture: supermarkets had the supply chains that allowed food to be made and sold 'fresh' within a couple of days. We also had a public that would pay for ready-prepared food that was posher than the frozen TV dinners of the US.

Microwaves were developed using the radar technology used in the Second World War. At first, microwaves were useful for defrosting deep-frozen food: the first model to hit the mass market in 1976 was a Toshiba introduced with the tag "The Unfreezer". The use of microwaves developed alongside chilled ready-meals. I try ready-meals every so often and (with the exception of some of the Indian meals, which seem to be made with more care and with flavours that, like the curry kept overnight in the fridge, can improve on the shelf), the meanness of most of these packaged foods affronts every culinary instinct in my body. Industrialized food certainly accounts for part of the English taste for ersatz food: the pretend lasagne; the 'brown' bread which is coloured with caramel as a substitute for the removed wheat germ; the 'fruit drinks' that are mostly sugar and water with colouring to give a fruity look. Packaged food robs us of freshness and it robs food of identity: once you start to mass-produce, you cut corners and end up somewhere else.

A huge amount of money is invested in promoting this sort of food. Heinz baked beans were trialled in the north of England. They did not take off, so C H Hellen, the head of Heinz in Britain, reintroduced them 20 years later in the 1920s, declaring: "I am going to manufacture baked beans in England, and they're going to like it." He backed his threat with an advertising campaign. Industrialized food and advertising march in step together, the budgets in proportion to the scale of production, to promote foods far worse than baked beans, which have their uses. What do we support: other people's profits or our own tastes?

The food of an industrialized society has given us some gems, however. Whether we like it or not, industrialization has formed our tastes, and it has not all been bad news. Take fish and chips, a good-value dish that is still made by plenty of independent operators and which compares favourably with other take-aways such as pizzas and curries in terms of nutrition. Its roots lie in our industrialised society. Jewish traders in London used to fry fish because it tasted good and

Oakwood fisheries in
Roundhay Road, Leeds.
The shop has a
modernist frontage. They still
fry in beef dripping.

frying extended the life of fish on the turn. Meanwhile, a trade in fried potatoes grew in the industrial northern towns of the Pennines. Nobody is quite sure who first put fried fish with chips, but their spread throughout the country was very much a product of the mass market. Their growth in popularity centred on London and the northern cotton towns where wives and mothers continued to work, cooking space was small and budgets were tight. At the height of their popularity in the 1930s, there were at least 35,000 chip shops in the country. In some working class areas their density was as high as one per street. Even in the 1970s, Holbeck, in Leeds, had eight chippies in an area the size of a small village.

According to John Walton, an academic who has written a good history on the subject, *Fish & Chips and the British Working Class 1870-1940*, our taste for the dish is bound up with the industrialization of the fishing fleet. Fishing had been a small-scale, even cottage, industry until the advent of steam trawlers opened up fishing grounds further away, particularly in the Icelandic waters with their great catches of cod. It was the network of fish-and-chip shops, with their growing need for plenty of fish, which provided a market for these hauls. Confidence in the trade meant that deep-sea trawlers were built even in the Depression.

The effect of large-scale trade was, as ever, to iron out differences. In Edwardian times, Walton writes, there were local preferences for the particular fish that landed on the nearby stretch of shore. But in the 1920s and 1930s, as boats went out to new fishing grounds, cod became prominent and spread throughout the chip shops all over the country. Local tastes do exist. Yorkshire tends to eat haddock before cod, and Lancashire the other way round, and in Lancashire you see people eating gravy on their chips.

In the spring, I spent a couple of days on the southern edge of
England, on the Kent coast. At the time, news reports were full of
asylum seekers and the area bristled with the antagonisms of a border
country, but the Men of Kent have also, in the past, been alert to the
advantages of trade. Kent's hop gardens, with their garlanding bines,
became widespread under the influence of Dutch merchants, who
helped bring about the change from old English ale to hoppy beer.
Tracts outraged at this foreign trait were printed in the 15th and 16th
centuries and Henry VIII forbade his court brewer to use the new
ingredient. But brewers and drinkers took to hops because they acted
as preservatives and made the beer taste good. In time, foreign
influences become naturalised.

I was interested in getting a foreign perspective on English food.
Folkestone, a town that had sometimes been belligerent towards the
invading Channel Tunnel, felt like an interesting place to meet an
Anglophile Frenchman. Philippe Esclasse was working for the council
as a town centre manager. He first fell for England on a teenage
exchange holiday, mostly because of the fashion and music. When
he returned to live here in 1976 he described the food as "an absolute
disaster": there were limited shops and bland, over-cooked meals.
Sliced white bread and toasters were handy; the biscuits were
interesting (my teenage French exchange student went off to buy
presents of what she called "biscuits for cheese"); fish and chips, if
well prepared, could be "quite attractive". But overall: disaster. A visit
to Simpsons-in-the-Strand for steak and kidney pie, summer pudding
and trifle was something of a revelation: Philippe recognised English
puddings as a national treasure.

Two decades later, he thinks that standards have improved –
especially in London, with its dazzling ethnic mix – but he has two

major complaints: you have to be prepared to spend more than in France to get good food in restaurants, and high quality produce is not always easy to discover. Going around a food fair run by the food specialist Henrietta Green, Philippe noticed lots of foreigners who were equally amazed to find there was such a range of English food. When a chef is successful in England, he added, he moves on. In France, where chefs have a higher social standing, they are more likely to stay put as part of a community. I thought of what happens to good newcomers to the restaurant scene in England; almost immediately, people ask them whether they are going to expand, or start a chain.

Down the coast from Folkestone, I had dinner in La Terrasse, a French restaurant in Sandgate. My starter of scallops with slivered discs of truffle in the middle and a leek and truffle sauce epitomised good French restaurant cooking: refined food that avoided fuss, each part designed to enhance the flavour. The depth of French restaurant culture is apparent when you hear that the maître d' of La Terrasse, Joel Fricoteaux, trained for two years before he even started to work on the waiting side of restaurants, and before going on to take other specialised courses.

He has a file four inches thick of basic recipes, cuts of meat and other information to give him a solid understanding of the kitchen. Every day the students would smell little bottles of essences – tarmac, green pepper, lavender, violets, liquorice – to train their sense of smell to recognise flavour elements in wine. "Service is to do with the enjoyment of food and drink," Joel said – not an ethos always at the heart of English attitudes to waiting.

Modern British restaurant cooking has been so deeply influenced by French chefs that it might more accurately, in very broad terms, be called Anglo-French – though our food bears influences from many other countries as well. The spread of the French culinary culture owes much to the autocratic, semi-apprenticeship system of restaurants. The chef's brigade, by which the younger, or less-experienced learn the trade in the teamwork of a kitchen, under a head chef, is a system that passes on craft. In this way, chef 'family trees' spread out, the success of their shoots acting as living testimony to the quality of their rootstock. The ethos of the best French restaurant cooking, such as that of the renowned Le Gavroche set up by the Roux brothers in London's Mayfair district, is to pay attention to ingredients as well as technique. What interested me was how chefs were applying this principle to the produce of the English countryside.

Steven Doherty, one of the many alumni of Le Gavroche, was one of the first chefs to see the potential of cooking in a pub when he set up in the south of the Lake District. His culinary education was French but his setting utterly English: he runs a pub called the Punch Bowl Inn in Crosthwaite, Cumbria. In springtime, the valley is laced with the blossom of damson trees, fragile against the grey slabs of the stone buildings and walls. You can see Steven's attention to ingredients, and the elements of Modern British cooking, by the way he makes use of the fruit grown on these trees: in a compote to go with doughnuts filled with lemon crème pâtissière; to sauce duck; pickled to spice up cured meat such as the celebrated air-dried Cumbrian ham made by Woodall's in the western Lakes; in pear and damson crumble; in a purée to accompany panna cotta; in sorbets. French, Italian, English: Modern British.

He describes the flavour of Lyth Valley damsons, with their hint of almonds, as "profound".

The Roux brothers' philosophy is that ingredients are paramount; that you should buy the best and keep its character, and if you start with rubbish you will end up with rubbish. They have remarked that the English undervalue their own ingredients, such as the lamb, the lobsters and the abundant game that come from our woods, seas and moors: beautiful produce of beautiful landscapes. Steven sources many of his ingredients from the Lakes and Lancashire: a particular black pudding, Shorrocks' Lancashire cheese, bacon from Woodall's, as well as the air-dried ham.

As well as time spent at Le Gavroche, Steven worked with the French master Alain Chapel in his *auberge* near Lyons. This three-star establishment was the equivalent of a country inn, with stone-flagged floors and rough plaster on the walls, but with Baccarat crystal and fine linen on the tables. Families would come to eat there, and pay for the quality of food. Steven wanted to run a place where you could get a bowl of soup and a pint or seared tuna and a *premier cru* Chablis. English food works "up to a point", he thinks. He might roast lamb, but with garlic and rosemary. He likes crumble and pea and ham soup. Most of all he wants the best of all worlds: free-range Lancashire chicken with a dash of white truffle oil, Lancashire cheese and Cumbrian pancetta, or onions pickled in cider vinegar with brown sugar and bit of star anise, pickling spices and bay leaves. His setting is English and so are the tastes of many of the customers. He can sell grilled kidneys but not sweetbreads. A shoulder of fell-bred lamb may be cooked slowly with a *mirepoix* (note the French terms of fine cooking) of vegetables, stock, rosemary, thyme and seasoning, set in its juice until it is cold, sliced and served with a sauce of its juices that have been sieved, reduced and had red wine added. The Sunday luncher may then ask for mint sauce. This can be the downside of translating a French philosophy into an English setting: not everyone is speaking the same language. Because the Punch Bowl is a pub, and because of the area, Steven has to keep his prices down. He charges less than many a formulaic restaurant run as a profit exercise would charge, yet in his pub the prices buy the benefit of his training at Le Gavroche. The night I visited, a Friday, the pub was full. The food had a finesse that stood out in a rough-hewn setting and the room had pockets of the real pleasure and expansiveness that good food inspires: the people at the table to my left were laughing long and late and other customers stopped to thank Steven. He has acclaim, but not enough when you consider what he represents. I wonder if, in another country, Steven Doherty would be more celebrated?

Sadly, the number of damsons grown in the Lyth Valley has dwindled. I stood at the top of the valley with Peter Cartmell, who is trying to revive them, and he remembered a time when there was ten times the amount of blossom as there was that day: it just seems to have drifted away. Damsons are a touchy crop and difficult to pick. The growers were not getting enough money for them to bother, though there are possibilities of marketing them as a specialist food. The day after my meal at the Punch Bowl was Damson Day in Crosthwaite. Hundreds of people flocked to see the blossom and buy damson gin, damson chocolates, damson jam; there certainly seems to be a demand, if the farmers could work together to develop the market.

It is true: we do not, on the whole, seem to value and nurture our raw ingredients. Of all the odd aspects of English food, the most unfortunate is that an island race should, gastronomically, turn its back on the sea. No one on this long, thin island is ever more than 75 miles from the coast; we are surrounded by the cold waters that produce sweet, firm, plump fish. We land around 60 species and are envied by other European countries for the quality and variety of our catch. Yet most of our fish are exported and the mass market concentrates on a generic fish known as "white". As a nation, we dismiss what amounts to a cornucopia; we give it, in short, the fish finger. Perhaps this will change now that the fishing industry is clearly in some trouble due to low stocks. On the quayside of Padstow in Cornwall, where chef and restaurateur Rick Stein has done so much to sing the praises of British seafood, Spanish lorries drive up to take away the celebrated Cornish crabs. More than 80 per cent of the catch from Newlyn fish market will go abroad – partly because it includes species not eaten by the English mass market, such as monkfish and megrim.

But why don't we eat them? In his book on restaurants, *Modern Cooking*, Drew Smith remarks that the classic cuisine of Escoffier, which underpinned much English restaurant cooking until the 1970s, favoured Dover sole, turbot and salmon because their fillets could withstand the saucing and breadcrumbing and multiple manipulations of this style of food. It is partly the lighter approach of modern French cooking that has brought the likes of brill, John Dory and red mullet back on to restaurant menus; besides, they were, at that stage, cheaper than the over-subscribed 'classics'. But this is clearly a move at one end of the market, not in the mainstream. The other reason we export is that other countries will pay for quality, whereas the English culture favours cheap food. The English spend a smaller percentage of yearly income on food than any other

European country. Sometimes even the person who would pay dearly for an expensive dining table will object to paying £1 for a well-made pie to put on it when they can get a dull one for 60p.

The upshot of this is that people come back from holiday praising the delicious seafood without realising that it may well have come, like them, from England. We eat so many dishes from other cuisines, the impression arises that the seafood itself comes from elsewhere. Our native squid gets eaten as calamari; our shellfish becomes *fruits de mer*; mussels go into in *moules et frites*. English fish dishes amount to fish pie, fish and chips, fish fingers and fish cakes. All can be delicious, but do these generic names denote a certain lack of care?

We do not generally poeticize our food; we do not have very many equivalents of the French *vol au vents* ("flight on the breezes"), while in other parts of life, the English language is used with greater relish. The delicious names given to old-fashioned apple varieties says more about our horticulture than it does about our love of food. Two exceptions reveal an emphasis in our diet: some puddings are honoured with interesting titles – Poor Knights of Windsor, trifle and roly-poly – and products of the mass-produced have names dreamt up by marketeers. The Portuguese have delectable cakes called Angels' Breasts. We took to something else: Angel Delight.

Modern eaters, just like modern chefs, are influenced by foreign travel – or at least the modern eaters who go beyond egg-and-chips xenophobia. In the Suffolk village of Lidgate, I sat in a pub, The Star, owned by a Catalan. Wafts of garlic came across the bar, followed by the sizzle of sherry hitting the pan. Towards the end of lunch, I noticed a table being set out for the staff. They were going to get a dish of lamb with a blackcurrant sauce and a big salad. I asked Maria Teresa Axon, the owner, if they drank wine at lunch and she threw back her head in laughter. Of course there was a bottle on the table! We talked about the Spanish custom of taking a three-hour break in the middle of the day and then going back to the office at 4pm. It means they work until 8.30 or 9pm, when they are ready to go out and enjoy themselves. The English, meanwhile, take a sandwich at the computer keyboard and come home at 7pm to slump in front of the television. The Spanish example would be hard to translate to English life; it fits into so much else – the weather, what everyone else does, opening hours and so on. But the long midday break was a philosophy evidently shared, in part, by the full house of diners in The Star during that particular mid-week lunchtime.

Adopted influences, naturalised, have long been a part of the richness of our culture. We drink tea from China and India just as rhododendrons and Asiatic pheasants are part of the traditional English countryside. A sweet fruit paste called marmalade has been eaten in England since the 15th century. Named after the Portuguese word for quince, it was a solid block that was eaten as a sweetmeat, made from quince, oranges or other fruits which were cooked and concentrated. From the 18th century, the Scots were eating a thinner jelly containing little pieces of cut-up peel. The spread of popularity of marmalade came about as sugar became progressively cheaper and with it jams and other preserves. Marmalade, as any other preserved food, was easy to transport and followed the flag to become a talisman of native tastes.

The historic links between England and the West Indies are revealed in regional specialities such as the rum butter found in the Lake District, where the northwest harbours saw trade from the islands. The West Indies also partly established our taste for our favourite fruit, bananas. At the turn of the last century, the British government subsidised a company to bring in refrigerated cargoes of West Indian bananas to Britain. The story goes that the posher fruit sellers wanted to protect the more lucrative existing trade with the Canary Islands, so instead, the imports were sold to costermongers in London, Bristol and Liverpool, where they hit the streets with a price tag that the working man could afford. Within a year, bananas became a part of the diet of these cities. Bananas are still the best-selling fruit in Britain (and the politics of post-colonial bananas rumbled on into the 21st century).

The British Empire had, of course, a huge influence on our taste in food, nowhere more so than with Indian curries. Queen Victoria had a curry made daily in case of Indian visitors. The Anglo-Indian influence has filtered into our national taste buds in vibrant flavours such as Worcestershire sauce, first made in 1835 by the Worcester pharmacy Lea & Perrins to a recipe brought back from India. The mixture of plainness and piquancy, a balance of contrasts, such as sweet and sour, is a very English taste: think of lamb and mint sauce (thought to date back to the Crusades) or beef and horseradish. Piccalilli, served with cold meats, gets its bright-yellow colour from turmeric and mustard seed, two spices traded by the East India Company.

One of England's first Indian restaurants, London's Veeraswamy, was opened in the 1920s by an ex-Indian Army officer who had brought his cook back with him. The décor – flock wallpaper and brass – was intended to inspire nostalgia for the Victorian heyday of the British Raj, and it is a style that lingered. Indian restaurant cooks adapted the food to suit novice English palates. The influence of Indian cooking, one of the most fascinating and complex cuisines in the world, continues to develop as various communities and cultures make their culinary marks. Over the last decade, we have seen the spread of a greater range of regional Indian cuisines and top-class Indian restaurants.

I like Hansa's in Leeds, a restaurant set up by a woman serving the vegetarian food of Gujarat, in the west of India. The owner, Hansa Dabhi, a slight, casually elegant woman with a spirited approach to life, has brought together Asian women to use their home skills in a restaurant setting. It is a personal place, with black-and-white family photos on the wall; the door to the kitchen stays open. The food is cooked in a style that owes more to home cooking than to restaurant food, with dishes such as delicious banana bhajis and tender cocolcasia leaves coated in a mixture of chickpea flour, ginger, garlic, chilli, yoghurt and spices, then layered, rolled up and steamed. There are some interesting quirks of cross-fertilisation between cultures. Hansa uses mint sauce in one of her relishes.

Driving down Manchester's Curry Mile in Rusholme excites the senses, not just from all the savoury smells wisping from the doors (the Bisto Kid could easily be following a curry), but also for the long stretch filled with the sparkle of gold and colour that bursts out of the Manchester drizzle. After one meal, we were given Vimto lollipops, a nice regional touch. When I went to one of Birmingham's balti houses, a certain taste caught my attention. I blagged my way into the kitchen to discover what I had suspected: a big container of Marmite.

The more I looked at English food, the more I found that it bore the influence of other cultures across the centuries, from the hops in beer to the new national dish of curry. Look, for example, at an average vegetable patch. So much of it has crossed the globe over the centuries. The pork butchers of the north of England were strengthened by the influx of Germans leaving Germany and compulsory military service after the country was unified in 1871. English microbrewers are influenced by American microbrewers, who in turn use brewing styles from other European countries such as Germany and Belgium. We eat pâté and not potted meat. Cockney chefs can be heard bellowing French terms when the restaurant doors swing open. Look at many a menu: lasagne, spring rolls, Thai green curry, samosas. In all the rush for pasta and chicken satay, for all the different influences in the shrinking globe, what about our own native savours? What about ethnic English?

To see English food properly, I had to try to look with a foreigner's unfamiliar eye. In a hostel in a converted Methodist chapel in Zennor in Cornwall, I got into conversation with some German students who were backpacking around the Southwest, and asked them what they liked about our food. (I have to admit I felt more confident asking a German rather than a French couple, having too often heard a grudging Gallic admission that Stilton was the sole highlight of English food.) There was a long pause. Their impression of our cooking was, broadly: toast (nice); weird breakfasts (a universal way of defining foreign-ness); fish and chips (too greasy); and sandwiches with lots of salad (nice). As it happened, the hostel was at that time being run by Gabby Jackson who, as a television producer, had put Gary Rhodes into Disney-esque check trousers to tour the country serenading great native food. In Cornwall she had found beautiful clotted cream from Jersey cows, home baking and excellent pasty shops. The hostel breakfast included delicious back bacon, meaty sausages and real leaf tea. Her cakes were golden with butter and free-range eggs from the chickens that pecked around the chapel.

Zennor is a particularly atmospheric part of Cornwall; people here have deep roots. Far-flung members of local families still come home for an annual feast day in May. The Mermaid's Arms, near the chapel, which features in a short story by DH Lawrence based on his time in the area, sold a good pint of Sharp's. Down the coast in St Ives, a number of restaurants serve sparklingly fresh fish within sight of the sea. We talked of these things, and the German couple listened. "Perhaps we should reconsider your food," one of them said, before setting off on a rain-sodden walk. But you do not bump into such flavours; finding good food in England is a question of island hopping: step in the wrong place and you will end up in the tinned soup, or something equally dreary. The quadruple fault lines of bad English cuisine are the dully plain, the industrialized, the ersatz and, closely related, the pretentious: they are all out there. Good things are out there, too. In search of them, I next went to look at the countryside itself.

3 countryside

IT IS THE NATURAL
FRESHNESS AND VITALITY
OF NATURE, CAPTURED
ON A PLATE, WHICH
GIVES US SOME OF THE
MOST DISTINCTIVE OF
ENGLISH TASTES.

IT IS THE NATURAL FRESHNESS AND VITALITY OF NATURE, captured on a plate, which gives us some of the most distinctive of English tastes. England, to the foreigner, is as famous for its countryside as it is infamous for its cooking. Looking down on the country from a plane, returning from abroad, you are struck afresh by the closely woven texture of the land, the way it has been worked for centuries into a complex mesh of buildings, fields, woodland, shoreline and cities. Though we do not tend to think of it in this way, around 80 per cent of the land is connected with food production.

To start with the broadest terms, zooming far, far out and looking down as if from a satellite, England's most obvious physical feature is that it is part of an island, surrounded by sea. Standing on the coast, watching the sea relentlessly bash the land, it seems anything but a moderating force, yet the sea softens the extremes of our climate to make a damp, temperate land with, on the whole, an equable temperament. Compare it to other countries on the same latitude – parts of Scandinavia, Russia, Poland, Canada – and you start to appreciate the benefits of the sea and the Gulf Stream. Our mild succession of seasons, rainfall throughout the year and, usually, few extremes result in plentiful grassland to support livestock; hence the emphasis on meat and dairy produce in our diet. This kind of climate suits woodland, which in the past provided fuel to roast and stew our meats, bake and toast our bread and cook our puddings. Our climate also partly explains our style of beer. Other European countries used new methods and technology in the eighteenth and nineteenth centuries to solve probelms caused by extremes of weather, and made lager. The English, in more equable climes, stuck to the older way of making beer.

In the past, before the industrialization of food, the connection

between the land and the food that came from it was far more
immediate. Thomas Hardy's *Mayor of Casterbridge* is set in the West
Country of the mid-19th century, an era when the wheat fields
brushed the edges of the town and the fluctuations of the harvest
affected the fortunes and tables of its inhabitants in a very direct
way. These days, much of England's produce and livestock go through
centralized markets, abattoirs and supermarket depots to end up far
from the place where it was grown or reared. Around 34 per cent
our food is imported. You could argue that, on the whole, it is no
longer possible to find visible, local connections between field and
plate. But look hard: certain kinds of food can still tell you something
about the landscape in which they were grown. Tasting places can get
you under their skin.

Food can distil a place and register it in your mind. I once stopped
for a rest as I walked along the shingle beach of Dungeness, on the
south Kent coast. Walking on shingle is so difficult and so noisy. I
sank down, the smooth pebbles forming a seat, and listened to the
drone of bees and the grasses in the wind. The breeze brought scents
and the toot of the train on the narrow-gauge railway. Oranges, reds,
yellows, whites, purples, pinks, greens: there are 600 species of wild
plant growing here. The late film-maker Derek Jarman, who tended
his celebrated garden at Prospect Cottage, noted in his diary one
July Monday how the bees clambered hungrily up the "sour" green
Wood Sage.

Malcolm Finn is a honeymaker who harvests clear, golden Wood
Sage honey by putting his hives on Dungeness in the summer.
The area is a nature reserve and he knows the bees will not stray

into the oil-seed rape that produces an increasingly ubiquitous honey. What specific, local honeys offer is a link to the flora on which the bees feed. It might be heather from the Isle of Purbeck, the North Yorkshire Moors and the Northumbrian Fells. It might be fruit-tree blossom. Here in Kent, bee-keepers are paid to put their hives into orchards to fertilise the flowers in order to produce fruit. Honeys can be surprising. Some of the best come not from the countryside at all but from the backgardens of urban areas like Brixton. Jill Mead, the photographer of this book, and her partner Steve, have a hive on the roof of a block of flats near Tower Bridge in London which produces delicious honey. They found a website that details the plants that grow in London in every postcode, and rested more easily after seeing what was on offer in SE1. In Northumberland, I noticed some borage honey from a crop grown on the borders. Farmers were growing fields of the plant, not to scent the jugs for some gigantic Pimms party, but for pharmaceutical companies who use it to make the drugs used in hormone replacement therapy.

Learning how certain kinds of food relate to their environments can make you regard both with more respect. A good example is eel, which is sold in the pie-and-mash houses of estuarial London, occasionally fresh (they go off quickly) but more often as a hot-smoked fish. Michael Brown runs a smokehouse and restaurant in the Somerset Levels, a prime example of a place where you can enjoy food close to its landscape. Michael explained to me the life cycle of an eel, as far as it is known: an epic journey across oceans, rivers and brooks that ranges over thousands of miles and is full of both the scope of the globe and local poetry. Eels are spawned as larvae in the

Sargasso Sea, east of Bermuda, and then take three years to drift on
the currents of the Gulf Stream to the continental shelf where they
change into recognisable baby eels, or elvers. In the springtime,
these come up the rivers of northern Europe to live and grow.
At this stage, Michael explained, they move in schools of millions.
"There are three million to a ton and I've seen a river with well over
a ton," he said. "The water actually begins to move almost on top.
Locals used to say the water sort of swerved and swelled like a mare's
tail. They do this amazing 'rope'. If you put them in a bucket, they
will rope and the sum of the parts has a greater force than the
individuals. In a way, it is a bit like herds of animals running or
migrating in Africa."

   Having entered the river systems of Europe, the elvers live and
grow to maturity and up to 12, 15, 20 years later – no one is quite
sure – the mature eel turns into a silver swimming machine, leaves
European waters and returns to the Sargasso, probably using astro-
navigation, fixing on the stars then going down deep to motor back.
"It's just staggering," said Michael. "They go in their thousands."
This restless movement, this longing to go out to sea of the eels'
autumnal migration, is triggered by climatic conditions – typically a
wild, stormy night with a lot of rain when, it is said, apocalyptically,
the brooks start to run chocolate brown. This is when the eels are
caught for smoking. The adult eel, with its fat stored for travel,
makes for succulent smoked fillets. Michael gets his eels from
the rivers of southern England such as the Avon and the Test.
The shape of these rivers means that the eels are easier to catch
commercially than they are on the Levels, where the rivers can be
in permanent flood.

   Because he relies on harvests directly from the wild, Michael's business is sensitive to any changes in the eels' environment. He's the first to know the state of the elver and eel populations. When he started in 1975, one man could catch the same number of elvers in the spring migration as 40 men caught in 1998. Elvers used to cost £1 a kilogram; now it is £275, as scarcity has put up the price. One problem is the over-fishing of the elvers, which are sold abroad.

For locals, eels used to be a staple, fried in butter or eaten with parsley sauce. On a wall in Michael's restaurant (in a converted barn) is a beautiful piece of kit: 'Ernie's eel spear', which was used by a shepherd on the farm. It's a sort of Levels trident with a five-pointed metal head at the end of a five-foot wooden handle and would have been made by a local blacksmith in the same way as they made such ordinary, everyday objects as buckets. You can eat the smoked eel fillets with a beetroot salad, bread and horseradish at this simple, comfortable restaurant/café.

After lunch, I walked near Hambridge, in the heart of the Levels, with the river on one side and a rhyne, or ditch, on another. It is an elemental landscape of air and water, punctuated by stone church towers. A cold east wind ridged the water and the reflections. I looked at the surface and thought about what was beneath.

You cannot taste a place more directly than by eating the wild food that grows there. I once spent a spring and summer researching wild food for a television programme, and the flavours I encountered – scallops that had just been collected by diving, birch sap wine in a Sussex woodland, wild mushrooms in the New Forest – fixed in my taste buds for ever the true meaning of freshness and gave me a deep respect for people who know the land intimately. Wild food is closer to hand than you think: it's there when you smell the wild garlic while driving down a lane, or pick blackberries, or eat fish that is caught from the wild, rather than farmed.

One wild flavour that has entered into mainstream commerce is elderflower cordial, which used to be widely made by country people. Lord John Manners, a younger son of the Belvoir Castle estate on the Leicestershire/Lincolnshire border, used a home recipe as the foundation of his business. Belvoir cordial is made in exactly the same way as the original, except in big, old cheesemaking vats rather than buckets, and captures the green, floral essence of an early English summer. There are fewer hedges now and the Manners advertise in local shops for people to bring in blossoms. They have also planted fragrant field-fuls for a ready supply of organic elderfower. The flower heads are pulled down and harvested with the aid of walking sticks.

Of all the gastro-pleasures to be had in England, to catch a natural crop cooked by a good chef in its area has to be one of the greatest. In the autumn, I found my way to a dining pub on the edge of the New Forest, the Three Lions at Stuckton. It was a friendly place, with a menu on a blackboard that included zander, a freshwater fish with gastronomic potential, and interesting game. My starter was a salad of wild mushrooms: not just a few, but a plateful piled high with the flavours, textures and freshness of at least six varieties picked by the chef, Michael Womersley. He gets pigs which have grazed on beech mast in the Forest and game shot by experts. North of the New Forest, in Romsey, Mauro Bregoli, an Italian chef, runs the Manor House, one of those places that London chefs escape to on a day off. He shoots some of his own ingredients and the antlers decorate the rooms as trophies. He makes his own salamis, and bresaola which he sticks up the Tudor chimney to smoke. Mushrooms served at the

Manor House are found wild in the Forest: they offer a different
experience from eating the wild fungi from Eastern Europe,
imported by a wholesaler.

By reading natural-history writers and landscape historians,
particularly the books of W G Hoskins and Oliver Rackham's classic
History of the Countryside, I began to see how much of the English
landscape was created in the first place: settled man needed to grow
food. Our ancestors carved out their fields from woodland or drained
marshes to make land for growing. The water-meadows where I
walked near my grandmother's house near Winchester, and which
fascinated me with their waterworks, were designed to be
deliberately flooded every spring to provide an early crop of grass
to feed livestock. Roads I drove along in Kent ran on the old tracks
down which pigs were driven to summer pastures. The high-banked
walls of Devon lanes were double-ditch boundaries to mark out
fields. Some of the granite walls on West Penwith, at the far end of
Cornwall, have been there since the stones were cleared off the land,
probably in Celtic times. A famous formula was invented in the
1970s by Max Hooper: the number of tree and shrub species within
25 meters of a hedgerow equals its age in centuries. Beyond its
natural beauty and the variety of its species, the richness of an old
hedgerow lies in the knowledge that it has been used and appreciated
by so many generations.

   Above Dungeness is Romney Marsh, created by monks who
drained and ditched the land to make the fertile fields. For centuries,
the area was famous for the Roman-nosed Romney Marsh breed of
sheep. On the marsh itself, farmers could raise up to three times the

number of sheep per acre as they could on the nearby downs; the
sheeps' dung made the land all the richer. Most of the area has now
been dug up to grow more profitable crops; green lines of potatoes
sway like three-dimensional op-art as you drive past the fields. It is
a peculiar and mesmerising part of England, full of smuggling,
witchery and atmosphere. The legacy of the great sheep-grazing days
is evident in the famous Romney Marsh churches. Fourteen remain:
some slightly doddery, with tipsy floors and full of light falling
through clear glass onto whitewashed walls. These churches rise
from the flat land, their size and number inexplicable in such a
sparsely populated place until you think of the links between
Canterbury and the great, past profits of wool. In this way, farming
explains a place.

I spoke to two farmers who still graze lambs on the marsh. One,
Frank Langrish, grows on the 'poor' west end of the marsh, which
hasn't been ploughed up for more profitable crops. His Romney
sheep dot the landscape like daisies. He quoted a saying that where
sheep feed on the marsh, you could throw a silver sixpence as far as
possible and still see the glint because the sheep had grazed the grass
so short. This area has wonderful wildflowers in the late spring and
early summer, because it has never been ploughed.

The meat of Frank's sheep, according to a good butcher in
the area, Jamie Wickens of Winchelsea, is consistently excellent:
a testament to the skill of the farmer as well as the grazing. Jamie led
me to the Landgate Bistrot in Rye, where I ate a delicious piece of
Frank's lamb: sweet, full of flavour and tender. It was one of those
restaurants where they care about ingredients and the heart of the
place is in the taste of the food. Jamie told me about The Ypres
Castle, a pub known locally as The Wipers. The cooking was gutsy

and the place had character. There I ate some more of Frank's lamb.
On the way out, I looked at the view over the landscape.

I also met the auctioneer of the Rye fishmarket, Bill Drew, who
had a basic stall with a small range of very fresh fish, including a
couple of cod with skin the subtle colours of sulky Channel skies.
He owns a pub, The Inkerman Arms, a potato-or-chips-and-peas
place. It serves good beer, some local brews, homemade pies and fresh
fish at reasonable prices, including the local scallops.

All over the country, on my travels, I learned to trust these local
networks of people who were in touch with the countryside. They
all know each other; they rely on each other, in part, to keep going.
Such networks survive. Still.

Another farmer, Philip Merricks, took me to a piece of old
shoreline that runs through his land. Standing on this small ridge,
you could see how the marsh had grown, bit by bit; I felt right in
the heart of the place. These Romney Marsh sheep go elsewhere
to be fattened for market; the grazing on this particular patch would
not, on its own, fatten the sheep adequately and the more fertile
land is used for more profitable crops. The sheep are just a part of
the overall farm and Philip gets a subsidy for keeping this part of
the countryside as a nature reserve. Although he likes the idea of
local markets, and was very much a man of the Marsh, Philip also
threw the cold light of business on it: most farming fits into a bigger
system, and few farmers have the skills and energy required to market
and sell their own meat. Bureaucracy was against it, too, he said.

We went to a local pub where the cook had made a good soup
using vegetables from local suppliers. The meat came from a central
supplier and she was not sure of its origin. It is not always
immediately obvious how to taste places, but it is possible.

4 regional foods

IN 1999 A BOOK CALLED
"TRADITIONAL FOODS
OF BRITAIN" CAME OUT,
WHICH LISTED AND
DESCRIBED OUR NATIVE
FOODS. IT WAS, AS IT
SAID ON THE JACKET, "A
DOMESDAY BOOK OF THE
NATION'S TRADITIONAL
SHOPPING BASKET".

IN 1999 A BOOK CALLED TRADITIONAL FOODS OF BRITAIN came out, which listed and described our native foods. It was, as it said on the jacket, "a Domesday Book of the nation's traditional shopping basket". The book was part of a Europe-wide project, which immediately offered some interesting comparisons between our food culture and that of our neighbours. For a start, other countries were quicker to publish their lists than we were, or already had similar publications. The book was published in Britain by a specialist food press, Prospect Books, rather than the official participants, the Ministry of Agriculture, Fisheries and Food, and Food from Britain.

One of the problems encountered by the author of the English part of the volume, Laura Mason, was the difficulty of defining such English foods, as instructed, by specific regions. She had to argue for the inclusion of such national classics as hot cross buns and Christmas pudding, even though they did not have a specific regional origin. As early as the 12th century, she says, England had a much more centralised administration than other European countries. Then, of course, there were such homogenizing forces as agricultural improvement, industrialization, transport and modern retailing.

The way the broad trends of agriculture tie into diet is clearer in other countries with stronger, less nationalised food cultures. Some of Mason's European colleagues, particularly the Italians, faced far fewer problems with identifying the regional origins of their traditional food. To take one very broad example reflecting agriculture, northern French traditional dishes use butter and southern French cooking is based on olive oil, but beyond this, there is real pride taken in the range of products particular to a place. The links between region and food in England are less straightforward.

Bread offers an example of an everyday, staple food with a
history that reveals England as a trading nation where long-standing
international supplies have profoundly influenced what we eat.
When archaeologists examined the stomach contents of the first
Lindow Man, the Iron Age bog man found near Wilmslow in
Cheshire who captured the public's imagination in the 1980s,
they discovered that the last meal he ate had been a flat bread
made of wheat, oats, rye and barley flour, cooked on a fire.
Particles of heather from the fire had made their way into the
bread and he had drunk water with sphagnum moss in it. We
moved on.

Bread can be made from barley, oats and rye, but our preference
is for that made from flour milled from wheat with a high
amount of gluten (the protein that stretches and holds as bread rises
in the oven). English wheat, like those of other European countries,
was historically comparatively low in gluten. Between 1740 and
1830, the English population doubled. Elizabeth David, in *English
Bread and Yeast Cookery*, recounts how, at the end of the 18th
century, we began to import some wheat from North America,
where the growing conditions of the great grain prairies produce
wheat with more gluten. The net result of this trade, she argues, is
part of the reason for our taste for tall, light loaves. After the repeal
of the Corn Laws in 1846, the spread of railroads in America,
and an ever-growing population, imports of corn from North
America increased. They accounted for more than 50 per cent
of our flour after the Second World War. Today, new varieties
allow us to grow corn with higher levels of gluten here; we
mill around 80-85 per cent of our own flour, but the majority of
the rest still comes from North America, to be used in bread.

*Malcolm Finn and his hives
on the edge of Dungeness,
producing Wood Sage honey
that is very much part of
its place.*

In her book, Laura Mason describes how England divides roughly
into two zones along the watershed of the River Severn and the
River Trent. Above the line are higher and wetter landscapes to the
north and west; to the south and east lies lower, drier land. These
divisions, as she points out, historically affected the staple crops.
Wheat has long been the grain for bread in the southeast, but
historically other crops – barley, rye and oats – were used in other
parts of the country. Oats were traditionally a staple crop in the north
of England because the number of hours of daylight and the amount
of rainfall suited it better than wheat. These differences largely
disappeared as food became more centralised. Even by 1815 the
average loaf was made from wheat. But I remembered my fellow
judges in the dock pudding competition talking about how good
oats were in biscuits. Until recently, you could still find very isolated
remnants of the traditional northern oatcake in different forms in
Lancashire and Yorkshire.

Betty Wordsworth, the last traditional northern oatcake maker, has
recently stopped production at Stanley's Crumpets in Barnoldswick,
Lancashire. The technique is labour intensive and involves 'throwing'
the mix from a trolley on wheels onto the bakestone below. The
long, thin oatcakes could be eaten warm – used "like a wrap or a
chapati" as another maker said to me – or dried, when they look like
pieces of chamois leather. Betty used to sell around the markets, and
to pubs and clubs, where they were eaten in combination with meat
as 'stew and hard'. "I fought against closing," Betty said; at 57, she has
decided to retire for health reasons. "I loved the job. It was such a
happy little place." Schoolchildren used to come and watch her work.
The business could almost be run partly as a tourist attraction, she
said, to hold its own as an independent, traditional enterprise against

the might of the supermarkets. However, she has not found anyone willing to take over because of the work involved.

Another baker, David Nicholson, the grandson of the founder of the business, just outside Bradford, has had the traditional equipment made using drawings from patent documents. But the regular oatcake maker uses a less time-consuming method, though still to an old family recipe. "Of course, these days, time is of the essence," said David.

Thankfully, Laura's book has plenty of examples of traditional foods, indigenous to their area, that are thriving. Staffordshire oatcakes, like circular oat pancakes, are more widespread than the Yorkshire ones, probably because they are easier to make. You can come across them as part of good-value pub lunches in the pottery towns. Seeking out regional food can feel a bit like mushroom hunting: once you know what to look for, remarkable and beautiful forms emerge from the gloom. Yet if you are stuck on a mental motorway, toiling round the average supermarket, road-blind and trolley-caged, you will see very little.

Whitstable, on the north coast Kent, has been famous for its oysters since the time of the Romans. They grow well here because the shallow, estuarial waters are fed by two rivers – the Swale and the Medway – and the nutrient-rich waters provide plenty of food for the phytoplankton on which the oysters feed and fatten. The town has long attracted Londoners, most recently to the Royal Native Oyster Stores beachside restaurant, but there are other places, too, including the splendid Wheelers, which looks like a Victorian parlour. I was intrigued by the way oysters are affected by their environment.

The Seasalter Shellfish Company has a hatchery on this stretch of coast where millions and millions of oyster spat are produced. At this stage of their development the young oysters look like piles of glamorous gravel. I tasted two fully grown Pacific oysters which both began life here; one was raised to maturity in Whitstable and the other in Cumbria. They tasted different partly due to the nature of the different waters in which they had grown. Their character had been influenced by their environment.

The native English oyster, which is flatter with a round shell, in contrast to the more common Pacific oyster, used to be far more common in the days when Dickens described his characters feasting on them with such gusto, and when Whitstable became famous for its oysters. At that time, they were even added to pies to add bulk and flavour to the meat. Our native oyster beds have been decimated over the course of the late 19th and 20th centuries by disease, cold winters and over-fishing. But native oysters still exist and are worth seeking out.

One place they still breed in the wild is on the Fal Estuary in Cornwall. If you walk along the coast from the waterside Pandora Inn near Mylor Bridge to the headland that looks onto the Fal, you can still catch the magnificent sight of Europe's last sail-powered fishing fleet as its boats dredge for oysters on this stretch of water. The fleet is a great example of 'conservation by inefficiency', since the fishermen can work only at set times, without motor power and between October and March. Some of the oysters are relaid in the Helford to grow at the Duchy of Cornwall Oyster Farm in Porth Navas, an atmospheric place where you can go along with a bottle of wine for a shellfish picnic by the quiet, oak-tree-lined water.

Tasting a food in its place, or even just seeing where it comes from, makes a profound connection that echoes in your mind whenever, and wherever, you eat that food again. This is how regional foods have come to life in my mind and my mouth.

Regional foods arise from the products of the landscape, along with other factors such as trade routes. To strengthen our sense of regional foods, it is important to look at the contemporary use of such products, as well as their past. Cornwall's celebrated stargazey pie, with its pilchard heads poking out of a sea of pastry, is an example of a regional food which may still be made on special occasions, but feels a little like an historical curiosity left stranded on the shores of time. More relevant today are the pilchards themselves. These are mature sardines of a different species from the South African and Pacific pilchards that come tinned in tomato glop; recently they have been packaged by Marks & Spencer as 'Cornish sardines'. They are salted and sold at the Pilchard Works in Newlyn.

The exhibition here is a model of how a display can link a food to a particular area and way of life, and how a small focus opens up a whole new view of a place. Stargazey pie originated at a time when pilchards were a staple food because large shoals swam around the coast of Cornwall. Special spotters looked out for the shadow of a mass of fish in the water and raised the fishermen for huge landings. The pilchards were not all eaten locally: from the 1850s to the beginning of the 20th century, 10-12,000 tons of pilchards would go abroad each year, mostly to Italy.

They still cure the pilchards at the Pilchard Works in Newlyn, in time-honoured tradition, and Italy is still the main customer. It gives me a little surge of pride to think of the villages of northern Italy receiving salted Cornish pilchards, packed into old-fashioned wooden boxes; the pride deflates again when one recalls that they have nothing like the same status in their own country.

Pilchards no longer swim along the coast in such huge numbers. Nick Howell, who set up and runs the Works, used to rely for his supplies on the Scottish trawlers which came down to fish off Cornwall. Now he has persuaded local boats to catch them, lending them specialised cotton nets and guaranteeing a decent price to get them to take on the work. The Pilchard Works has kept going in spite of modern hygiene regulations. At one stage the workers were told to change the hessian mats they used for absorbant pads, like the ones you get in the bottom of packets of meat in supermarkets. The fish rotted. There was, after all, a reason for methods that have lasted centuries.

Look at any regional speciality and it will tell you something about where you are. Growing up in Wiltshire, my greedy child's eyes would search out the lardy cake in baker's windows. The sticky, glossy cakes, made with lard and layered with dried fruit, were a special treat – and still are. Only as an adult, and living elsewhere, did I wonder why they were so relatively common in Wiltshire. According to Laura's book, other areas had versions, but lardy cakes are most associated with Wiltshire, Oxfordshire and Berkshire, which were areas of pig farming, hence the spare lard in the area that went into the cakes. Pigs still have vivid connections in Wiltshire. On the Wiltshire/Oxfordshire border is an organic pork producer, Helen Browning, who has 120 Saddleback sows and has formed a group of farmers who sell organic meat under the Eastbrook Farms' Organic Meat label. The meat is also used to make Duchy Original sausages and bacon.

In Calne, Wiltshire, you'll find a butcher, Michael Richards, who has long made proper pork pies and other pork products. In the days before railways, Calne used to be a strategic resting point for pigs being driven from Ireland to the London market. The area naturally became a good place to start a bacon business: the weaker pigs did not have to be driven so far, losing weight with every mile, but were fattened-up and turned into a transportable, less perishable product. One of a family of butchers in Calne, George Harris went to America in 1847 and saw how they used ice-houses to cure the meat even in summer. He imported and patented this particular method of curing in brine in iced premises, and it became 'the Wiltshire cure'. At their height, Harris sent tins of meat all over the world. Because of the factory, there was a by-products plant in Calne which took waste from other abattoirs, and on a very quiet day with no breeze, residents say you could sometimes walk out of your house and reel back from the smell. As a child, I would dwell ghoulishly on these tales. Not so romantic, but still, in the past, a part of the place.

You can still get proper Wiltshire-cured bacon and hams at Sandridge Farm in Bromham, just outside Calne. The pork is put in vats of different cures; the Devizes cure includes a local beer, Wadworth's 6X. Production is local — very local: they grow their own cereals on which the pigs are fed and spread the pig muck on the ground to fertilise the soil so it does not need artificial chemicals. The bacon and hams are exceptional. They also do hand-cut pork scratchings which are too good to be legal.

Another bacon-related Wiltshire strand can be seen in sauces. A

*Gloucester Old Spot pigs
reared by Andrew Hudson
and sold by Tavern Tasty
Meats, a rare breeds farm
shop near North Walsham,
north Norfolk*

man called William Tullberg lived in Calne and worked in the bacon industry. Because he had to do so much tasting, he often wanted a keen bit of mustard on his meat. The packet mustards and other sauces on sale were usually full of artificial flavourings and preservatives. Reading the diaries of John Evelyn, William got the idea of making some mustard himself. His experiment, conducted in a bucket, was the start of the first English-produced commercial wholegrain mustard. The company he set up, Wiltshire Tracklements, still makes its high-quality products – mustards and other sauces, or tracklements, in Sherston, near Calne. You see them, with their distinctive labels in William's script, in the good butchers and delis in the area and across the country. William's favourite lardy cake, incidentally, comes from Hobbs House in Chipping Sodbury, Avon.

Further into the West Country, high rainfall and southern warmth make for lush pastures and a land of dairy produce. Walk down some of the lanes in Devon on a summer's evening and the very air feels buttery. On the M5, coming into Devon, I remember parts where the motorway turned pink. The concrete was made using chipping from local quarries and kept the tinge of the stone in the area. By these pink patches of road, the grass really did seem greener, and the buttocky, bosomy round hills started, in my imagination, to look like scoops of ice-cream as I anticipated the rich pleasures to come.

County Cheeses, an excellent shop in Tavistock, has three whole counters full of cheese. When you walk in, you might assume they come from all over Europe, but they are almost all from the southwest of England. One Devon pub, the Nobody Inn at Doddiscombsleigh, has a vast cheese menu – pages and pages of the stuff – again with a

West Country bias. It is the abundance that impresses; the restaurant menus are filled with the words 'sticky', 'clotted', 'creamy', 'buttered'. Your imagination – and arteries – are filled with the lusciousness of the area. There is even a place called Butterleigh.

Those on the lookout on the coast of north Norfolk, their minds keen with appetite, will soon spot the local mussels being flagged up on roadside signs, or know to choose them from the menus of good pubs and restaurants. In the summer, you will also see marsh samphire, the salty 'sea asparagus', on sale, or take some for free – "enough for a feed" as the forager's phrase goes – on the marshes on the coast. You cut it just above the base so as to leave the root system: it is one of the marshland plants that helps to hold the land together. The coast is also known for its crabs, called Cromer crabs, that are caught and landed along this stretch. In June, in a good deli on the quayside of Wells-next-the-Sea, I saw pots of sea-lavender honey and, through the window, the purple haze of the flower spread across the marshland.

Now, you could say that mussels can be found all around England, crabs in other areas, samphire on other shorelines, and sea-lavender honey elsewhere in East Anglia, but that does not take away from the distinctiveness of these finds in their places. They are as much a part of north Norfolk as the views, the birds and the salty smack of sea in the air, and they are a contemporary way to define regional food. They may be served in dishes influenced by other cuisines and with flavours not from the area; you may eat the crab in chilli-spiked crabcakes using Thai ingredients and techniques, or you may eat one on the quayside, boiled, picked and sold from an English seaside stall.

A holiday-maker with a
Cromer crab and a cuppa
in Wells-next-the-Sea,
Norfolk.

But either way, they have a connection with the place.
It is the clued-up people in the area – chefs, food producers, shop-keepers – who know the produce on their doorstep, have the contacts to get the best and can bring to you these flavours with the indefinable, lively sparkle of freshness on the plate. They, too, are part of the region.

One widespread regional tradition still thrives across the country. Local breweries provide much more than just a pint; the best add to the character of their region. A great deal of brewing has been crudely industrialized and debased, but there are still about 35 regional and 400 smaller breweries operating around Britain.

East Anglia, with its dry climate and soil, has a tradition of growing top-quality malting barley. Not surprisingly, Suffolk is an area that is particular strong on beer. Adnams, brewed in the coastal town of Southwold, and the Nethergate beers from Clare are two that I have enjoyed. There are those who say Adnams' bitter has the tang of the sea, in the same way that Laphroaig and other island malts have a briney note of old sea ropes. Mmm. This is probably a matter of suggestion, especially if you are drinking it in a classic Suffolk coastal pub. The head brewer, Mike Powell-Evans, thinks this impression arises from the unexpected 'citrus marmalade' character of the hops. Their yeast is also distinctive. Beer is largely water, which varies greatly around the country, depending upon the rocks through which the rain has filtered. Regional brewing styles were based partly on the qualities of the water. The beers of Burton-on-Trent, for example, became famous for their clarity, sparkle and bitter edge. The local water is high in particular salts, especially gypsum, which gives the beer a strong fermentation and gets the most from the hops. Beers in other parts of the country can be 'Burtonized' by adding minerals to the water in order to reproduce this effect: again, showing how regional products can bear various influences.

These breweries own estates of pubs, in most cases near the brewery, and these add to the character of a place. You know you are in Adnams' or Harveys' or Bateman's country (in Suffolk, East Sussex and Lincolnshire, respectively) by the signs on the pubs, which mark out their territory in the same way that supporters' red-and-white striped football shirts are part of Sunderland, say, or Arsenal shirts cluster around Highbury in north London.

Each brewery has its own personality which you start to notice in small ways. Timothy Taylor, based in Keighley, West Yorkshire, has long been famed for its beers (especially the superb Landlord), and there also tend to be coal fires in its pubs. I noticed, on a winter northern pub crawl around Timothy Taylor's pubs, that I was happy from my taste buds to my toes. Holt's of Manchester has been among beer drinkers for a no-frills policy which helps to keep prices unbelievably low. A local legend goes that Holt's used to give bus passes to its sales reps instead of petrol allowances. I have no idea if this is true or a regional joke. Walking around Manchester you'll see a number of packed Holt's pubs with permanent low prices flagged up outside – down to £1 a pint – and full of people emptying glasses, though the interiors were far less spartan than I had expected. Adnams has a renowned wine business and, as well as offering 20 wines by the glass in the Crown in Southwold, the brewery makes an effort to train its tenants in keeping and serving wines.

Another spin-off for consumers, and for other regional trades, is the increasing amount of care that these regional breweries take over their food. This helps make locally sourced, good food more widely available. For example, Timothy Taylor's pubs get their bacon and black pudding from Scaithes, another traditional producer in Keighley. I sometimes settle down to local, meaty sausages with onion and beer gravy at the John Harvey Arms near the Harvey's brewery in Lewes.

I once had to loiter around supermarkets in different parts of Liverpool to find locations for a television programme, working out the feel of each neighbourhood by peering into baskets and talking to customers over the vegetable stands. Obviously, the posh supermarkets sold a different range of food from the discounters in less prosperous areas. Yet it was impossible to discern the overall character of the place – what made it Liverpool – from the food I saw in those baskets which was pretty much the same as anywhere else in England. The next time I went to Merseyside, however, I met a microbrewer and went to a pub to drink his beer. I came away feeling that the man, the beers and the pub could not have existed anywhere else but in Liverpool. Two small details of a city, but vivid ones.

Phil Burke runs the Passageway Brewery in a lock-up on the south side of Toxteth, towards the Albert Dock, an area you would not stumble across as a visitor but worth driving through for its atmospheric Victorian warehouses – especially if you have a taste for *film noir* locations. In the 18th century, this part of the city was inhabited by merchant seamen, and there are plenty of yarns about naval press gangs who would try to get men on board ship when they lay drunk in their beds, and how word would spread among the dockers until there were running battles along the streets. The Victorians covered the place in big brick warehouses to cater for the seven miles of docks that thrived when Liverpool was the second biggest port of the Empire. The big brick building with a great tower is Cain's, the Liverpool brewery which, after many years, has been restored to use as such. I like Cain's beers, but in this case I was going to see somewhere smaller, with an interesting brew of cultures.

The Passageway Brewery owes its origin to a strongly rooted culture in another country: Belgium. Phil Burke was inspired to go to Flanders to try the famous Trappist brews after seeing a television programme presented by the beer writer Michael Jackson. He now makes an annual pilgrimage to the birthplace of St Arnold, Belgium's patron saint of brewers and bakers, where he fills a container full of holy water from an Artesian well. The first time Phil and Steve Dugmore, the co-founder of Passageway, went to the holy well to get the water, a priest came up and asked what they were doing. When they explained, he took them into a chapel and showed them a glass cylinder "like a big joint", which turned out to contain St Arnold's leg bone. They knelt, feeling touched by the surreal, as the priest said a prayer. Back home, as Burke was about to pour the holy water into the mash tun, Steve spontaneously told him to say a prayer; now he never brews without this added ingredient – the prayer of St Arnold, in Flemish. Kevin the security guard, before he got to know Phil and his brews, thought there was witchcraft afoot when he overheard the Flemish mutterings over the steaming cauldron. The brewery has two statutes of St Arnold, one holding a mash paddle, the other a wicker basket, known as a stuikmand, used by Belgian peasants to take bottles of beer to the fields.

An important part of the character of the beer comes from a strain of yeast from a Belgian monastic brewery. In his initial approach to the monks, Phil impressed the Father in charge of brewing with a certain arcane bit of scientific knowledge he had picked up from a rare book on brewing borrowed from the well-stocked Liverpool City Library. Thanks to Liverpool Council, Phil managed to get his magical yeast.

Now, would another city, with less of a belief in public services than Liverpool, have had this unusual book? There's something in the way Phil tells the story, and the cultural catholicism of the tale, that ties the Passageway Brewery to Liverpool. It is Belgian in influence but Liverpudlian in style - not least because that's where you drink the beer.

I went with Phil to the Baltic Fleet, a pub on the edge of the warehouse area and near the Albert Dock, where they sell Passageway beers. It is an atmospheric place, shaped like a wedge of cheese with a rounded point, surrounded by pavement and originally with eight entrances. Like a number of old pubs, it remained standing when the surrounding buildings were knocked down: pubs are sometimes the only old buildings to survive in an area, being too profitable to demolish. From the cellars, a tunnel goes down to the waterfront, possibly from smuggling days, and the walls of the pub are washed with images of the sea: ship crests, salty faces in old photographs, launches of grand old boats. It used to be a dockers' pub and got its name from the Baltic fleets that stopped here in Liverpool. There is still a saying in the north to describe a cold day: "It's Baltic out there". The area nearby, the Albert Dock, has been turned over to very good museums, including the Liverpool Tate, but there is still a working chandlery near the pub, whose owner drinks here. Simon Holt, who runs the Baltic Fleet, is in his early 30s. He sources his food as carefully as his beer. He sells pies made of meat from Welsh Black cattle, and the same breed appears roasted on Sundays; he serves good sausages and unpasteurized farmhouse cheeses. He has restored the interior carefully, without spoiling the atmosphere, and has won a Merseyside Pub of the Year award from Camra.

Simon's family were West African traders, in the years after slavery ended, and the pictures on the walls belong to the past of the city and his family. He could have gone into the bowels of a bigger business, but instead chose to set up independently, in search of a smaller operation with a genuine personality. The Baltic Fleet is a pub with good food, good beer and a distinctive atmosphere – a place that could not be anywhere else but here. I sat in the end room with its big windows and merry fire, looking across to the Liver Building and drinking a pint of Phil's refreshing beer.

There are two famous pub buildings in Liverpool. One, the Philharmonic, is on Hope Street, the street that has the Anglican cathedral at one end and the modern Catholic cathedral at the other, with the Everyman Theatre and the Philharmonic concert hall in between. The other is The Vines by the Adelphi hotel. Both have everything going for them in terms of position and looks. Both were fitted out by the master craftsmen who worked on the luxury ocean liners built in Liverpool, and were said to be truly stunning places to visit. When I spoke to seasoned beer-drinkers in Liverpool, they did not recommend either, apart from mentioning the red marble urinals in the Philharmonic's gents. I was curious to see why.

The Philharmonic had giant art deco thistles (gold on coffee cream) mosaics, stained and engraved glass, elaborate cornicing, detailed wood-carving and snugs named after composers. It was a breathtaking, arty-tart of a boozer. The Vines had chandeliers, a zodiac on one ceiling and the ornate, elegant opulence of Edwardian baroque. Both pubs were sensational and, on a mid-summer lunchtime, curiously lacking in atmosphere. The back room at The Vines, a brass-and-mahogany palace, was locked up, although they obligingly let me in. The Philharmonic has since changed hands and serves real ales. I hope it is – as it sounds it is – on the up: it had felt like opportunity squandered.

The most famous old pub in Leeds, the narrow and splendid Whitelocks, always seems to have a buzz about it, even though it is tucked down a yard. Other Leeds pubs, like The Adelphi, right by Tetley's brewery, have as much stand-up Victorian pride as the splendid town hall. Leeds pubs are not the only places to drink in the city. You can monitor the amount of disposable income in a city by counting the number of thriving café-bars. Leeds, in the centre of the country, attracted enough business for the financial ball to get rolling: farewell post-industrial decline, welcome to the caffè-latte-and-bottled-beer generation. In this new generation of places to drink, it is the independents which give the character to the city, not the lengths of chains. Call Lane, near the Corn Exchange, is wall-to-wall café-bars, from the mellow Arts to the hyper-cool Norman, where a door with the appearance of a tortoise's shell turns out to be made of pieces of toast behind plastic. Not all such bars serve interesting real ales, however.

Laura Mason makes another valuable point in the introduction to her book on traditional foods: that English food suffers from a lack of strong definitions. "Who has bothered to describe [British food] in terms more precise than the grossest impression?" she writes. "Who questions the logic of sausages that contain little meat, chocolate of infinite impurity, or ice-cream constructed of pig fat? A little definition would help. For too long we have closed our minds to the meaning of words. Our stomachs bear the consequences."

It takes detective work to root out regional foods; you can't always identify the genuine article, its provenance and manufacture, from what it says on the packet, and there isn't always someone to ask. A trustworthy system of labelling would help. There is some movement towards adopting the French system of *appellation contrôlée*, which defines food by an area of production or a defined method of production. In 2000, there was a Cornish pasty summit. Pasty makers from Ginsters to the Women's Institute discussed possible definitions of the product.

If the definitions take quality into account, it could mean that a market is created for consumers and producers interested in a higher standard, and locally made produce. Whether that means the meat and vegetables in a pasty come from Cornwall, or the pasty is made in Cornwall, from ingredients not necessarily from Cornwall, was an issue under debate. Because of supplies it was decided to go for the latter.

Lancashire cheese is an example of how a traditional regional food can become industrialized and lose much of its personality in the process. You will find a mass-produced form of Lancashire on the shelves of most supermarkets: a block of white, moist, salty cheese made in a factory. Traditionally made Lancashire takes you to a whole new level of pleasure and character.

Lancashire cheese, it is said, should be made within sight of Beacon

Fell, the local beauty spot that rises up northeast of Preston. Before the Second World War, it was more common to make cheese on the farm. Cheesemakers were banned from making Lancashire during the war when, to harbour resources, all milk had to go to factories to be made into hard cheeses or sold as liquid milk. They never really recovered. Now there are just nine businesses and only two make the cheese with unpasteurized milk. But Lancashire cheese still has stronger regional roots than other specialist foods. Much of it is consumed in its own county. Restaurant chefs favour particular kinds, and some label them by producer on the menu. Good shops, markets and the exceptional regional supermarket, Booths, often have Lancashires from more than one producer on sale. They also sell various strengths, which differ depending on how long the cheese has been matured. and are sold as mild, creamy, tasty and strong. Local preferences and the variety of tastes on offer make Lancashire cheese a food that is very much a part of its area.

Chris Sandham makes pasteurised Lancashire with much pride and attention to detail. His grandfather, who started the business, had another saying about Beacon Fell: "If you can't see Beacon Fell, it's raining; if you can, it's about to rain." Rain is part of the nature of this moist cheese. Lancashire lies partly on sandstone, which retains moisture well, producing good pasture, which means good milk. They say that in hot weather, the Lancashire grass will be green and lush for longer than in other parts of the country.

What is important, beyond the rain, is the nature of the grass. Chris Sandham buys some of his milk from cows grazing on organic pastures where, rather than spraying herbicides, a man goes out every day to keep the weeds down. Chris thinks the quality of this grass makes a real difference; in blind tastings, shoppers find it creamier than cheese made from conventional milk. Ruth Kirkham, who makes the most famous of all Lancashire cheeses, says the family still farms "in the old-fashioned way", using very little fertiliser on the grass. In the winter, when the animals can no longer eat grass, they pay for a superior product from a local feed merchant.

Lancashire cheese is made by keeping half of the milk from each day and adding it to half of the milk from the next day. It is this slight maturing of the milk which adds flavour to real Lancashire. In the winter, when the cold weather means the milk will not spoil so easily, the Kirkhams even stretch this process to three days, thereby adding yet more taste.

Unpasteurized milk in particular changes from day to day, according to the time of year, the weather and cows themselves. It is the skill of the cheesemakers to know their milk and adapt their craft to suit the raw ingredients. "I'm after milk that is as rich in butterfats, proteins and rich and creamy and bad-for-you as you can get," says Graham Kirkham, with a grin. "I can make some ace cheese out of that." Instead of buying in a starter (the bacteria that encourage the curds and whey to form), the Kirkhams have a monthly brew in a saucepan which they top up with milk every two days, set on a stove to warm up, and then cool it down. It takes an hour and a half every other day and is less uniform than a pre-prepared starter, but they believe it gives more character to the cheese. Their unpasteurized cheese will vary each day. This is part of the pleasure of eating it: your senses are alive to subtle variations rather than dead bored by a consistent but dull commodity. The challenge the cheesemaker faces is to make cheeses that are consistently good when each one is not identical: a hard task that requires experience.

The taste of individuality you get from these Lancashire

cheesemakers is a matter of craft, and also of character. Producers have their own quirks and styles. Regional food is enriched by reality: what actually goes on rather than a perceived rural idyll. Sandham's, for example, is made in a dairy just off a busy road of a ribbon-development village: hardly the fairy-tale farmyard setting you might imagine. The village noticeboard is outside a Chinese take-away and there are suburban gardens and a railway behind the dairy rather than green fields of lowing cows.

Chris Sandham's grandfather was a tax collector for Preston Council. Back then, the house used to have shutters on the windows to lock out people looking for DIY tax rebates, and he would always take a knuckle duster and a club when he set out because of robbers waiting in the nearby dip in the road. After he had a row with the council, he was left with two small children and no income, and started making cheese because his wife was from a farming family and knew how to do it. Talking to Chris, it was the small details that added to my sense of the place. You need to be strong to work in cheesemaking. Some of the truckles – barrel-shaped cheeses – weigh more than 20kg and Chris remembers that one of the workers, Bill, had such big calf muscles he had to split his wellies to get them on. Some supermarkets sell small pieces of the cheese wrapped up in plastic, but unless you have seen a truckle, you cannot picture the true identity of a Lancashire.

The two remaining unpasteurized Lancashire producers are both found down a twist of lanes in the middle of peaceful countryside, the kind of place where where you get that feeling of travelling 'off piste' on unmarked roads. There would be no reason to go down to the delightful spot where Shorrocks is made, except to go to the nearby pub, Ye Horns Inn, which has the cheese on the menu. The dairy, right by the milking parlour, is small, with a few old-fashioned cheese presses and lengths of muslin. It feels at odds with the modern industrial age. Missus had an all-American tan, dark glasses and shorts; Mister came over with farming on his hands, making an effort to sit down during his working day. We talked about the pressures on specialist producers and he harrumphed about being judged by a rookie buyer from a supermarket at a big cheese show. They also told me how a public health inspector had gone around the markets suggesting sellers might like to have separate boards and knives for pasteurised and unpasteurized cheese, even though it is not required by law, or, indeed, necessary. Be that as it may, Shorrocks' market sales had fallen and they were looking for more specialist outlets. I had been encouraged by the spread of good Lancashire cheese within the region, but this was a sinister sign that the local choice might be narrowing.

Very close to the Shorrocks, almost back to back, are the Kirkham's. Up until the 1990s, Kirkham's was sold through a wholesaler and was called, anonymously, 39. It has subsequently been championed by, amongst others, Randolph Hodgson of Neal's Yard Dairy, won the accolade of Supreme Champion at the International Cheese Show in 1995 and is much sought out by name. Graham Kirkham is an ex-mechanic. His mother, Ruth, is a plain dealer with a determined chin and a smile. They both hooted with laughter at the nicknames she gives the cows which go according to their characteristics: one is called Sparrow; another Mouse because it always goes back to clear up the last feed nut; another, Tatty Ears. Mrs Kirkham talked about meeting Prince Charles at the British Food Awards and how he spent some time talking to a pig farmer who had gone out of business. She noticed he wanted to keep talking to the farmer for as long as possible, and then longer. "You can tell when someone's really interested and not just pretending," she said.

A factory product is made by pressing buttons and computerized readings; real food is made by people who use hard-learned skills and pay constant attention to what they do, who take a pride in making something exceptional. What I learned from talking to these producers and seeing them in situ was that each had their own ways, their own character. Place, weather, soil, grass, craft, producer, seller and customer: these all had their parts to play in this regional product.

Many of the regional foods that have survived have done so because of strong links beyond the limited local market. Morecambe Bay shrimps became more than a cottage industry when railways brought tourists to the area who ate potted shrimps on holiday and bought them to take back home. Rail links made possible a regular trade selling to London. You still see Morecambe Bay shrimps on the menu of traditional fish restaurants such as Sweetings, in the City as well as in more modern ones such as Ransome's Dock in Battersea.

The Lake District, so long so popular with visitors, has a proportionately higher number of regional specialities than other less beautiful parts of the country. The survival and fame of Grasmere gingerbread, Cumberland sausage and Kendal mint cake, to name but three, have been partly due to the tourist trade. Stilton was named after the place to which travellers and traders came and bought the local cheese. Cheddar was named after a town to which visitors came to see the famous gorge.

A modern form of tourism throws another lifeline to regional foods. Many of the people I spoke to said gastro-tourism was on the rise. For their customers, a long weekend might involve a walk, a visit to a garden or a house, shopping, a trip to a pub and eating well. There are encouraging signs that the National Trust is making an effort to source foods locally and serve some regional foods in its restaurants and tearooms. The food historian Sara Paston-Williams, as well as teaching historic food courses to Trust caterers, has made sure that cream teas at the houses in Cornwall, where she lives, serve Cornish splits using the proper soft-crumbed bun rather than scones. Mass production may have taken over, but there is a counterforce of people who, increasingly, are 'eating England'.

Philippe Esclasse (mentioned in chapter two, Cultures), as a Frenchman travelling around England, describes us as a land of tribes from the way atmosphere and accent change as discernably as the countryside, in a short distance. We tend to lose sight of these differences. As I travelled and talked to people about food and drink, I became excited by the way they led into the detail and intimacies of a place – cities as well as landscapes – to show how they were distinctive. Food and drink became linked into social history, place, nature and living culture in a way that revitalised my whole notion of English food, and of England itself. It was a subtle shift, but for me a profound one. Knowing just a little bit about what I ate and drank added another layer of life and pleasure to a place; equally, my platefuls became all the richer for the associations with the surroundings. The country was pieced together, gradually, in all its subtle variety, until England became the sum of real parts rather than a vague, airy generalisation.

There are signs that a sense of regionality is being revitalised. Peter Paprill, a Cheshire-based regional foods merchant who gives talks under the title, 'The Cheese Detective', says the people in his audiences are stirred by stories that link products to a place, and at such moments of connection, he is aware of nodding heads around the room. Laura Mason told me she had sometimes felt depressed by the lack of official interest while she was researching *Traditional Foods* in the mid-1990s. Since then, she believes that people have become more engaged in the idea of regionality, even if it is not as highly developed a concept for us as for the French and the Italians.

Food producers who cannot compete with economies of scale, and consumers, bored or frightened by industrialized food, are turning to specialist markets. It makes sense to use what is already there, what has roots in an area and a familiarity, even if a vague one from the name or past tastes. Perhaps we shall not see the extinction of traditional foods, but a strengthening.

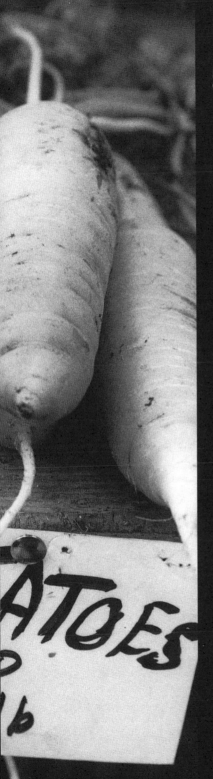

5 local foods

TRAVELLING AROUND
ENGLAND WAS AN
INSPIRATION AND A
PLEASURE. BUT IN
ORDER TO HAVE A REAL
EXISTENCE, AS A LIVING
PART OF CULTURE,
DELICIOUS, DISTINCTIVE
ENGLISH FOOD AND
DRINK MUST BE PART
OF DAILY LIFE.

TRAVELLING AROUND ENGLAND WAS AN INSPIRATION and a pleasure. But in order to have a real existence, as a living part of culture, delicious, distinctive English food and drink must be part of daily life. I had to seek out the nourishment and character of what was on my own doorstep, in Lewes and the surrounding countryside of East Sussex. This happens to be where I live, but these foods and issues could apply in many places, with their own local variations.

During the writing of this book, I packed my cooking pots and books to move from the hydrocarbon high of the Holloway Road in London to the elegant green curves of the South Downs. Once there, I looked at the food available to me with fresh eyes, simply because everything was new. Lewes, the county town of East Sussex, has a flint-knapped high street and views of chalk hills at the ends of the streets. The flints of the old houses, the pattern of the streets and the views tie the town into the surrounding countryside. I was intrigued to discover whether the same sort of connection could be made with the local food and drink.

In the past, Lewes thrived because it sat in the midst of productive farmland and straddled trade routes. Corn from the fields and sheep from the hills were brought into the town from the surrounding countryside and taken up the River Ouse to the port of Newhaven. There used to be a weekly cattle market and a big sheep fair in the autumn. Like so many livestock markets around the country, Lewes' cattle market closed in 1992 and the annual autumn sheep fair stopped way back. The old web of local markets and wholesalers has been largely superseded by new methods of distribution. These days there are fewer buyers, and they buy on a far larger scale. I came across a small livestock market in Rye, further along the coast, on the Kent border, and on market day the buzz in the town was palpable.

But many of these old meeting places for farmers, which brought the countryside into the heart of the town, have gone forever.

It is hard to tell, on first appearance, that Lewes was ever a market town at all. There are two main shopping areas. The uphill half once had four butchers, a bakery, two grocers and a fishmongers; now it has mostly clothes shops, second-hand bookshops, charity shops, estate agents and solicitors. There are some unusual independents, two food shops and not many chain shops. The buildings are beautiful and the crown court has the usual rum characters and sharp-eyed lawyers outside. Yet this part of town only just avoids the hollowness that comes when a street loses the comings and goings, and chit-chat of the customary shoppers doing daily basic food shopping.

A row of shops further up the hill includes a butcher and a greengrocer. Down the hill, in what is now the centre of town, is Cliffe High Street, which still has many independent shops. It is these two stretches that make you feel Lewes is still a real town, with streets that have life and movement other than the cars driving through.

There is a certain amount of local food to be had in Lewes. It is not always obvious, or labelled, and it is spread out among the independent shops; finding it revives the dormant instincts of hunter-gathering. Shopping has become such an anonymous, weekly trudge around the supermarket aisles that the old skills of seeing what is new in, what looks good, what's freshest and what's a snip are falling away. But the rewards of shopping like this are paid in flavour, and the local Lewes shops are still busy, still offering an alternative to the town's two supermarkets.

There are three independent greengrocers in the town. Bill's down the hill has a good range and a colourful café, and Swanborough Nurseries grow some of their own produce, including flowers, which are often well priced. My regular greengrocer is two minutes' walk away and is run by Vera. She has the spread people expect: the Dutch tomatoes, imported beans, lots of spuds. But she also sells high-quality goods like French greengages, and, crucially, both organic and non-organic produce from a number of local and regional suppliers. Organic basil is grown in the walled garden of Glynde. With the cool, sunny days of September come cobnuts from Kent and several varieties of plums. Later, there may be quinces from a tree in a nearby village. The superb Jerusalem artichokes used to be grown locally by an old boy through a canny contact, though circumstances changed. Never mind; another good supplier was soon set up. In February, Vera brightens the gloom with a display outside the shop that might run from red-cheeked mangoes to bright-pink forced rhubarb to the orange glow of Seville oranges and bunches of pink and red tulips. Her organic onions strengthen the base of many dishes; the bags of salad herbs are green vitality. Each time I go in, there is something new, some temptation to divert me from my list. What delights me most is that this is not a posh shop that sets itself apart as boutique food. It is run by an 'ordinary' greengrocer who takes a pride in what she does. Long may she last, and others like her.

I had struck a quiet seam of gold, for next door to Vera's was a good butcher's shop. It sells proper free-range chickens, quite unlike those fake free-range which are kept in a huge numbers in a barn with a door open somewhere in the distance. There is a ox-shaped clock advertising the Sussex breed. Some of the lamb and most of the beef are local, although not labelled as such; it is simply the custom of butchers like these to buy what is good and local, if possible. You are always aware, in the background, of the craft of the butcher's trade – the sawdust, the knives – and, hanging from steel hooks, the carcasses, which will end up as chops, steaks and roasts. On my way to get the paper, I will pass one of the butchers with a pig on his back going from van to shop, and as I wait to be served in the shop, perhaps buying one of the pork pies for my lunch, I'll watch a side of pork being divided into belly and loin on the scooped butcher's block, or see where the chunks come from for a stew. You can play the sequence in your mind of the animal turning into cuts and then rewind it, speeded up, so the cuts leap back to become a whole again. The vegetarian may cringe, but to recognise that meat comes from an animal is to value it more, to give it respect.

When you go regularly to local shops like these, fleeting pleasures come your way, according to season and the quirks or personal connection of the shop-owner. The display in my local cheese shop, Say Cheese, as well as showing off Sussex cheeses such as Golden Cross and Flower Marie, will occasionally sprout a puff-ball or some ceps brought in by someone in the know. Just being in these shops means you pick up snippets of gossip past and present. I remember overhearing that one of the doughty old ladies who had just been served had helped the French Resistance movement in the war.

The most visible source of local produce is Lewes' Victorian brewery, Harvey's, which sits in the middle of the town by the River Ouse. With its black-and-white building and old tiled roofs, it is an attractive factory that seems to give the town an engine: the clouds of steam and rolling metal barrels are a solid, industrial presence amid all the flitting consumers. Before the 19th century, the rhythms of the brewing year tied it to the agricultural seasons. The ingredients for beer – barley and hops – were grown in the countryside around Lewes. The brewery hired from the ready supply of local labour that drifted between farm work in summer and brewing in winter, when cooler temperatures made the yeasts in the beer more predictable. This system changed as technology improved. In the mid-19th century, there were no fewer than nine breweries in Lewes. You can see the skeletons of maltings around the town. With their wide floors and sturdy columns, they are handsome buildings which convert well to modern uses. One houses the record office, another is partly occupied by a video shop.

In a roundabout way, it was the new monthly farmers' market, set up in June 1999, that made me realise that this was still a town with a living food culture. On the first Saturday of each month, around Cliffe High Street, shoppers carry plastic bags bursting with springy kale and the flourish of carrot tops. People would mention in passing some sausages they had found, or a meal they had pulled together from discoveries. The stalls are an enjoyable diversion, an event, a chance to talk to the growers, a reminder of freshness and seasonality. What I realised was that some of the same sort of produce was on offer already in the local shops, day in, day out.

Increasingly, food comes from centralised depots, following mainstream arteries leading from farms to supermarkets, run according to economies of scale and mass production with not much time devoted to flavour, character and difference. But good, fresh, local produce still spreads into Lewes through a number of smaller producers constantly pumping in supplies. Less than before, but Lewes is still connected to the surrounding countryside through its veins.

In October 2000, however, disaster struck. Floods caused serious damage to Cliffe High Street when the Ouse broke its banks; what had been a busy shopping street was obliterated by a sheet of blank water. Nature ignored man just as man had ignored nature, and we were shocked. Harveys barrels floated down the river; the centre

of the town was cast adrift. When the drama, waters and hyper-
ventilating rumours of typhoid subsided, we were left with a
nagging fear: that this vital, quirky part of town was less viable than
it had been before. At the very least, many of the independent shops
would not open before Christmas and thus lose a bumper part of
their annual takings. Would they bother to re-open or take the
insurance money and the chance to do something else? With much
perseverance, many of the independents seem to have picked
themselves up and survived. Harvey's produced a flood memorial
beer, Ouse Booze.

If this part of town does not revive and thrive, Lewes will be half
the place it was: we will be left more to the bright blandness of the
chain stores rather than the interweaving, varied, idiosyncratic buzz
of the independents. The floods made it starkly clear how important
they were to the spirit of the town.

Beyond Lewes, I made small loops around the countryside to see
farm shops and other producers who sold from the door. Food is
such an excellent excuse to explore; it's the ultimate consumer
pastime. I found a tabletop near one of my walks which had freshly
laid eggs. In Hastings I wandered amid the tall Victorian fishing
sheds, known as 'shops' and built to store nets. They are this shape
because there was only a limited space on which to build. I walked
along the shore with fish and chips hot in my hands and bought a
squid to take home and cook. I visited Seaford, my venue for wet,
winter days when indoors turns stale and I need a five-minute gasp
of ozone and stormy seas. This time I found a fishmonger, Rolf's,
run by two brothers who were the 13th generation of fish-sellers

An honesty shed on
Dartmoor monitored
through a CCTV camera

in the family. The iced counter was open to the street. They had
fat lemon soles, some line-caught, wild sea bass and a single,
beautiful eel that had been caught in a fishing competition and was
destined to be smoked. The local plaice plump up in November,
the brothers told me, because they feed on the mussel beds getting
ready to spawn, and this was a good time to buy. I cooked one
that night with mushrooms and a white sauce made with a slug
of Chablis.

In a hidden valley in the Downs, Breaky Bottom must be one
of the most beautiful vineyards in England. You drive on a rough
track over the top of a crest, the car sucking in its breath so its axle
does not touch the ground, and it suddenly appears below you. The
vines etch the contours and the wine is made in an old flint barn.
I have a glass sometimes in The Ram at Firle, a pub that sits at the
base of the Downs quite near Breaky Bottom, and as I drink, its
aromatic verdure, subtly keen, fits into the landscape.

Even as I enjoyed my discoveries, I felt how vulnerable these
businesses were. The fishing fleet in Hastings is unusual in that the
boats launch off the beach. A man in the local fishing museum told
me that the local fishermen were scraping by and some were not
repairing their boats. The Rolfs say they think they will be the last
generation of their family to sell fish. Breaky Bottom was flooded at
least 24 times in the winter of 2000/1. The winemaker, Peter Hall,
finds it hard to sell their wines in Lewes, except through the Harvey's
brewery shop.

Sometimes as I walk around the supermarkets, the local food
I value seems like a trickle of water next to the mass-produced
torrent – a trickle that was drying up. But that trickle had a gleam,
a vivid and refreshing sense of life. And those local shops – they were

busy. If local foods and shops are valued, they will survive. If we want them, if we value them, if we enjoy them.

Lewes is on the smooth slopes of the South Downs. One favourite regular walk takes me through a green lane, across a couple of roads, through a cornfield, past a childrens' home, past detached houses with lush gardens, the close, varied knit of the occupied English countryside. And then, suddenly, the Downs rear up, majestic. "Whale-backed", the writer Hilaire Belloc called them, and in a certain light, at dusk, they have that dark massiveness. Each part has its own character: Firle Beacon, like a seductive sloping shoulder; the quiet stretch above Alciston where, in autumn, swallows gather in the shelter of the hill, waiting to set off south; Mount Caburn, where the paragliders seem like huge neon butterflies catching the air currents.

I enjoyed the Downs, like so many, for exercise and relaxation and it took me a while to connect this place with the lamb on my plate. In fact, the clean, lithe, bare form of these hills is due to centuries of grazing sheep. Rabbits are picky eaters, cattle tear the grass up and their weight churns up the soil. But the lighter sheep, nibbling away, have created and maintained the springy downland turf that is so good to walk on, or to lie upon in the summer with a book and a bottle of beer. Even within a single square foot, there can be up to 40 species of plant forming a textured weave. This diversity is due to the constant, indiscriminate munching of the sheep; no single stronger species gets a chance to dominate the other plants. On the warmer southern slopes, chalk grassland too steep to plough up for profitable cereal crops is speckled with wildflowers in the summer. The whites and yellows of spring are joined in high summer by blues and purples of wild thyme, viper's bugloss and the symbol of the Downs, the round-headed rampions which look like asteroid Ascot hats. In the sun, you can smell the wild thyme when you run your hands over the ground.

When I got to know the Downs better, I could see how they had been marked by the presence of sheep over the centuries. Shepherds' tracks, now used by walkers, criss-cross the slopes. Running around the contours are ribbed corrugations where centuries of animals balancing on the incline have nibbled up and down hill. These lines, so noticeable in frost and dew, are said to be the stretch of a sheep's neck apart.

A string of villages sit near the springs at the foot of the Downs. As ever, the names of the local pubs give clues to the past. In Firle, The Ram. At Fulking, near The Shepherd and Dog, is a fountain where the villagers washed their sheeps' fleeces snowy white for market. In St Michael and All Angels church, Berwick, Duncan Grant, Vanessa Bell and Quentin Bell painted an English nativity attended by a South Down sheep, the breed of these hills, with a characteristic teddy-bear face. Instead of gold and myrrh, they have painted a Sussex trug full of carrots and onions that could have been dug from a village vegetable patch. The shepherds in the painting were shepherds in real life and carry the local Pyecombe crook. These shepherds and their huts were a feature of this countryside within living memory.

It was near Lewes, within an aria's swoop of Glyndebourne, that an 18th-century farmer, John Ellman, improved his flock by breeding, giving them better wool and more meat. The result was the South Down breed, which was used in the breeding stock of many sheep around the world. Sheep provided the lightbulbs of the past: strips of sacking were rolled up, dipped in melted sheep fat, or tallow, and hung up to dry up. If you repeated the process up to 25 times, you had a tallow candle. The houses must have smelt like rancid kebab shops.

I lay on a hilltop one day halfway through a walk, watching the sheep move across the opposite slope. They were drawn, like white filings to a magnet, to the extra food the farmer had brought, and I thought of how they animated the landscape, of the millions of sheep that had grazed the Downs and how they wove into the daily lives of the people who lived among them. And stories. I remembered one of a local publican who got drinking with some farmers one market day and woke the next morning as the owner of a flock.

Some 50,000 lambs a year still come off the South Downs area, many from the lower slopes and lowland. Of these, a tiny proportion, less than one per cent, will be the South Downs breed pioneered by John Ellman. Since the 18th century, breeding has been further refined to get the maximum yield of lean meat and lambs. Only a tiny part – three per cent – of the hills is covered in the distinctive Downs chalk grassland.

Thousands of walkers come to the Downs to enjoy the springy turf and wildlife; thousands visit the top of Ditchling Beacon to eat ice-cream or go for a stroll. They are drawn to places as elusive and vulnerable as snow, which are disappearing in the heat of modern life. Most of the rest of this land has been ploughed up for wheat and other subsidised crops. One conservationist I met admitted that there is a beauty to the sweeps of flax and oil-seed rape that stripe the hills like flags, signalling whatever is making the money. But these crops are not always best suited to the land, and the soil needs artificial input to make them grow here. Bit by bit, they take away the character of the place. The old system was to graze sheep upland and then bring them down to be put in pens, or 'folded', on the lowland. Their dung manured the soil and made it fertile for crops. It was a logical but labour-intensive system and it did not survive.

It is not just sheep breeds and land use that have been rationalised; so has the whole food chain. Many of the sheep raised these days on the Downs will go to Wales or Cornwall, or wherever there is another big abattoir with a supermarket contract, to be slaughtered and processed. The lamb you eat in pubs along the South Downs may well have been raised in Wales. There is a transport network that takes Welsh sheep down to the southeast, some to be killed and eaten in England, some to be exported to the Continent. The empty lorries may load up with lambs from the southeast to be slaughtered in the big abattoirs and processing plants in Wales. At such places, the animals enter vast structures at one end and come out chopped up and clingfilmed. From here, the lambs from the South Downs could end up anywhere in the country. There is no way for the consumer to tell where the lamb on the shelf has come from. As far as a customer could tell, they might even end up in the Lewes Tesco.

Throughout the centuries, farming has periodically gone through times of profound change; we are in the middle of one such shift. Farmers are having to get bigger, go part-time or add value to their goods. In the case of meat, this may mean selling direct to the public rather than losing the retailer's cut. Some of the good small local farmers are making a seismic mental leap from farming livestock fed into a big system to becoming food producers selling direct to the public. In the local shops are leaflets advertising half-lambs for the freezer. A farmer with a campsite on his land persuades holiday-makers to take freezer packs home to eat through the winter.

David Burden is a modern Downland shepherd who works as a relief milkman for his day job and keeps 220 South Down sheep and a few cattle in six different places around Petworth, in West Sussex. It is a method of patchwork farming which fits into commuter countryside. "I have to be opportunist," David says. "If someone I know says they want a suitable patch grazing next week, I have to move the sheep to it." At the point were people want to 'discuss terms', he tells them: "I'm one of the virtuous poor and you let me graze your land and feel good." So he keeps going. His family have been in the area since 1327 and his knowledge is rich and resonant.

We go to one of his patches. The old barn with tied beams is all the more beautiful for being a working place, full of the kind of bits and pieces that might come in useful sometime. The sheep graze in a field in front of the Downs, which are furry with trees in this part of West Sussex. David is less of a purist than other South Downs breeders I met: some of his sheep are black, a trait that is frowned on and bred out because black wool can't be dyed different colours and is therefore less valuable. David had a ewe which he thinks produced his black sheep but kept her on because she was so prolific: 14 lambs from six pregnancies.

We drive on, past an old poorhouse built in the 18th century to feed and put to work the poor of 12 Downland parishes, and which was sold recently for a vast sum. We drive to a big house converted into flats, next to which David keeps some more sheep. Range Rovers and commuters in four-wheel drives pass us. Everyone waves and smiles. "People don't see a lot of shepherds round here," says David. Some of the residents apparently check with the local butcher that they are not buying meat that they have seen grazing.

We get on to the vexed question of how David's meat is sold. The local abattoir closed in 1991 and the local livestock markets have all gone. Property is valuable in this part of the world. Smaller-scale, local selling becomes less viable when the distances travelled increase. The net result is that a lot of the best meat produced around here is not sold through shops. Under current regulations, David is allowed to sell an animal alive which can then be killed privately and eaten at home. That meat does not have a health stamp and cannot be sold through a shop. A regional brand for South Down sheep is being developed, which will be a chance for meat produced by people like David to reach the wider public. He is keen for it to work. Schemes like this, he says, originate under pressure; without them, farmers like him face annihilation.

This wider, co-ordinated effort to get lambs from the South Downs area branded and sold locally, to recreate a local market for the meat, comes not from the farming community or supermarkets, but from conservationists. They are worried because plant and animal populations have declined drastically with the disappearance of habitats due to modern farming. It is an intriguing development. The farmer and the conservationist cover the same turf, but come from different cultures. The conservationist wants habitats for wildlife; the farmer wants to produce as efficiently as possible for profit. Yet farmers say they also see themselves as conservationists, as "the guardians of the countryside". It is farmers, after all, they say, who know the land most intimately and who have in their hands its present and future.

Broader forces are also at work. More European Union money is to be shifted from simple production to agri-environment schemes. It will be a slow process, but such subsidies, though still a fraction of the total amount of subsidies, should have more of an impact on how the countryside is farmed. Today, farming and conservation must move closer together. Between them they must find and share common ground if the consumer is to enjoy protected beautiful countryside and local, less-intensively produced food which has taste, identity and pride of place.

Such is the vision. Phil Belden's office at the Sussex Downs Conservation Board has an Ordnance Survey map across one wall, the greens and contours and symbols of the slopes, woods, fields and water of the countryside he covers. He wants to get together a collective of farmers and shops to produce a branded South Downs lamb. The plan reaches into many corners of Sussex. Local landowners with country houses open to the public, for example, can see the potential of selling locally branded lamb to visitors.

Restaurateurs and hoteliers also see a market. In a survey of 23 local butchers and chefs, 22 said their customers were asking for local meat and that they were anxious to find supplies. Some independent butchers already flag up locally produced meat and report good sales. Even with a premium price, there are plenty of people, post-BSE, who want to feed their children and themselves with meat that has an identity and a provenance. Ten million people live within an hour's drive of the South Downs, the nearest you can get to a proper open space in the southeast. Phil Belden is convinced that if these people really made the link between this landscape and the sheep, they would want to buy the South Downs brand.

It sounds like an attractive proposition. The scale of the project is initially ambitious: not to have a few niche products but to get into the supermarkets. Phil needs bigger sales to ensure a viable future for the Downs as sheep-producing countryside, yet the stumbling blocks to the scheme are huge. What he faces is nothing less than a whole system of food production that is now geared to the big boys. "We're a yacht in the English Channel facing an oil tanker," Phil says. "We've got to move from being a yacht to being a motorboat, at least, so we can draw up alongside it and shout. Otherwise we'll just be knocked over."

His work continues. And in other parts of the country, other schemes are starting up. It could be the beginning of a movement to keep English farming going in the landscapes such farmers helped to create. By investigating the provenance of the lamb available and trying to find South Downs meat, a consumer in the South Downs plays his or her part in keeping alive the distinctiveness of the area.

6 growing and farming

EARLY ON IN MY
TRAVELS, AFTER WALKING
AROUND FIELDS AND
INVESTIGATING HOW
FOOD WAS GROWN, I
WANTED TO GO BACK TO
MY ROOTS, LITERALLY.
WITH MY PARTNER
GORDON, I STARTED TO
KEEP AN ALLOTMENT...

EARLY ON IN MY TRAVELS, after walking around fields and investigating how food was grown, I wanted to go back to my roots, literally. With my partner, Gordon, I started to keep an allotment while we were still living in London. It was our chaotic first attempt at growing. The first day, feeling far too clean and shiny, we went to see a friend who had kept a plot on the site for a couple of years. He gave us some leeks with luxuriant green tops and then we walked to our patch. It was a neighbourhood without walls, where everyone's business was open to view.

At that time of year, mid-March, many of the allotments seemed to share the same features: horse manure and straw, leeks, perennial herbs and a few winter greens. The sky was blank as sugar-paper and the ground sullen. Yet, even now, every plot had its own personality. You could tell there must be an old BT phone factory nearby because a number of improvised greenhouses were made out of dismantled phone booths, the discarded corporate logo on the plastic hovering like a protecting angel over seedlings as they warmed in the shelter. Our plot was a mess, with brambles and a big, mysterious mound. There seemed to be a lot of pieces of crockery in the earth and I wondered if we were digging over remains from the Blitz. Bits of bone fertilised my sprouting imagination. For the most part, it was a straightforward, down-to-earth pleasure we found that day, weeding our patch, with the smell of the soil as we worked outside.

Over the coming months, the allotment emerged as a place different from the rest of London life; nobody walked past without acknowledgement, and we never left without bagfuls of food – mostly, it must be said, grown by other people, who were unfailingly generous about giving us produce – and tips. Our own successes were a source of pride and joy: there is a photo of me holding a wonky, earthy parsnip aloft as if it were a school swimming trophy. We listened to all the advice of our neighbours; all the vegetable gossip of this old-fashioned street. But growing, like cooking, is best learned by experience. The day came to dig up our first potatoes. Gordon pushed down on the "T" of the pitchfork handle to detonate an explosion of earth; a rough dozen of dirty diamonds flew from the ground. A good scrub, a pan of salted water and we ate them simply that night with butter. A mealy creaminess spread through my mouth, so dense with flavour that every forkful craved attention. It was one of the best platefuls I had ever eaten.

The allotment affected my *Eating England* trips in three main ways: I went out of my way to find freshness, I became more interested in the detail of how things were grown, and I was more appreciative of the growers.

Organic producers tend to be easier to meet than conventional farmers. They have had to evolve an ethos of direct selling because the distribution systems of supermarkets don't suit small-scale growers any more than they do those who raise livestock on a small scale. Organic food does not use the sprays that limit spoilage and increase shelf-life. While conventionally farmed food can be shifted around depots and bought fortnightly to sit around the house without going off, organic food is more alive in every respect – including its potential to decay. A swift supply chain is therefore imperative to capitalize on the freshness and flavour of food that has not been artificially treated to last a long time. For the consumer, buying organic may mean adapting the way you shop, but you will know when food is really fresh, because it shows when it isn't. After a while, you start to feel suspicious of produce that does not go off.

Jan and Tim Deane were pioneers in England of bringing organic foods fresh to local people, direct from the producer. They live far down deep lanes, directly in the cleavage of bosomy Devon hills. To make a living, they eventually realised they needed to build up a local network of regular, committed custom. The answer came from an idea used in the US: vegetable boxes. In 1991, they began to produce weekly boxes, good enough to make people radically rethink their shopping habits. They grew melons, celeriac, squashes and other produce to make the boxes interesting and varied. Two hundred customers bought boxes from them, within a ten-mile radius of their land.

Since the Deanes started their business, vegetable boxes have become a movement. More growers' co-operatives have formed. Increasingly, veggie boxes are bought by people who are engaged by the whole argument of local production versus large corporations, and who want to buy less, or not at all, from supermarkets. Grahame Hughes, in Bunwell Street near Diss in Norfolk, now sells around 500 vegetable boxes a week. From the end of June to the end of March, everything possible is sourced locally: in his boxes he packs very fresh greens, beans, mange-tout, spinach, broccoli, cabbage, carrots, onions and other vegetables alongside fruit grown in England, as well as imported oranges, grapes and lemons.

As well as buying in from local suppliers, he grows tomatoes in big glasshouses behind his packing hut. Right at the start, he grew organic tomatoes for a supermarket. The first year, at the height of the season, he got one swift phone call that simply cancelled his whole order because the stores were over-supplied. His carefully grown tomatoes, £1,500 worth, were left on the vine ready to rot. Vegetable boxes have kept people like Graham going. Because he knows roughly what the demand will be, he can plan what he grows. Now his business is less subject to the decisions of large, distant masters.

Matthew and Louise Unwin, at Longwood Farm in Tuddenham St Mary, Suffolk, were mainstream farmers growing carrots, onions and potatoes for supermarkets and a large oven-chip manufacturer. They sprayed before planting, they sprayed during growth and they sprayed after harvesting so the crops would not spoil in storage. At a certain point, Louise realised she did not want to feed her own children with the food the farm produced.

Matthew's reasons for going organic were hard-headed. He saw that the trend was for bigger and bigger farms and that he was on the bottom rung of the ladder and had no control over the prices he got for his produce. The Unwins became organic and set up three shops – one on the farm and two in Spitalfields Market in East London – which allowed them to stay a relatively small operation and yet retain some control over production and price.

When conventional farms become organic, the high-maintenance blonde of chemical agriculture turns into a woman who must speak for herself. The Unwins' land is on Breckland Heath, where the light soil needs a good fertilising boost to produce vegetables. When they became organic, the land would not support such a greedy crop, and they started to keep livestock, principally chickens and pigs, with some sheep. As well as providing meat, the animals fertilised the fields with their manure; on this land could grow barley for animal feed and to sell, and lucerne to further enrich the soil. You can see where the chicken huts have been because the crops spring up most vigorously in rectangles all over the field.

Organic farming is labour intensive and skillful. Every day, the Unwins have to put the chickens into their huts; a friend who has large poultry-production units can stand in her kitchen monitoring a computerized control panel that automatically adjusts the humidity or air supply as necessary. Neighbouring farmers thought the Unwins' sheep would have a lot of problems without the standard 'six-in-one' vaccine, a preventative shot against six potential problems. If the Unwins' sheep get a particular disease, they deal with it individually, as it comes up, which means they have to keep a sharp eye on the animals.

Matthew says he now thinks far more about the long-term effects of chemicals on the land. As a boy, he saw farming become more intensive and reliant on new technology. His father kept pigs outdoors, then indoors. Now Matthew has come full circle and the pigs are once more rooting around in the mud. He believes the old skills should be maintained, in a 'back-to-the-future' approach, so that there is an alternative method of production, should the intensive approach prove to be unsustainable.

The name of one particular farm was familiar to me from the milk I had been buying for a couple of years. Manor Farm milk, read the cartons, made in Dorset. Some organic milk and dairy products are imported or part of a large conglomerate. My milk clearly came from a particular place and I was curious to understand more about what I was buying every day. Manor Farm in Godmanstone is run by Pam and Will Best, who turned organic in the mid-1980s, having run their farm conventionally for 15 years. During the conventional years, the annual delivery of fertiliser arrived and was dumped in a corner of the farmyard; over the year they dragged the blue bags up to the fields to put on the ground. "It felt artificial," says Pam. At the time, a craze for aerial spraying of crops coincided with a rash of sore throats in the valley. The Bests, like the Unwins, had young children, who focused their mind on the world they were handing on, and the immediate health of their offspring.

The Manor Farm packaging is not adorned by cartoon cows but by photographic images of grass and clover. Clovers fix their own nitrogen in the soil and boost fertility. They are not easy to grow, but if you nurture them, they reward you with productivity. Clover is at the heart of the business. The farm is in West Dorset in a valley north of Dorchester. It is not a rich place in terms of agriculture; the land is 'hungry': low in phosphates and with poor topsoil. In order to farm organically, the Bests had to build up the microflora and fauna in the soil to make it as rich as possible without artificial input. Instead of treating the earth like anonymous blotting paper, they had to find varieties of grasses, herbs, and other plants, in addition to clover, to maximise the soil's natural potential.

Besides the cows, the Bests grow Maris Widgeon, a long-straw variety of wheat that is favoured by local thatchers (organic straw lasts well). Each year, a team builds the wheat into ricks the height of a house. The sheaves are laid almost horizontally and built up in a spiral pattern, so that each rick-structure is upright, with the stalks kept straight for the thatchers. The ricks stand at the top of one field: simple, practical, almost monumental, unofficial land art whose beauty is in its functionality as well as in its aesthetics. The fields are peaceful places to walk around, full of life.

The Bests' wheat is sold to a mill near Shaftesbury, and some of it returns in the form of organic wholewheat loaves sold by Leakers bakery in nearby Bridport. The Bests have brought other obvious benefits to the valley. They encouraged another couple, Hugh and Patsy Chapman, who grow organic vegetables, to settle in the area, and sold them a field. The vegetables they grow are sold via a box scheme, at a very tempting stall by the farm and at Dorchester's farmers' market in Poundbury.

Milk is even more perishable than vegetables. The relentless daily production means that there is not much slack in the lives of the Bests. Diversifying and keeping a mixed farm that relies on fewer chemicals multiply the skills and documentation required. Pam describes weekends as "a chance to catch up with paperwork". Organic producers like the Bests have had to build up their own ways of making, branding and selling their products. The care they take is evident at every stage, from the way the animals are treated with homeopathy to the way the milk is pasteurised but not homogenised, thereby keeping more of the micronutrients that make it special.

When you buy Manor Farm milk, do you know or care about the skills, the risks, the ricks, the quality of the soil, the careful pasteurisation, the homeopathic treatments, the independence, the valley's association with organic produce? When you know a bit more about the places and people, when you fully appreciate what you have bought, food loses its blandness and anonymity. There is a greater degree of trust and pleasure to be gained from buying from good producers in this way.

It is worth saying that the Bests sell some of their milk through Waitrose – that's where I discovered it – and this has been an important part of their trade. Waitrose gives them credibility as producers that has attracted other business. Pam says the buyers who come to the farm don't just visit the dairy; they want to walk around the fields, getting to the heart of what organic farming is all about.

On the other hand, buying organic or, that difficult category to define unless you have local knowledge, 'nearly/uncertified organic' from a farm shop or a farmers' market is about getting local, seasonal produce at its peak. You get a chance to see where the food grows or who grows it. Many producers go out of their way to encourage you to look around, organise farm walks and produce leaflets and newsletters. They are often delightful places to visit. At Marshford Organics in Northam, near Bideford in Devon, the air was alive with bird-song. It would be hard to buy food fresher than the produce grown and sold here. Vanessa Ebdon, who runs Marshford with her husband, Dave, gets a lot of cooks coming to the shop because they appreciate freshness. Perry Court, another farm shop (non-organic) in Bilting, near Ashford in Kent, had three tables of apples when I visited. Over the season they sell a hundred different varieties. The room smelt attractively musty like my Grannie's shed. Heidi Fermor, the owner, is developing a seasonal database so she can let the local papers know when the new varieties are out.

Some organic producer shops have noticed a fall in custom as the supermarkets have gone into organics. This is a serious threat. It is the smaller, independent shops that operate on the right scale to show a commitment to the web of local grass-roots operators and co-operatives. I have been less than impressed by the wan imports I have seen in supermarkets, compared to the sappy vitality of produce gathered in by smaller operations with local contacts. Demand for organic produce outstrips native supply, but as the bigger buyers move in, will the movement keep its principles? The word 'organic' may seem like a lifeline in stormy seas, but not if the concept gets watered down. The answer is to buy as locally or as close to the point of production as possible, or to find a shop, or box scheme, run by people whose standards and approach you trust.

People who live in the midst of farmland describe the gradual deadening of the air as the birdlife disappeared from the 1970s onwards, an eerie sort of silence that you could identify only if you had known the life before. The decline of farmland birds has coincided with the rise of intensive agriculture. Pesticides, herbicides, the removal of hedges and other farming practices lead to the loss of habitat and feed. Many blame modern farming practices for the decline of species such as the skylark that are held as quintessentially English. From the car, you may see cows in green grass. Perennial rye grass, to give an example, has spread across English fields. Boosted by fertilizers, it grows so vigorously it does not allow competition from other grasses and may be cut for silage several times a year, before the seeds form. This efficiency has resulted in less food for insects, which in turn provide food for the birds. Not so green, this grass.

The Royal Society for the Protection of Birds has the second biggest membership of any charity in the UK. More than a million people take an active interest in birds in this country. Yet, day after day, these same people may unwittingly buy produce which could, indirectly, be detrimental to the bird life they wish to support. Can you imagine the consumer power if the switch clicked and people made the connection?

In the past, the RSPB has lobbied for environmental schemes which concentrated on the field margins. They have supported grants for hedges and 'conservation headlands', the unsprayed, unplanted stretches at the edge of fields. The impact of these schemes remains, not surprisingly, marginal. The society is now getting more interested in the rest of the field. In a project with potentially far-reaching consequences, the RSPB has bought a typical lowland arable farm in Cambridgeshire to investigate whether adjustments to mainstream farming methods can increase bird life.

The history of Hope Farm, as the trial farm is called, charts the changes in agriculture in the 20th century. It started as a mixed farm. The livestock fertilised the ground for crops; the crops fed the livestock. The excess produced from this self-supporting system — the meat, the eggs, the milk, the crops — were sold. Since the Second World War, farming became increasingly specialised. First the dairy cows went (in fact, before the war), followed by the pigs and chickens. A small beef herd survived until the 1980s, but then it went, too.

From Victorian times to the 1950s the farmland was roughly a third permanent pasture, a third temporary grassland and a third arable. Now it is almost purely arable, growing whatever subsidies encourage: currently oil-seed rape and wheat that will go into manufactured bakery goods. About 90 per cent of all the work is done in three months of the year — July, August and September — when one crop is harvested and the next sown. Up to a dozen people used to work the land, but now it takes just one; other work is contracted out, with labour and equipment shared between farms to lower costs. You can see why agriculture has gone the way it has: efficiency is a much-prized quality, not least by the farmer who reaps the profits. Yet we have also reached a point at which we are questioning whether efficiency is everything — or even sustainable in the longer term.

The RSPB hopes to discover at Hope Farm exactly how farming

affects bird life and how to reverse the decline in numbers. In one experiment, small patches of fields have been left unsown to see if the openings will attract skylarks in to nest, without causing weed problems or substantially lowering yields. In another, they are reducing the amount of ploughing (which, after all, means less work for the farmer) to see if leaving more seed on the ground helps keep birds alive over winter. Time will tell whether these experiments will be successful, and whether they will then influence other farmers. But like other agri-environment schemes, the project signals a shift in the focus of farming from pure productivity.

As producers start to show more shades of green, environmentalists are taking a closer look at production. Tim Beech manages two sites for English Nature on the South Downs. One of them, Mount Caburn, is the Iron Age hill fort where I would lie watching paragliders catch the air currents. One side of the fence is a conservation area where Tim grazes sheep to maintain the grassland and its swathes of wildflowers: purple scabious, sheep's bit, autumn gentian, bird's foot trefoil, the round-headed rampion, wild marjoram, thyme that you smell as you walk or sit down looking at the view. On the other side of the fence is a field which is simply mown once a year; some flowers grow here, but nothing like the same lush spring of life on the ground where I lie dreaming. Tim is one of the conservationists who would like to move further towards farming, to combine conservation of the South Downs with selling the sheep for profit. "Chalk Downland was produced by farming, and in a sense it needs to be maintained by farming," he says.

What Tim Beech is doing on Mount Caburn is known as

conservation grazing. The aim is to use animals – ponies as well as sheep and cattle – to keep unfarmed land of environmental interest clear of scrub. Volunteers or conservation workers may be able to come onto a site only once or twice a year to clear the ground, if at all, but an animal can graze constantly.

Bill Grayson is another conservation grazer in Silverdale, a beautiful slip of land which lies north of Morecambe Bay in Lancashire, so called because the limestone flashes white in outcrops amid the woodland. On a still night, the moon turns the bay into a silver mirror. Bill keeps sheep on the shoreline and cattle on the fields above. Even more of a challenge, he also keeps cattle on Warton Crag, a bit of limestone that is a nature reserve and a popular place for walking. In the past, sheep and goats would have grazed the land, but it has been largely ungrazed for 50 years; as a result, it is overgrown with scrub and bracken. Bill has put five cattle on the ground in an attempt to keep the place under control.

The Crag is a jungle, head-high with bracken, and it is about as different from a plain green field as you can get. Finding the cattle felt at first a little like a Lancastrian version of hacking through the Congo. It is easy to see the difference the animals make. The first patch we went through, which had been fenced off to keep the cattle out, was just a mass of scrub with dead bracken litter below. Where the cattle had been allowed to feed, niches had opened up and, as we walked, wild strawberries and violets peeked through by our feet.

The violets are the food of the caterpillars of the rare High Brown Fritillary butterfly. The plants need light to grow, away from the shade of the bracken; the caterpillars need the violets if, later, the butterfly is to dance, bright chestnut, around Warton Crag in the summer. When Bill and I reached the cattle among the undergrowth a sudden swarm of flies buzzed in a swirl, attracted to a fresh cow-pat. Bill came up with a delectable statistic: each animal can produce, every year, 20 per cent of its body weight in insects by providing them with dung for food. The insects, in turn, are food for birds. Violets, caterpillars, butterflies, insects, birds, cattle: such are the connections made possible by bringing animals back to the Crag.

There are problems with this kind of grazing. The cattle must browse the bushes and the ground rather than solidly munching their way across a field. Bill is not quite sure why the animals do not eat the poisonous bracken, but thinks it is probably because there is a relatively low number of animals per acre and so they are not forced to eat everything. He also goes out regularly to give them supplementary feed and check on the animals' well-being.

You need a strong instinct for conservation to be bothered, and he admits that people who tend to come into conservation grazing, do it for a while and stop, to be replaced by others. On the other hand, Bill doesn't pay rent for the land and he gets some subsidies for converting the land to organic. He sells the meat from home, to people who come from across the country to visit this beautiful spot and take home a freezer pack. And he is paid for conservation work. For Bill, it is a question of juggling several sources of income. It is a labour-intensive, complicated way to make a living, but it is possible.

An advantage for the consumer is that many conservation grazers favour native breeds, which were bred to be raised slowly on a diet of grass. Continental breeds such as Charolais and Limousin came into favour because they can grow big quickly by being fed barley. Native breeds such as the Devon Ruby, Sussex, Aberdeen Angus and Welsh Black accumulate a greater flavour and succulence than the fast-grown, lean beef of Continental breeds. British scientists have found that meat from grass-fed animals has more flavour and higher levels of fatty acids, which have proven health benefits for consumers. As Prof Jeff Woods of Bristol University concludes, what a marketing opportunity for British farming.

One place that gives a vision of how things used to be is the Parsonage Down National Nature Reserve on the edge of Salisbury Plain. Visiting there feels like taking a step back in time. The land was acquired by the Nature Conservancy Council after the farmer died without descendants in 1989, aged 93. He had run it as a traditional mixed farm when other farmers in the district had turned to arable crops. It is like a prairie, with cloud shadows moving over the wide open spaces. The main surprise is the sheer quantity of wildlife: not one sparrow-hawk but four; not just a few birds but big flocks; acres of wildflowers. The chalk landscape, fine and smooth as china, has 150 species of plants, including fields full of orchids flowering in late spring and early summer. The 300 acres of grassland comprise 80 per cent herbs and 20 per cent grasses. The air is alive with swallows.

Roger Marris, who farms the land to maintain its flora and fauna, says the place changes from week to week with the flowers. He grazes England's oldest breeding herd of native Longhorn cattle, which are amazing-looking beasts with horns curved round almost like a bone bob: Mary Quant bangs crossed with African warriors. There is clearly a market for such special meat; marketing it properly would help ensure the future of this special place. A good rate of production has not yet become the priority of conservationists, however.

On the other side of the fence surrounding Parsonage Farm is an area that has not been managed. The grazed side is full of flowers; the other is thorn, gorse and scrubby wilderness.

So much for birds and flowers. But what about people? One of the most beautiful places in England is the Lake District. Even against the scale of the soaring fells, it is impossible not to notice the sheep that dot the slopes. You notice them in a different way when you learn how they are farmed and when you feel the vulnerability of this tradition – and when you realise how a way of life that produces good meat can be sustained if we make closer connections between what we eat and a specific environment.

The sheep breed of the Lakes is the Herdwick. Beatrix Potter was a keen Herdwick farmer and left her land to the National Trust on condition that Herdwicks continued to graze there. The story goes that they are descended from a flock of 40 sheep that were washed ashore from a Norweigan vessel wrecked off the coast in the 10th century. Their name comes from the Old Norse, *herd-vik*, meaning sheep farm, and the double meaning of the word is appropriate. Flocks are 'hefted' to a particular farm: that is, they have a homing instinct which brings them back there after free-ranging over the fells. Flocks are sold along with the farm as a living part of the capital of a place. Gathering in the sheep, for shearing and so forth, involves days of covering the slopes. The sheepdogs are trained not to rush the animals over difficult terrain and to keep an eye on the sheep without losing their own footing on the crags. It is a very tough, skillful tradition of farming. Those who follow this way of life currently continue it under immense pressure.

Hill-farm incomes have sunk so low that the farmers in the Lakes, even before foot-and-mouth, were facing a period of "restructuring", a word that has a sinister ring. The farms could get bigger and spread the fixed costs: one way to cope with declining profits is expansion. Or they could produce less and, by joining agri-environment schemes, get compensation for having fewer sheep – there is concern about over-grazing on the fells. Neither option is straightforward. The majority of farms have common fell grazing: there are 20 to 30 farmers, for example, with grazing rights on the fell Blencathra. It is difficult to get all parties to agree. Another approach is to add value to the sheep by marketing the breed and selling directly to the consumer. This involves a big mental change: farmers see themselves as breeders and farmers, not as meat producers. Ten years ago, when this idea was suggested, it met with a frosty reception, but now its time has come. It has to come.

I went to two farms which are at the forefront of direct selling. Joe and Hazel Relph are at Yew Tree Farm, in Rosthwaite in Borrowdale, on the route of the coast-to-coast walk near the Cumbrian way and right in the centre of extremely beautiful countryside. Hazel has already diversified, as tradition goes, into farmhouse bed and breakfast. She has also opened the unfrilly Flock-In Tearoom, where she serves such food as delicious Herdi burgers made from their Herdwicks, homemade mint and rosemary jelly, Borrowdale tea bread and pints of tea. She has three women baking to keep her in cheese, bacon and chive scones. "We are farming tourists," she said, with her dry-stone wit. The Relphs sell their meat fresh from the tearoom and by post, and through Hodgson's butcher's in Keswick, which sells meat from within a five-mile radius of the shop.

Joe farms 650 acres of enclosed land and has grazing rights on
800 acres of fell. He gets the sheep in for five main gathers: lambing
(April), shearing (July), spaining, or taking the lambs away from their
mothers (late September), autumn dipping (October), and tupping
(late November). The only way to get them in is on foot, which can
mean walking 20 miles in a day. The farming traditions have not
changed for centuries for a reason: there is no other way to do it.
Joe gets up at 5am in lambing time and, for eight weeks, finishes
around 11pm. It is rare, even in the dark of winter, for Joe not to
have a 12-hour day: he is out even more in winter to check on
the animals.

There are only two families in the valley with offspring to take
over from their parents. The Relph's own daughter has decided not
to continue. Joe has seen the pressures on his way of life mount up.
The paperwork has become enormous and the returns have shrunk.
He is worried that younger people will not see a future in farming
on the fells. Property prices are high – so many of the houses now
are non-farming holiday homes – and you have to pay for a quota
to keep sheep. Will the people prepared to learn the skills be able to
afford to take on the farms? There are many stories of older farmers
putting off retirement because there is nobody to take over. Joe is
worried about richer farmers coming into what they think is an
idyllic way of life without the knowledge, skills and stamina to do
the job. The risk is that they will run down the flocks. If a flock with
a hefting instinct goes, the traditional way of running that farm
suffers a body blow.

Eric and Sue Taylforth are based in dramatic, rugged Great
Langdale. Eric describes getting the sheep off his terrain as "like
trying to gather a pepperpot: they can run off any side". They can

go up hundreds of feet, drop hundreds – and then go up again. The Taylforths have also suffered from falling prices (though these low prices do not seem to be passed on to the consumer) and have taken matters into their own hands. Eric tried to persuade the chef at a local timeshare operation to buy local, but he continued with New Zealand lamb. Then he took it to the Britannia Inn, a good pub in Elterwater, where Eric's lamb was put on the menu as "Langdale Herdwick lamb reared on the fells at Millbeck Farm" and became a best-seller. Staff take bets on how long it will take to sell out: the record is 40 minutes. Eric sells to other local restaurants and gets his animals slaughtered at a small abattoir, Airey's, which is more of a farm than a factory. I stayed at the Taylforth's bed and breakfast and ate some of the meat for supper. It tastes exceptional, especially the fat, which has an entirely different quality and length of flavour from the run-of-the-mill lamb.

"I would like to see us, in the next five years, selling 50 per cent of our own stuff," Eric says, referring to the way farmers are starting to sell directly these days. "We have got to change. We can't carry on with the way it is going." He has seen a dramatic change in the people coming to the area. Twenty years ago, most of those who came to the Taylforth's dale were climbers who never spent much money. Now there are visitors with large disposable incomes who want to know where their meat is from, especially for their children. Eric is working out how to sell using the internet, and noticing that people will now drive further or make more of an effort to get good meat. It seems only right that the millions of people who come to the Lakes should support and enjoy a prime product of the area.

If Herdwicks are the product of the particular farming conditions of the fells, the peculiarities of geography give Wakefield a very different tradition. In a natural frost-pocket are the rhubarb forcing sheds of Yorkshire. The crowns of rhubarb are grown outdoors before being taken indoors to grow quickly in the warmth. These dark sheds are as eerie as goblin caves, the silence broken by the soft 'pop' of the leaves unfurling from buds. Lit by candles, rhubarb sheds carry the atmosphere of underground work. The low ceilings were once kept up by pit props and the rhubarb was kept warm with the coal from this mining area. Shoddy, a waste product of the local wool industry, is still used as a fertiliser. It all fits into the area, especially when you step outside in freezing February and hear that rhubarb flourishes in Siberia. Forced rhubarb has brought this English taste back into vogue and its bright-pink stems bring native colour to a dim time of year. There are now tours of the sheds between January and March.

I wanted to look at other fruit and vegetables we eat and, in particular, one that is a staple of the English home: frozen peas. Peas start to lose their sweetness the moment they are picked. At the Birds Eye Lowestoft freezing plant at harvest time, the control room is like a sci-fi B-movie version of NASA. Banks of computer screens flash up pea-green times and figures. For 50 days of the year, the operation runs 24 hours, seven days a week to bring in the pea harvest, ever monitored by the tick of the clock. The mission: to get the peas from field to frozen within two-and-a-half hours. The lorry drivers talk to each other on CB radios about traffic conditions; the worst days are the wet ones when the holiday-makers do not go to the beach but drive around looking for something to do. Peas drum down like green rain: go, go, go. A loading container was developed so that the first peas picked would be first to be frozen, saving vital minutes. If one batch comes too late, the peas are downgraded and sold more cheaply (about five per cent a year). Time is sweetness; time is money.

The East Anglian and East Yorkshire farmers like growing peas as part of the rotation of their crops because they fix nitrogen in the soil and make the land more productive. When I arrived at a field near Norwich to see the harvest, half the field had been picked and the breeze smelled of just-picked peas. After a couple of days it smells sour; from the moment the pea is picked, a process of decay sets in. Immediately after a field is harvested, locals arrive with plastic bags to get any pickings that the harvesting machine has missed.

The trick is to pick the peas when they are just ripe. Before dawn, David, a field manager, walks through the plants in a semi-random zig-zag line, taking samples as he goes. He squeezes a pea between finger and thumb to see if it shoots out of the skin like a bullet (too hard) or squidges just the right amount. The sample is then tested by the comically named 'Tenderometer' in the factory, to back up his 'finger-test' results. If the field is ready to go, a viner – the pea equivalent of a combine harvester – goes to work. The machine strips the pods off the plants with spikes and scoops them into a rotating drum, a bit like a spin dryer, which tumbles the pods so they are bashed open but the fragile peas inside are not crushed. The peas drop through holes in the drum and the opened pods fall behind the viner like cuttings behind a lawn-mower. These are left as green manure or used as silage by the farmer. The peas then fall in a green gush from viner to lorry and are taken straight away to the freezing factory. What makes this harvest unusual is that everything is controlled from the factory; it is the factory that gives the signal for the picking to start, as soon as there is the capacity to freeze the peas within the allotted time.

Frozen peas are useful because they catch the sweetness of the pea before it disappears. I was intrigued, going around the factory, to catch the scent at the stage when the peas are part-cooked to kill the enzymes. This is a distinctive smell that I associate with packet peas. Some of the peas I have bought from greengrocers have been disappointing because they are not so sweet, though they do not have the slightly sterilised taste of the frozen ones. Precious but rare, unless you are a grower yourself, is the experience of eating peas straight off the plant. I ate some in the walled Norfolk garden of an exceptional organic grower called Pat Kemp. The flavour stopped me in my tracks. You do not know all aspects of the words 'sweet', 'green' and 'pea' until you have sampled peas fresh from the garden.

One of the problems English growers face is the challenge from overseas. Birds Eye frozen peas may not be organic but at least they are still grown in England, at a time when the cheaper land and labour costs of other countries encourage imports. This is a huge challenge for British farmers. Orchards still spread over Kent, but when you hear that Chile and China, with their cheap land and labour, are planting up vast areas of apple trees, you start to fear for the future of our home crop. English apples are unusual because the growing conditions here are marginal compared to the climates of other countries. Our apples grow more slowly but this is part of what gives them their taste. We have specialised in Cox's Orange Pippin, an aromatic, cream-fleshed variety that is relatively difficult to grow, but which has a superb flavour.

There was a great flowering of apple varieties in Victorian England, thanks to nurserymen producing for specialised production rather than for the mass market. They wanted to excite the eye and the palate by creating fruit with ruby-red skins, or flesh that tasted of pineapple. Apple breeding involves a certain amount of luck, since the progeny of the pips from an apple will not be identical. If a good variety appears, it is propagated by grafting rather than growing from the pips. In Australia in the 19th century, so one story goes, Anne Smith, who had emigrated from Sussex, threw some apples into a creek. A couple of decades later she ate the fruit from a seedling she found growing there. The family founded an orchard on this tree and from there a business which eventually took the apple around the world: Granny Smith. Many of our older varieties are now seen as 'uncommercial' – that is, they are not suitable for mass production. These apples were developed to suit particular areas with particular soils and growing conditions. In a less artificial world, these qualities could be useful. And who knows what will be needed out of the gene pool in the future? Brogdale, the National Fruit Collection near Faversham in Kent, keeps and promotes a huge 'library' of fruit, with more than 2,500 varieties of apple alone on show.

East Malling in Kent is one of the most famous horticultural research stations in the world because around 75 per cent of the world's rootstocks for apple production came originally from the breeding and selection programme developed here. They are constantly trialling new varieties. The centre was set up by fruit growers who pooled resources to develop new varieties for the commercial market. At the moment it takes between 20 and 25 years to get an apple onto the market, between 12 and 15 years for a raspberry and seven to nine years for a strawberry. Each year around 13,000 strawberry seedlings are planted as potential varieties. These will be gradually whittled down, through progressive tests and field trials, to one or two.

You begin to see why breeders' eyes light up at the mention of genetic modification technology: it offers a box of tricks which can cut the time this process takes substantially. Part of the process of picking fruit varieties is taste trials, which routinely include representatives from big buyers such as supermarkets. Tasting is subjective and notoriously hard to monitor, but if one variety provokes dissent – if one person loves it and another hates it – it will be dropped. Buyers are after consensus. Above all, the fruit must be commercially viable. Home gardeners benefit from the fall-out of the trialling process: some varieties that are deemed uncommercial for big growers nonetheless make it onto the market for gardeners who care about flavour rather than how the fruit will withstand transport and storage.

East Malling is trying to find ways for our fruit growers to survive in a global market. They are looking at niche markets, which will add value and quality to offset higher production costs – for example, more sophisticated forms of pest control for organic apples. They mentioned other work, being carried out in Holland, which considered other aspects of orchards: the environmental benefits and the way they fit into the rural economy.

I went to see Peter Hall, a Kent grower who grows organic and conventional hops and a 100 acres of fruit – again, organic and conventional – using some of the state-of-the-art pest control which is coming into farming. He also builds up an income from environmental farming with grants for stewardship of the land: planting hedges, digging ponds, looking after footpaths and so on. His land is near a village, Marden, with a railway station and there are plenty of commuter-belt families in the area who want to go for walks in the countryside at the weekend.

Across one of the fields is the Millennium Avenue, created by each of the village groups planting a tree. I walked around here, sheep on one side, a pear orchard on the other, trees, wildflowers and the ruffled blue ridge of Kent's wooded horizon as a backdrop. Many of the Kent hop fields have gone, but not here. It felt like a particular type of beauty had been saved by a viable modern form of farming that offers a number of values other than pure quantity of production.

Our soft fruit is a bit safer from competition from imports than orchard fruit because it is more difficult to transport. Raspberries, for example, have to be ripe before they can be picked and have a particularly short shelf life – one reason you see fewer raspberries on sale than crisp, dull imported strawberries ("nice if you like carrots," as an English grower said to me). After the raspberries destined to be sold fresh are harvested by hand, machines vibrate and shake off the rest. The fruit that falls is even riper; perhaps this explains why raspberry jam often seems to have more taste than other kinds.

The raspberry has evaded mass production and early picking. Not so the strawberry. The origin of the modern strawberry is an example of a global mixture: the large South American strawberry was crossed with the delicious little Virginian strawberry by a botanist in France in the 19th century. English market gardeners then improved this hybrid to form the basis of most modern varieties. Spanish strawberries, grown quickly and picked slightly underripe so they travel better, will never compete with the taste of the locally grown crop. Kent and Worcestershire became centres for strawberry production because the land was suitable and because they were close to the markets of London and Birmingham.

New markets are opening up to that vital and all-too-neglected aspect of food: flavour. I spoke to one strawberry producer in Kent, Stephen Wellbrook, who has gone for a specialist market including wild strawberries and old-fashioned varieties. The Cambridge Vigour variety he grows is very juicy and it is the texture that is the biggest surprise. They were bursting with succulence and generosity: like a soft, juicy, delicious kiss. Stephen's wild strawberries are picked with great care; it is a very labour-intensive and expensive process. Within their four-day shelf-life, some are flown across the Atlantic to be picked at by the sleek rich of the film industry at Universal Studios.

These strawberries occupy an interesting niche. In French markets, particularly delicious strawberries are labelled by variety and sold at a premium. Wouldn't it be wonderful if the same could happen here? There are signs of greater interest in labelling by variety; you could describe it as a sort of 'branding with meaning'. The more consumers care about flavour, freshness and the environment, the more breeders, sellers and restaurants will respond.

The outbreak of foot-and-mouth disease in 2001 exposed many of the underlying issues about farming to a wider public. The RSPCA had long campaigned against the excessive transportation of live animals, for example by speculating dealers and, more generally, because so many abattoirs have closed down due to the costs of implementing regulations after BSE. Foot-and-mouth made such issues headline news. It remains to be seen if this outbreak, and so much of the surrounding debate about environmental issues and rural policy, will be a catalyst for positive change. Hold on to one fact: policy-making can seem so far away, but as consumers we vote with our money.

7 food producers

PRODUCING REALLY
GOOD FOOD – BE IT
PORK PIES, FUDGE,
PICKLED ONIONS OR
BREAD – IS LIKE ANY
OTHER CRAFT. A GREAT
AMOUNT OF CARE,
EFFORT AND SKILL
GOES INTO IT.

PRODUCING REALLY GOOD FOOD – be it pork pies, fudge, pickled onions or bread – is like any other craft. A great amount of care, effort and skill goes into it: the materials must be right; every step of production needs supervision, judgement and correct technique. Good producers use knowledge and skills that may have accumulated over generations. The end result will be more interesting than something that has been mass produced. It will also cost more. The central question is how much we appreciate what goes into good food and see 'value for money' rather than 'cheap' and 'expensive'.

After a couple of years of interviewing smaller producers, I came to have a great respect for their endeavours and achievements and have also become fascinated by what keeps them going. They are often in beautiful places, working with the land, using interesting raw materials. They are generally self-employed or part of a small, personal business. But how do they cope with the bureaucratic obstacles that are particularly onerous for the small operator? The craft-food producer's work often requires two contrasting qualities: a dynamic, alert intelligence and a patient, painstaking diligence. Any number of university degrees are put to nurturing the earthy practicalities of food production. What motivates them?

One theory was put to me by Richard Waterman, who owned a deli I visited in Bristol. Richard went out of his way to praise his suppliers, to the extent of rating their stock with stars stuck onto his shelves to applaud the best. He thinks good craft foods come from two sources. First, there are traditional businesses, often family-run, with skills and recipes that may have been handed down the generations. These people continue using the same methods and bother with the details because that is what they have always done and it works. Then there are the individuals with a burning passion, who follow their own inquiries in a quest to master a chosen craft, sucking in established traditions as they do so from a number of sources. Such people go the extra distance to maintain an outstanding standard because nothing less will do.

As I went around England, listening and eating, both strands of Richard's theory proved to be true. Neil Boustead's Toffee Shop in Penrith is a fine example of a traditional business; his products got a top star-rating at Waterman's deli. He makes just two kinds of toffee – treacle and butter – and three kinds of fudge (plain, chocolate and mint) using time-honoured methods. Neil personally stirs his copper pans every day by hand, starting work at 5.30am to do so, and always uses the same equipment, the same proportions, the same kind of sugar and even the same brand of butter. Each toffee is wrapped individually by hand, though it takes five women 20 minutes to do a trayful. The butter fudge is found in some of the best delis in the country and the Toffee Shop's mailing list is a who's who of the great, the good and the greedy of England. Biting into a piece of Toffee Shop fudge, the word becomes almost onomatopoeic: a slight "fud" of firmness and a long, slow 'jjjjje' of smooth-dissolving-spreading-buttery-sugarbliss. Would he ever be tempted to make a change? "I wouldn't dare," Neil replies. The technique and ingredients, bought by his in-laws from a lady with an established business, have been the basis of the company's success. If it ain't broke, why add raisins?

Stephen Muller was born to a life of pickling. He runs The Little Pickle and Spice Company in Oldham, Lancashire, which has a good reputation among chefs for its piccalilli. He also makes tasty, crisp pickled onions as well as other pickles, chutneys and sauces. He went into the family firm after leaving school and worked on as the business was swallowed up by progressively bigger companies, as were the other Oldham pickle makers, in a localised 'pickle war'. Stephen eventually decided to buck the trend towards bigger and cheaper production by going back to the old methods and selling a better-quality product at a premium price. People said he was mad. "There's no room for little pickle-makers any more," someone said, unwittingly giving the new firm its name. "If you sell to the supermarkets," Stephen said, "you might sell a lot, but nobody makes a great margin nowadays." He has stuck to the proven ways of making a good pickle. He believes, for example, that brining the vegetables overnight is crucial; others just put them into saltier vinegar to save time and money. "We need people with fresh ideas, but they should also have respect for the past," he says.

I drove along the coast of Northumbria looking for kippers. Every year, great armies of bullet-headed herrings swim down the east coast, in the past tracked on sea by fishermen and followed on the shore by migrant Scottish women. The women moved down the coast to where the fish were being caught, and salted the fish in barrels as they were landed. It was a brief season, with many fish caught in a short time, and ways were developed to preserve the glut. Kippers were invented in the small harbour town of Seahouses on the northern end of the grand, empty stretch of the Northumbrian coast that leads up to Scotland. There was already an established smoked-salmon trade in the area, to make second-rate salmon, thin after releasing their eggs, more attractive by brining and smoking. These fish were called 'kippered' salmon (the word deriving from the Dutch word for spawning) and were sold on to London. In 1843,

a man called John Woodger started to experiment using the same techniques on herring. In contrast, the herring were in their plump prime, before spawning, as they passed this part of the coast. The rich, lacquered kipper was born.

In the shop at Swallows Smokehouse in Seahouses you can still see the fireplace on which the travelling 'herring lassies' cooked when they stayed in the building in the 19th century. Around a hundred black-and-white photographs line the walls of the shop, freezing the statuesque ghosts of the past. The women are up to their shins in heaps of fishy silver, the natural wealth of the sea (not that it made the workers rich) and the harbour so full of boats you could walk from end to end over the water.

Kippers were made along the eastern coast, especially in Lowestoft. They were easy to transport by the new trains and became staples of grand Victorian and Edwardian breakfasts, as well as the working man's table. It was in wartime, when food supplies were short, that corners were cut and kippers became a cheap commodity made from second-rate fish. C L Cutting, in his book on preserved fish (*Fish Saving, a History of Fish Processing from Ancient to Modern Times*), has a theory about the decline in standards. The herrings came to be kippered, he says, outside the season, when they were not at their best. Also, kipper-makers took up American methods, using milder cures, smoking the fish for shorter times and dying the pale flesh brown to disguise the fact they were not real, oak-smoked fish. The trend went towards high-volume, low-quality production.

Then, in the late 1970s, disaster struck. The herring population crashed and fishing for them was banned for seven years. The herring fishermen on the northeast coast had to buy different equipment or go into other work to make a living, and the kipper-makers, squeezed by the narrow margins of mass production, could not absorb the cost of buying herring from further away. Of all smokehouses along the coast, two traditionalists coped best: Swallows and Robsons, down the coast at Craster.

Both smokehouses, on the day I visited, had layers of racks of herrings waiting for the sawdust to be lit into smouldering fires below. The walls were covered in the treacly lava that coats old-fashioned smokehouses. Others have switched to stainless steel, but the traditionalists say the deposits add to the flavour, like the tar in the stem of an old pipe. Robsons now use Icelandic fish, frozen at sea, for consistent quality. Herring are still caught along the Northumbrian coast, although their migratory patterns have changed. They tend to be found further north, where they are caught in bulk by ships with nets one fisherman described to me as "the size of a football stadium". The majority are sold for export rather than to the specialist smoking trade.

Alan Robson, the third generation in his family to make kippers, 'christened' his son Neil with a herring scale and has taught him the trade the time-honoured way. You can buy their kippers at Waitrose, but they look at their very best straight out of the smokehouse all a-glisten, before chilling congeals the natural oils. Alan and Neil send kippers all over the world to ex-pats who yearn for the bone-old tastes of their homeland.

At the turn of the century there were 24,000 independent bakeries in England. Bakers rose before dawn or worked in day and night shifts; the craft of making proper bread requires the dough to rise for several hours, developing flavour and the gluten that stretches and holds when you make bread. To get fresh bread in the morning, you had to start early. In the 1960s food technologists launched the Chorleywood Breadmaking process, which enabled the dough to rise in minutes rather than hours, cutting out labour and also, unfortunately, flavour. There are family bakers who still bother with proper bread, though numbers are dwindling. One example is Herbert's in Montpelier in Bristol; here, they make old-fashioned organic loaves that are raised overnight, as well as weekend specials, such as four types of rye bread.

There are also fine examples of Richard Waterman's other type of producer, the self-taught, inspired individual. Paul Merry is an Australian who works as a consultant specialising in baking and building wood-fired brick ovens. I talked to him as he was setting up a bakery attached to a house in Long Crichel in east Dorset. The bakery was in an 18th-century coach-house and stables which have been beautifully converted (the owners are architects). On the inside, pristine stainless steel sat alongside the handmade details of the past, such as patterned brickwork. To one side was the oven, a big beast, and all around were wire racks of bread and the faint sound of creaking as the bread cooled and the crusts cracked.

Paul was 25 when he took to baking after a law degree. At this time, he was living with potters and weavers and became absorbed by how crafts could survive in a modern industrial society. After wandering around the world, he fetched up in London in the mid-1970s and started working in a family bakery underneath the Earl's Court Road. It was the kind of genuine old-fashioned business which, even in the mid-1970s, was starting to get scarce, pushed aside by industrial baking. Officially, he worked at the bakery one night a week, but he went down other nights to learn the trade and stand yarning with the other bakers as they worked the dough, which was left to rise for four hours. "It was because I had the passion that I hung around the Irish and English under the Earl's Court Road," he says. After a spell in Scotland when he learned on the job as a novice in charge of a 20-tray oven, he went back to Australia to set up a village bakery outside Melbourne. He ran it for ten years, then became a consultant and returned to England.

Once Paul got into baking he realised that to make the best bread possible, he would have to use a brick oven. Brick gets extremely hot and bakes the bread in retained heat, emitting rays in a different way from metal. So it was that he learned to make not just the bread but the ovens as well. The Long Crichel bakery is the result of modern patrons, who see food as a rich part of life. Like the combination of steel and old bricks, the style of the business is both progressive and traditional. When I visited, they were setting up the place with tried-and-tested designs, with three banks of drawers below the work table so they could weigh up dough and put the raw loaves in these compartments to rise. They use a mixing machine that has a wonderful old dough hook like a whale's tail, found second-hand in a trade magazine. You can get facsimiles made in Italy, but they are not the same as this original, probably made 50 or 60 years ago. I watched Paul, an articulate and inquiring man, discuss with the log man how to place the wood so he could walk easily among it. "So much of a craft is how well you organise things," he said. "How you move from A to B with minimum movement."

Paul wants to set up a British Association of Artisan Bakers to help strengthen this form of baking. What he finds distressing is that children growing up today have no yardstick by which to judge proper food. They are losing even the simplest of skills, such as cutting bread off a loaf. Bread – the staff of life – is symbolic of a whole attitude to food. A supermarket executive once said to me: "What matters most about bread is that it is fresh." He did not mention ingredients, craft, nutrition – or flavour.

The word "passion" is casually bandied about. In fact, passion is an extremely difficult quality to live by, and nobody in food production proves this point more than cheesemakers. Every day the easily spoiled milk arrives to be turned into cheese; at each stage the cheesemaker must accommodate daily variations of milk and microbes. This form of passion requires attention, patience and physical strength to keep it going.

Many of the great cheeses of England are still made by businesses built on farming family traditions – the Kirkhams, for instance, with their Lancashire cheese. The 1980s and 1990s spawned a new breed of cheesemaker, who created their own cheeses and gradually built reputations. Many of these newcomers were new to farming and used goats' and sheeps' milk because they are free from the expensive quotas put on cow's milk to limit production.

Graham and Josephine Townsend illustrate the sort of care and way of life that go into making good cheese. They met at Oxford, always wanted to do something agricultural and, in the 1970s, left a nice house and a maths professor's salary to set off for Devon in a little white van with a very pregnant goat, four beehives and three young children. They travelled through the night when the bees were dormant. At that time, the countryside was littered with food producers who had grown too quickly and collapsed; the Townsends knew they had to be patient and single-minded to survive. They needed to find one product they could do better than anyone else.

The cheese they arrived upon, Vulscombe, is particularly labour-intensive. Milk starts to turn into into solid cheese by two methods. It can be curdled quickly with rennet or (the Townsends' method) heated and soured in a controlled version of what happens when you leave milk on the doorstep. Then it is drained and gently pressed. Each small, 170g cheese contains three pints of milk.

Not only did the Townsends make cheese, they also kept goats to produce the milk. They built up the flock over 15 years from their one original pregnant nanny and half-a-dozen carefully selected stock they bought in, until they reached a hundred animals. Goats are animals bred for warm climates; their wool is designed to shed heat rather than retain it, so they had to be brought in every night. Even if it was wet, they had to go outside or they became, as Graham says, like fractious schoolchildren. There was always something to do – milking, feeding, hand-rearing the kids.

For 14 years, Graham went up to London once a fortnight to do some mathematics work to bring in money. On these days, he would get up at 5am and milk the goats. There would invariably be a tight race to the station, negotiating the cows in the lane. He would work on the train before delivering up to 300 cheeses, stacked up in boxes of 60 and carried in stout bags made of drill, to various cheese shops (the support of Jeroboams in St James's, London, has been crucial). He would then work for a full day, lecturing and moderating A-levels and, if the day had gone well, get back at 7pm to milk the goats and clean the vat, before collapsing into bed – and getting up early to do the milking the next morning. The figures were extremely tight and the mathematician had to find ways to make them add up in practice. For each cheese sold, for example, two pence went on straw.

Straw is important for good husbandry, but rare in the West Country where not much wheat is grown. Each year the Townends made ten acres of hay that they used to feed the goats, getting to bed at 4am after cutting and baling while the weather was dry. Every detail is still done with care. Jo selects the most perfectly shaped bay leaves from the garden to decorate the tops of one of their cheeses.

In the last few years the Townsends have had to compromise. After a heart-breaking decision, they decided to give up the goats. Part of the life of the enterprise clearly disappeared when the animals left, but it was the only way they could continue without suffering from total exhaustion. The link with the animals is important because cheesemakers need to be sure of the quality of the milk. When I asked Graham why they continued at all despite all the work and effort, despite only having one holiday together, on Exmoor, for their silver wedding anniversary, in all these years, he said: "You don't want to be beaten except by your own free will." They also have a home and a life with deep roots and beautiful, secluded surroundings, and they have achieved a dream, through their own endeavour and care.

There is one force that can break the finances and the spirit of the cheesemaker, or any other food producer: regulations. Regulations should be there to protect the public, but too often the rules can seem to fit into the demands of box-ticking rather than the consumers' interests, which include choice, quality and flavour as well as safety. Some say this culture is changing, but you still hear plenty of stories about how regulators, especially the inexperienced, can prefer ultra-safe uniformity to individuality. Everyone in this litigious world is concerned with risk, and regulators only have to make noises for producers and sellers to have to jump. After new temperature regulations came in, for example, many restaurants stopped offering unpasteurised cheeseboards. They found that, if they were to follow the regulations (or some environmental health officer's interpretation of them) to the letter, they would have to keep all uncut cheese in the fridge and throw away any cut cheeses after a few hours. In other words, a cheeseboard would be utterly impractical. It only takes a powerful officer even advising a restaurateur of the possible risks for the whole delicious affair to seem not worth the bother.

Some brave food producers have challenged the validity of such regulations. "I follow the advice of a builder friend," says one. "When an EHO [environmental health officer] tells me to do 21 things, I say, 'Certainly; but first please could you be so kind as to send me a copy of each regulation'."

The classic York ham used to be made in farmhouses for Christmas feasting. They are hard to come by now and I was delighted to find an example in a family butcher's, Radford's, in Sleights, near Whitby in Yorkshire. Andrew Radford, the fifth generation of the family who has owned it, has around a hundred hams hanging up maturing in his shop. When you pick out a ham, your name is written on a tag and tied to the leg. You can also buy thin slices of the deliciously intense meat from the counter. The local health officers have muttered about the natural mould growing on the outside. "If they ever told us we couldn't make them any more," Andrew said, "they would have to take me to court." Few are so strong-minded. I tried to find a Bath chap, the rolled and cured cheek of a pig that looks something like a mini-ham, and finally tracked down a producer. Apparently, the health officers had said they would continue to test the chaps until they found something wrong.

It is a fiddly food to prepare; they did not make very many anyway. Now, they have given up.

The problem can be that regulations designed for mass production and big businesses put a disproportionate and often needless strain on small, artisan operations. Regulators at every level, far away from the actual making of the product, cover their backs with reams of paperwork. Robin Congdon, one of the most experienced cheesemakers in England, often gets stacks of forms from wholesalers and others who want to prove he has taken 'due diligence' to ensure everything they sell is safe. Demand for Robin's cheeses outstrips supply and so he simply refuses; they still continue to buy his cheese. The newcomer setting out in cheesemaking would not be in a position to do the same.

During my travels I happened to catch a cheesemaker who was setting out with determination and enthusiasm on the route of making the best cheese she possibly could. Sue Proudfoot, married to a farmer in Cornwall, was mucking out a stable one day when she was suddenly struck by the realisation that she was coming towards 40 in an era when job certainty was a thing of the past. Not a person comfortable with leaving things to chance, she thought of all the milk they produced and how she had on her doorstep a wonderful chance to make something good and something of herself.

I can visualise Sue as we talked, an energetic woman in a blue hairnet running her hands and a pink plastic shovel though the curds as they turned into creamy, smooth globules the size of golf balls. She talked of starting out, her hopes, her isolation, the help she had got from cheese-sellers, the struggle and her motivation. She is a spirited woman, prepared to surmount obstacles. At that point, she was considering making unpasteurised cheeses because these had greater potential for flavour. I tried both pasteurised and unpasteurised versions of one of her cheeses, Trelawny, and the latter, at that stage, had longer, stronger, subtler flavours. She was facing the decision of going ahead with her recently established business or changing direction to do something exceptional.

The week after my visit, a negative visit from the local environmental health officers seemed like a set-back. She took advice. In the end, she decided to stick with the pasteurised cheeses she already made, and which were already gaining a good reputation. "If you are making something unpasteurised," she said, "you are leading from the front and you can fall a long way. I'm trying to make a living in a rural community. There's no point in having a fantastic product with no business."

Perhaps good food producers have a special position as we move into a post-industrial age and people are more prepared to pay for well-made foods. These producers, who make a great deal of difference to the amount of choice, pleasure and character available, may thrive. Some of them will continue to make unpasteurised cheese.

But will enough new individuals come into craft foods, given the costs and hurdles of regulations to people when setting up their own small businesses? And what of the independent, family firms that have kept going, day in, day out, as they have done for decades? Perhaps rules designed for mass production will become so onerous that these producers, for all their worth, will be the last generation to bother. No one wants well-made craft foods to become so rare that they are the privilege of the rich and the lucky few. Their future depends on consumer power and the recognition in government that smaller producers, collectively, matter.

8 shops

WAITROSE ARRIVED IN 1977 IN THE WILTSHIRE TOWN WHERE I GREW UP. THE AISLES WERE BRIGHT, WHITE AND WIDE. YOU SWEPT ALONG MAJESTICALLY BEHIND A GLIDING TROLLEY, PAST LENGTHS OF SHELVES ROLLED OUT IN MULTI-COLOURED RIBBONS OF KIWI FRUITS, TARAMASALATA AND CHEESY PUFFS... A SPACESHIP HAD LANDED IN MARLBOROUGH.

WAITROSE ARRIVED IN 1977 in the Wiltshire town where I grew up. The aisles were bright, white and wide. You swept along majestically behind a gliding trolley, past lengths of shelves rolled out in multi-coloured ribbons of kiwi fruit, taramasalata and cheesy puffs. There were sliding doors and an escalator to the car park. A spaceship had landed in Marlborough. We talked of it as a destination: it wasn't 'doing the shopping' but 'going to Waitrose', and the twice-weekly market suddenly seemed a weighed-down affair with its disorderly queues and bothersome bag-juggling. Waitrose smelt so good: not of foods, exactly (though perhaps there were bread smells) but of newness. The colours were brighter, the world smarter. The overall impression dazzled.

Twenty-four years on, supermarkets still dazzle me with their white light and apparent choice, but now I see past these. My local greengrocers, for example, quite simply have a better choice of fruit and vegetables in terms of quality and range, as well as being competitive in price. Some supermarkets bother more than others. Booths, in the northwest, is a shining example of a chain with many regional, high-quality products. I spoke to several picky customers and small producers who had nothing but praise for them. Waitrose has some good lines, as do other supermarkets. But on the whole supermarkets offer a far blander choice than the good independents.

From one perspective, it is no good disparaging the standardisation and anonymity of supermarkets: that is part of their appeal in the first place. No need to talk, to ask for cuts of meat we cannot name, to bother with transactions that disturb the lull of dull routine. Just a purse at a till and a succession of opened doors: shop, car, home, fridge, cupboard. Nobody, apart from our neighbour in the queue (whom we need not acknowledge) will know that we eat ginger crunch creams or Mr Men fudge yoghurts or deep-frozen onion rings or four-cheese pizzas. It is the city of shopping; invisibility in crowds. Parking. Simplicity. So seductive. No wonder we fall for them.

But as supermarket spaceships landed all over the country, and as their acres of car parks descended, the small independents felt the chill of the spreading shadows.

Like most people, when it comes to change, I am a gradualist. Like other people who are reconsidering their shopping patterns, over about six years, my shopping habits have altered. It was not so much a question of falling out with supermarkets as falling back in with small shops.

The first shop to delight me into leaving supermarkets was one that sells cheese. Good cheese is a living product that continues to mature in the shop, the microbes transforming the cheese from chalk to ooze, from plainness to riches. A cheese like Cheddar can be matured for a more than a year and keep producing new flavours that roll onto the tongue, on and on, sometimes with an extraordinary and luxuriant length. To find cheese with this potential, you need the skill and care of a good cheese-seller who, like a curator of the edible, picks out and gathers in the cheeses from many small makers and looks after them at all stages. A truckle of cheese, cut into small pieces and enclosed in tight plastic is a noble beast muzzled and denatured. No, more than that: it is dead. A good cheese shop allows a cheese its pride.

I was very fortunate in living around the corner from one of the most exceptional cheesemongers in the country, La Fromagerie, just off Highbury Fields in London. The owner, Patricia Michelson, is a truly passionate advocate of real food and the small producer. The feel of the shop is that of a fantasy cheese museum with wooden shelves displaying the variety – more than 200 kinds – that comes from the cheesemakers' craft, transforming mere milk into so many textures, tastes and shapes. There is a strong sense of seasonality in the shop. Next to the cheeses will be cherries or figs or tomatoes or walnuts, underlying the feeling of change and harvest that comes from natural produce. When milk from animals fed on the spring grasses gets going, La Fromagerie can have up to 45 goats' cheeses on sale; in the autumn and winter, the Vacherin Mont d'Or arrives and I always associate its spreading gloss with candlelight and a pre-Christmas fug edged with winter sparkle.

Patricia began buying cheese when, on a skiing holiday, she came across a particularly good Beaufort, a nutty Alpine French cheese, and brought some back to share with friends and restaurateurs. Encouraged by their response, she started a small business maturing cheeses in her garden shed. The shed became a stall and the stall became a shop which now supplies some of the cheeseboards of the top restaurants in London. Some of the cheeses in La Fromagerie, particularly the French ones, are otherwise sold mostly within a 20-odd mile radius of where they're made. Patricia is a great hunter-gatherer who makes regular trips to France and Italy to source good suppliers. She has set out a Greatest Hits of British Cheeses on a dresser, displayed so you can really look at them, rather than peer from a distance.

Patricia is helped by the French shop manager and *affineur*, Eric Demelle, who has two cheese caves beneath the shop, one of which is two degrees warmer than the other, to allow the harder cheeses to mature better. In here, Eric nurses his cheeses to readiness, turning, watching, washing with potions that impart flavour. On the day I went down, he uncorked a prune grappa which we sniffed with greedy noses as he told me he was waiting for the right cheese to come along for it. On another side of the cave, a whole frame of goats' cheeses awaited his attention, some wrapped in chestnut leaves. I wondered what explained their particular shapes, having learned that Ticklemore from Devon has its bumps and oval shape from being drained in plastic colanders, and that the Townsends' idyllic Vulscombe, with its carefully picked bay leaves and other decorations, first got its shape by being drained in small baked-bean cans.

La Fromagerie opened my eyes and taste buds to variety, character, seasonality and quality. Patricia also taught me the role of the shopkeeper as a commercial curator at the centre of a network of good suppliers, selling to consumers who sought out quality or introducing cheeses to anyone open to exploring the world of taste. At weekends, you often have to queue in La Fromagerie, but anyone with eyes is never bored. There is always a surprise: dried fruits covered in chocolate; green walnuts; an apple juice called Tiddley Pomme. I went to see the maker, a former architect who lived in a house covered in old metal advertising signs by a broad sweep of the Severn in Gloucestershire. He made cider in a dusty shed that used to be the stables of a temperance hotel and sold bacon and pork from apple-fattened Gloucester Old Spot pigs.

The cheese-seller as advocate of quality has an honourable tradition in this country, particularly the late Patrick Rance, with his shop in Streatley, Berkshire, who wrote the pioneering *Great British Cheese Book,* and Randolph Hodgson of Neal's Yard Dairy, who has specifically championed British cheeses. The aesthetic of his Covent Garden shop is one of truckles, and producers' names are flagged up.

A CHEALE THAT HAS NO SOME GO! SMOOTH, STRONG
A SMELLY!
£1.54 100gms
£6.99lb
FULL FAT SOFT CHEESE

SHARPHAM

SHARPHAM
Elmhurst

ELMHURST
A MOST DELECTABLE
CHEESE WITH
ADDED CREAM.
A TRULY RENEWAL
EXTRAVAGENCE!
£1.55 100gms
£7.03lb
FULL FAT SOFT CHEESE
✓ UNP

HELIGAN
A MIX OF COWS &
SHEEPS MILK WITH
ADDED CREAM &
A HINT OF LEMON
WHAT A WONDERFUL
RECIPE.
£1.31 100gms
£5.95lb
FULL FAT SOFT CHEESE

CELESTE
OUR VERY OWN
SOFT & SCRUMPTIOUS
CREAMY CHEESE.
HAVE A GO - LET
IT FLOW!
£1.16 100gms
£5.26lb
FULL FAT SOFT CHEESE

NANTERROW
YOU JUST CAN'T STOP
EATING THIS CHEESE.
SO SOFT & CREAMY IT
JUST MELTS IN YOUR
MOUTH
1.3
S

SLEIGHT
VERY SOFT AND VERY
FRESH GOATS CHEESE.
EXCELLENT TEXTURE WITH
AN UNBEATABLE CLEAN
PIQUENCY. PLAIN OR!
£2.
FULL FAT SOFT

Cheese

Cheese

heese

Cheese

EMLETT
WHAT A DIAMOND OF
A CHEESE. FIRM YET
SOFT WITH A MELLOW
FLAVOUR
£3.20 EACH
FULL FAT SOFT CHEESE ✓ UNP

LITTLE
RYDING
A 'BRIE' STYLE
SHEEPS MILK CHEESE
FROM SOMERSET.
CAN BE EATEN
YOUNG & FIRM OR
RIPENED UNTIL
GOOEY!
£4.20 EACH
FULL FAT SOFT CHEESE
✓ UNP

TYMSBORO
A PYRAMID GOATS
CHEESE ROLLED IN
CHARCOAL RIPENING
TO A RIDICULOUSLY
SILKY TEXTURE.
10/10 ON THE TASTE-
OMETER.
£4.60 EACH
FULL FAT SOFT CHEESE ✓ UNP

Finn

Funn

FINN
A TRIPLE CREME
CHEESE WHICH WILL
MAKE YOU FAT NOT
FINN! WHAT THE
HECK - ENJOY.
£1.49 100gms
£6.75lb
FULL FAT SOFT
CHEESE ✓ UNP

Jeanine's Lemon Curd

Ragsto
Hand made
mature goats milk c

*Carefully labelled cheeses,
complete with tasting notes
and details, in Country
Cheeses, Tavistock*

Around the country there are other cheese specialists who care about what they do and are well worth seeking out. Many cheeses, after all, are designed to keep, so you only need to go every so often and the effort is repaid with inspiration and flavour. Cheese is like chocolate: a good one is so packed with taste that you eat rather than gobble and it takes just a small amount for bliss point to hit you smack in the mouth. An artisan cheese may seem expensive, but it is far better value for money. "Don't cheat, don't cheat, don't cheat on the cheese" as the promotion jingle went, but surely this should be about quality and not just quantity.

In Chester, at The Cheese Shop, Carole Faulkner has around 200 cheeses, 80 per cent of them British. Her passion for native and organic produce comes from her upbringing as a farmer's daughter, growing up on a traditional mixed farm where they raised their own crops to feed the livestock. In the 1950s, she marched to the Houses of Parliament with six fellow agricultural college alumni to protest against the new – and, to her mind, unnatural – practice of feeding cows with animal remains.

Not content with the quality of wholesalers' deliveries, Carole has two vans to collect the cheeses from around the country so they do they do not get too cold and are handled carefully. She promotes and encourages small producers, though health regulations have done away with the really small ones: she used to sell a cheese made by a blind man who lived on an island off Ireland and left his cheeses wrapped in braille paper under a bush for a friend to row over and collect. Aside from cheese, Carole is such a fan of Womersley Hall products that she had customised shelves made to fit their bottles of vinegars.

In the West Country, Elise and Gary Jungheim of Country Cheeses in Tavistock have been instrumental in the revival of cheese in the area, encouraging both buyers and makers. From the producer's point of view, the feedback from sellers and customers is often vital encouragement and helps them to improve what they do. Elise and Gary feel that, by giving out pieces of cheese to taste and talking to their customers (it is a very friendly shop), they gradually encourage people to appreciate what riches they have so close to home and to see good cheese as an everyday pleasure rather than a dinner party event. "The different people coming through the door are what it's all about," Gary says.

I like The York Beer and Wine Shop, where two former scientists have left their microscopes initially to follow their passion for two end products of microbial action – beer and cheese – doing monthly trips around the country in a van to collect products from small producers. They have a small glass counter of cheese among the hundreds of beer bottles. People come in with plastic containers for the draught beers; it is a very down-to-earth place, far from the chrome boutiques of 'posh' food and drink. Food in England would certainly be far duller without cheesemakers and cheesemongers.

If supermarkets are most successful at packaged foods, they are least successful at the most spoilable food of all: fish. Have you ever seen a supermarket fish counter which consistently sparkles with freshness? I often think of a remark made by a Spanish woman who, when she first went into an English supermarket and saw the fish counter, said in disbelief: "These fish... they are *dead*!" At the other end of the scale, the good fishmonger positively entices you to buy with fish shown off in every shade from pearl to gleaming grey, from pale rose to deep coral and every taste and texture from meaty tuna to the soft skeins of skate wings. One shop in my area, Monteum in Shoreham-by-Sea, has a policy that any fish that shows a mere whiff of age is fed, sometimes by children in the queue, to the lobsters in a tank at the side of the shop.

The daily variables of the catch do not, on the whole, fit into the supermarket juggernaut. It takes training and knowledge to be able to pick the best fish, to care about it enough to store it properly on ice. It takes pride to get rid of it before it starts to droop. The good fishmonger goes down the line to get the best quality from the market or specific boats. John Strike runs an admirable fishmonger's, Quayside Fish, right on the harbour of the blustery south Cornish port of Porthleven, and he or his deputy go to Newlyn market to buy. The market is open to the harbour and the sealight gleams on the white bellies of the fresh fish. The boxes of fish are lined up like bricks and the buyers gather round each catch with the auctioneer.

After looking around for a while, you start to see that the catches vary in quality according to the boat. Some of the fish look slack already; others are "stiff-alive" as John put it. Newly caught fish can be dragged along in a trawl for hours and stored poorly for days before they are brought to shore. Or they can be landed quickly, put on ice and be on sale in the market within 24 hours. We came across a box of dark, greeny-grey turbot, caught by a boat with a good reputation, and 45 boxes of John Dory which everyone had been remarking upon. "Gorgeous fish," said John and you could sense his excitement. He believes that boats that bother with their fish haven't been rewarded by better prices; there is less incentive for these people to take care, although some still do, just as in any other walk of life.

John was a teacher whose collar started to feel tighter and tighter each day in assembly. He left and started to take people out on his boat to dive wrecks, or go crabbing or mackerel fishing. The boat needed repairs, and to make some money he went to Newlyn one day and bought a box of mackerel, put them in the back of an estate car on plastic sheeting and drove miles before he could summon up the courage to knock on a door. The first woman who opened the door said she hadn't seen such beautiful fish in years. What would have happened if she had turned up her nose? The customer's reaction and enthusiasm matter, too.

John's shop, close to the sea, stirs your sense of where fish come from. There are lemons and bottles of wine and cookbooks and hot-smoked fish you can take away to eat on the quayside. You get the same sense of connection by going to the fish stalls along the south coast or in places like Aldeburgh or Dunwich: that this is wild food and the customer must also get what comes in, and pay the price depending on the day.

Economies of scale are repugnant when they hurt sentient animals. I really believe that if people knew the details of factory farming there would be, in this nation of animal lovers, a far higher percentage who would think twice about what they ate, and for many reasons other than health scares. The conditions in which battery hens are kept are more widely known than other animal welfare issues and there are plenty of free-range eggs sold. Yet even as cafés advertise free-range eggs, they make no mention of the origin of the bacon on the same plate. Pigs can be kept in unnatural conditions, on concrete floors without enough room to move, without opportunity to rootle.

The British pig industry, encouraged by supermarkets, has made improvements; shoppers buy cheaper products from abroad. Don't blame the supermarkets: blame the shoppers.

I had to face up to my own role in the equation in an unexpected way. For three months I tested chicken recipes for a book. The chicken I used was from a supermarket and in that nebulous category that was 'better than battery' but not proper free-range, by which I mean animals that have a real access to move around, not those stocked in large numbers in big units. I was aware of the issues, but I needed so many chickens and my budget was tight. I'm afraid I think I justified using second-rate chicken by the fact I did not eat all the food: such was the nature of my deadline and the number of times I cooked the dishes that some went into the bin after tasting. It was possible to push the issues to one side.

It just so happened that at that time the chance arose to go inside a fairly intensive chicken farm. While I was there, standing amid a flurry of feathers, I discovered that these birds were sold in just a few places under a particular label; in fact, by some coincidence, these were the very birds I had been buying day after day for weeks to test my recipes.

How did it feel, standing in that flock? So strange that it was hard to know what to feel. The birds spread far further than it is possible to imagine, shuffling around; the dead ones were picked out daily. They were no longer animals, but bits of semi-animated matter. I could hear the strain in the farmer's voice, though: he knew what to feel. He was no ogre, just a man under a great deal of pressure to heave up numbers and cut costs to the point where he was clearly uncomfortable about the state in which he kept his animals. Each chicken made him so little money, once he had deducted 'bed and board', that his margins hardly worked out. We left the building. Suddenly, an alarm went off. The farmer ran, flinging a "must go" behind him, without even a goodbye. He was normally a courteous sort of chap: it was clearly an emergency. I went to get my coat and asked his wife what had happened. The generator that pumped oxygen into the sheds had broken down and within ten minutes or so that huge sea of birds would start to die. Alongside heat distress and suffocation, they would suffer from the fumes of their own excrement because birds like these, ready to go to the shops, are so packed in that they trap the gases below them, unless there is sufficient ventilation. It was this detail which brought into focus why the whole idea of factory farming, the whole experience, was so intensely repulsive.

I learned something else. Don't blame the supermarket or wherever you buy factory-farmed meat; don't blame the farmer; don't blame 'the customers'. Blame yourself.

Once I had made a real connection between the fact that meat came from animals, my reaction was not to become vegetarian but to eat less and better meat and certainly to respect it more. Some Buddhists think that if you eat meat at all, you should eat it from the largest possible animal, as it takes fewer lives to feed more people. I still eat meat; I still eat sprats as well as cattle. In the back of my head, though, the switch has clicked that these are not commodities.

In Exeter, I went down Magdalen Road, a street where there were still small independent shops managing to survive, partly by promoting themselves together as a place for good shopping. At one end was Piper's Farm, a modern type of butcher's shop. For a start, it did not look like a butcher. The meat was displayed on plates and there were great branches of bay and fronds of fresh herbs. It had the lightness and variety of a modern deli and the cuts were different: they looked like food rather than bits of meat. Peter and Henrietta Greig, the brains behind the operation, proved to be a countryside breed of radical who had gone back to the beginning and worked out a different way to produce and sell meat. They set up a business that really did follow meat through the whole process, from gate to plate. From the start, their two main principles were to produce and sell meat that was really good to eat, and to help to sustain the network of family farms and the rural community.

The meat that they sell in the shop and by mail order all comes from small family farms that produce the meat to the Greig's specifications: slower-growing breeds fed on natural local produce. The animals are allowed to behave as farm animals, and are killed in a small, local abattoir and hung properly to produce well-flavoured meat. Peter taught himself to butcher, initially carving up the carcasses with an axe, knives and a frying pan. He used practical logic to follow the seams of the muscles and put the cuts into the frying pan to check if the whole piece had the same texture. Interestingly, the method Peter eventually arrived at turned out to be not dissimilar to the French method of butchery. Crucially, tenderness comes from proper hanging. If the meat is not rushed into plastic but left to mature, it tastes its best.

The real starting point for the Greigs was that they used to farm chickens intensively. Battery farming used to be a good earner: they could make a net profit of £50,000 a year on just two acres of land. But they had to shuffle through the birds because if they picked up their feet they wouldn't be able to put them down again. At times they had to carry thousands of dead birds out by hand: 3,000 died in one night when a ventilation problem meant that the birds faced the same problems as those of the farmer I had met.

Piper's Farm is the Greigs' means of providing an alternative to this type of mass-produced intensification. They landed in mid-Devon in an area where the soil was good enough for small farms to make a living. Here, small family farms still existed that could form part of an informal network. On the Greigs' own farm, the sheep have pink fleeces from the red of the soil of Devon. This is also the colour of the Red Ruby cattle. Red rubies, dark rust, dried blood, cooked cherries: the colour of the soil varies and when you come away from Devon, you find it weeks later, perhaps a smear on a Ordnance Survey map or a dusty red mud mark on a coat. In one field, this soil produced the most delicious-looking hay I had ever seen: a luscious mix of mineral-rich meadow grasses that were deep-rooted to get their goodness from the ground. They grew slowly, relying only on natural nitrogens that are fixed by the clovers rather than by high-input chemical fertilisers.

Peter, Henrietta and I drove around the lanes, past Clyst Hydon's village hall, which still has 350 events a year, past the church where four of the six young men and women who brought in the plough for the Bless the Plough ceremony produced for Piper's Farm, past some anonymous chicken sheds that look perfectly normal – until you have been taken inside one. Part of the problem of factory farming is that it goes on behind closed doors. Even some apparently open systems have their problems: you may see pigs outside in the countryside and think all is well and good. But while the sows rootle through the mud, their piglets may be taken away from them at three weeks and reared for your plate in more intensive, indoor systems.

We drove to some of the farms that work with Piper's Farm. There are no official contracts, no formal co-operative. Existing farms keep their independence but dovetail part or all of their production into the Piper's way. We went to a chicken unit where there are 200 maximum in a flock compared to the 25,000 in each of the many sheds you can get in an intensive system. Piper's Farm wants animals to be stocked in numbers and at a density where they can behave naturally. We saw some pigs in an old cider orchard where Peter pays the farmer to keep them and provides the feed himself. We went to a malty-smelling feed mill, called Sargent and Sons, the only one left of the three feed mills in area, and there used to be many more than this. Sargent and Sons are getting more people to grow locally for them. We go to the slaughterhouse, a small abattoir which enables family farms to keep producing animals. So many of these have gone, too.

All this shows the tapestry of a local community and how food can be part of winding lanes, not just juggernauts on motorways and a chain of impersonal factory floors that are price-driven by accountants hundreds of miles away. I write about Piper's Farm at length because it helped me to understand how a shop's influence and connections go back a long way behind the counter, and that we, the consumers, are the last link in a long chain when we walk through the door.

If Piper's Farm is a modern kind of butcher, T M Ewbank in Appleby-in-Westmorland in Cumbria is a classic, old-fashioned establishment. Malcolm Ewbank, a third-generation butcher, wears a long white apron and moves about with that steady tread of custom:

cutting a steak off the rump, flattening it with the broad side of a
cleaver, curling it round to make a neat parcel, wrapping it in
greaseproof, throwing in a couple of sausages as he puts it in a bag.
Greeting people as they come in to collect orders, saying goodbye.
The legs of lamb are wrapped in lacy shawls of caul fat to keep them
moist as they cook. The only time Ewbank's sells poultry is at
Christmas. "I stick to my own trade. I don't sell tins or anything else.
Nowadays there are too many people dabbling in other folks' trades,"
Malcolm says. The shop is very spare, with pale blue paint on the
upper walls, a broad, low wooden counter and a metal rack at the
back with wads of greaseproof paper and cleavers hanging from it.
The window display is equally simple: white tiles with a number of
proud pieces of meat. The family uses its own cattle in the summer
and local meat the rest of the time, with a preference for native
breeds because they have more flavour.

Post-BSE, people are thinking more about where shops get their
supplies. This trend also, from the consumer's point of view, accounts
for the popularity of farm shops and farmers' markets. Farm shops
really boomed in the freezer-era of the 1970s, when people would
come for pick-your-own. Now, fewer people can be bothered with
bending and stretching, and Sunday shopping takes up one of the
prime times when people used to pick. Farm shops have evolved.
Now the emphasis is on ready-picked, ready-prepared food, and they
are turning into alternative supermarkets with fridges of meat and
shelves of bottles, tins, packets and pots. One line of thought goes
that farm shops are in a far stronger position than delis to challenge
supermarkets, primarily because they can match two of the most

attractive features of supermarkets: parking and enough space to stock a wide choice of food.

One of the best farm shops in the country is Alder Carr at Creeting St Mary in Suffolk. Here they grow really good produce, letting the fruit and vegetables fill with flavour, rather than pumping them up with water; they also make 14 flavours of ice-cream, including a very popular gooseberry and elderflower. With crafts on sale and a restaurant, it is a place worth an outing. The owners, Joan and Nick Hardingham, had to set up a shop when the infrastructure of wholesale markets was no longer viable for smaller growers because the supermarkets were buying directly from bigger farms. Joan's concern is that enough people care about the quality of food to allow the traditional skills of growing to keep going.

On the same site as the farm shop, Joan also set up a monthly farmers' market in 1998. Since it has started, the number of sales in the shop itself has increased from under 30,000 to 41,000 a year; people who come to the market realise that they can buy good produce here all the time, not just on the third Saturday of the month, when the market runs. One benefit of farmers' markets could be to break the belief in the one-stop shop. My biggest hope is that the markets will thrive and that they will encourage people to shop otherwise at independents, that it will become a regular habit, not an occasional event.

I also have a fondness for traditional markets where the stalls have real individuality. Many stalls may be turned over to frilly loo-roll holders and cuddly toys, but there are also still traditional markets in

more out-of-the-way rural areas such as north Devon. I liked the
one in South Molton. In such old-fashioned places, the Women's
Institute stalls sell little wonky courgettes priced in small bundles
next to the pots of lemon curd and sugared cakes. I talked to a man
who remembered an old market in the Lake District. "It was like
a beehive," he said. "The farmers' wives used to tramp over the hill
with plucked chickens, vegetables, plums. They had stalls of butter,
eggs, tiny flower arrangements. It was the most marvellous sense of
occasion." It provided money for shopping, a break from household
chores and a chance to see people and have a natter. Younger farming
women have set up their own businesses – cakes, breads, jams –
which will bring them more of an income. South Molton market also
had an excellent olive-seller with good links to the Continent. I came
away with local vegetables, two cakes, some organic bread and a
bottle of exceptional French walnut oil.

Markets are one way, as a visitor, of being amid the buzz of a place.
Bath Market is a delightful building and this is where you go to see
where Bath people shop, away from the boutiques. Leeds' Kirkgate
Market, with its lovely painted metalwork, is a top place for people-
watching, and has the rather ghoulish spectacle of a butchers' row,
where the men stand in the doorways holding trays of meat and
shouting against each other. All around are faces fixed on the hunt for
a bargain. In Newcastle-upon-Tyne, if you park in Eldon Square car
park you walk through a mall, a modern underworld where the
unnatural light dims natural colouring so you see only the bright
goods in the shops. Then go through to Grainger Market, a Victorian
covered market with a domed hall like a railway station, and life and
individuality begin again. Goff's greengrocers had a wall of fruit a
foot high, bands of colour – green, orange, yellow, red – in triangles

and rectangles. Along the row, a florist had set up buckets of beautifully arranged bunches at bargain prices. The coffee man was in earnest discussion with a regular. At Sarah's Tuck-in, people sat stirring their tea and eating stottie cakes, the flattish bread of the region. Two Geordie women shouted at either end of a stall, their overlapping, sing-song adverts pealing like church bells:

"YerBESTbananas, FOURpoundsforapound!"

"TWO colliesforfiftypence! LAST ofthebroccoli, threeforfifty!"

How do shopping patterns change? How do people decide they want to shop in places other than supermarkets? Gradually, perhaps. And as part of a slowly changing patchwork of shopping rather than an overnight conversion.

Over a number of years, I left the tartrazine fluorsecence, the small plastic envelopes of herbs and the sameness of the fruit and veg aisles. Delis and specialists provided more interesting cheeses and packaged foods; health-food shops and bakeries sold the bread I wanted; farmers' markets and farm shops topped me up with occasional inspiration and seasonal treats. I found meat was treated with greater care by good butchers. Fish became a great deal more appetising once I found where to buy it really fresh. I had drifted away from supermarkets and my habits became more grounded in the smaller shops. They are the convenient places now. I am, I admit, very interested in food; but it is also true that I became far *more* interested in food by shopping in such places. The first time you go into any shop that is unfamiliar it feels strange, and it can feel strange, too, that they are not impersonal places where you can just glaze over. Some organic carrots need parts cutting out; some real food has a shorter shelf-life. There can be a wait to be served. But overall, good, independent shops are far more interesting, far more alive. Far more entertaining, with all their quirks and personalities, quite apart from the quality of the food. People often talk of shopping anywhere other than the supermarket as a real chore. Where, they ask, are all the small shops? And sometimes I know that they live round the corner from a very good butcher or greengrocer. I know, also, that they would go out of their way for many other forms of shopping. For some, the problem is one of habit and priorities, in truth, rather than logistics. Habit, convenience and assumption are three difficult loads to shift.

At the start of the new Millennium, I stood in a field chatting with two farmers who were swapping subsidy gossip and eyeing up each others' harvest schedules. When we talked about local production the gist was: "This is the way it has gone. This is the way that it is." That may be true. All the same, I noticed it was hard to hear any enthusiasm in their voices until I asked about good local shops and they regaled me with stories about the butcher and recommended a local greengrocer.

I visited the butcher, where six proud carcasses hung from the gleaming bars. A Dutch man staying locally at a bed and breakfast came in for some dry-cured bacon. We talked about the beef, which came from cattle reared by a woman who was about to retire. "The last of a kind," the butcher said, referring to her skills of stockmanship. I went to the greengrocer's where they had local vine tomatoes and potatoes from the rich, dark local soil. The greengrocer worked hard to get a variety of good suppliers throughout the year. Then he told me that a supermarket was to open just down the road. You could see its shadow on his face.

At times like this, it is hard not to feel a slow, burning anger at the way it is so easy to drift with the tide: that we allow what is good to die off as we sweep along behind our trolleys, smoothed by gliding wheels, seduced by convenience. Convenience is something we treat as a god, with what sometimes feels like a lack of free will. Before we know it, the number of interesting independent shops and producers could so easily dwindle, and what seems like a great deal of choice could turn out to be very little at all.

From my perspective, failing to support the independent shops ultimately rips off the quality of our experience: to survive against supermarkets, the small independents have had to raise their game and offer the kind of quality and character that is hard to find in mass retail. It may be that shopping patterns shift, so that people do a big weekly shop in a supermarket and smaller 'treat' buys at the weekend; it may be that people buy bulk goods such as dog food and loo paper at supermarkets and meat and fish at specialists; it may be that a larger number of people switch to smaller shops all through the week. A small shift, repeated a few times, grows into a habit – and all habits are hard to break.

9 eating out

MUCH HAS BEEN MADE OF THE LONDON RESTAURANT 'REVOLUTION'. IN RECENT YEARS THE ENGLISH, MORE GENERALLY, HAVE STOPPED SEEING EATING OUT AS A TREAT AND HAVE BEGUN TO GO OUT FOR MID-WEEK MEALS WITHOUT THE EXCUSE OF A SPECIAL OCCASION.

MUCH HAS BEEN MADE OF the London restaurant 'revolution'. In recent years the English, more generally, have stopped seeing eating out as a treat and have begun to go out for mid-week meals without the excuse of a special occasion. Nowadays it's enough of an excuse that we just don't feel like cooking (and increasingly we do not). It's no coincidence that this shift coincided with an increase in the average income, whilst simultaneously the basic cost of living has gone down. There is just more disposable income flying around. When I talked to Tom Jaine, a former editor of *The Good Food Guide*, about the factors underlying the rise of restaurant-going, he pointed to the cost of a cup of Costa coffee. If someone is going to pay that much for a hot drink, maybe several times a day, is a restaurant meal so very expensive? At the other end of the scale, there are enough people prepared to dish out for the elevated cuisine of a Marco Pierre White to allow more top-class places to thrive. Both a greater sense of pleasure in food and more money have broken through an indigenous pain barrier about paying for food – in restaurants at least.

At the same time, there are murmurs that London restaurants are over-priced, over-hyped and impersonal. Food has become 'fashionable' and has suffered from the effects of favouring style over content. When I interviewed the food critic Egon Ronay for his millennium food predictions, he complained that chefs saw complications and twists as some sort of "virility symbol" and wanted "to be composers when they could not conduct". There is talk of a skills shortage amid this explosion of restaurants, of owners willing to over-promote young chefs before they have learned the basics of their trade. In cooking, as in other trades, certain skills are ebbing away: fish and meat come ready prepared from suppliers, for example, so there is less basic grounding in getting to grips with raw ingredients.

Spoiled as this sounds, I sometimes found myself sitting in curiously impersonal restaurants in front of some Fancy Dan concoction such as seafood perfumed with vanilla, and, to be honest, not really bothered whether I finished the dish or not. The whole experience of eating out can lack any charm or gutsiness or personality or heart.

What I learned was that the same principle applies to restaurants as to any other aspect of food: look for the individuals who bother – chefs such as Fergus Henderson at St John, Richard Corrigan at Lindsay House and Sam and Sam Clark at Moro – whose motivation does not stop at the bottom line. They make food so good you want to lick the plates clean and give you a satisfied sensation of fullness, instead of a heavy stomach and a hollow soul. Look, too, outside London. There has been a shift of attention to the rest of the country and the less-vaunted changes that have occurred in a quieter way beyond the M25. There have been excited reports of 'clusters' of good restaurants, around Ludlow in Shropshire, in Leeds, in coastal Suffolk. Perhaps this diffuse restaurant 'revolution' is more led by good produce than by chefs appearing on television; perhaps it is found in rugged pubs rather than designer-sleeked palaces. Perhaps it can be better value, too, and have more character and staying power.

An axiom of food is that a chef or home cook is only as good as the raw produce. It is one of those sayings that sounds so simple and turns out to be more complex in practice. Finding quality, day in, day out can ironically be more difficult in the countryside. In the capital, there are established supply networks for restaurants to rely on. Considerable effort goes into finding good ingredients and considerable art into letting their flavours sing out on the plate. At the heart of this new, quieter revolution outside London are chefs who have dug deep into their surroundings and managed to find the fresh, natural flavours of good ingredients. As often as not, they had settled in somewhere of beauty and, to build up regular custom, serve the food at a reasonable price. From the consumer's point of view, it is a revolution worth joining.

It used to be that much good cooking outside cities was found in country-house hotels which verged on the hushed side of peaceful and had too many cushions to be comfortable. A number of the latest wave of chefs (I use the term whether female or male, and the term 'cook' for home cooks, female and male) have set up in pubs, growing on the established roots of English custom. People are already relaxed when they walk in the door; they can come in for a drink, check out the menu and then decide whether to eat or not, or just sit at the bar with something simpler. Pubs are places where we do not feel self-conscious.

The important point about pubs is that they fit into the needs, supplies and character of the area. The Stagg Inn in Titley, Herefordshire, the first pub to get a Michelin star (in 2001) is still a pub that fits into its surrounding area and is not a stiff and starry sort of affair. The chef/proprietor Chris Reynolds has based the food on the best ingredients of the area, such as Hereford beef; the bar in the front room has a blackboard that marks up in chalk the name of whichever smallholder supplied the lamb, pork and beef on the table that day. At the back is a dining room with walls the colour of plum fool, wonky wood and old chairs.

My starter was a duck salad with Ragstone cheese and walnut dressing, in which the creamy, melting discs of breaded goats' cheese were the foil for the tender, perfectly cooked meat. Saddle of hare came with a beetroot gratin. It was the art of restraint: everything working to bring out the flavours and nothing else. The apple crumble parfait had the sharpness of apple and the texture of crumble. It was arranged to show off the streaks of green apple, the flavours and textures laid out for you to appreciate. Rural pubs need to serve food these days to survive. If they can do it as well as this and still keep attracting those who just want a good pint, we are, as they say in the States, "in gravy".

In Nidderdale, the quiet Yorkshire dale where I went to see the Blessing of the Lambs ceremony (*see chapter one*), Frances Atkins cooks at The Yorke Arms, a former shooting lodge-turned-pub-turned-pub-restaurant. She gets meat from sheep that have fed on heather at the top of her dale. Her mutton pie, with the meat cooked long and slow to produce a rich darkness, has the depth of mahogany compared to the rosewood of young lamb. She gets bilberries from the moor to go with local grouse, saucing the birds with the berries on which they fed. This, she says, is the cook's equivalent of finding gold. When she cooked in Scotland, she made a dish with three kinds of lamb, that had grazed on grass, salt-marsh and heather, and says that there was a slightly different flavour and texture to each one. The Yorke Arms' cheeseboard had 20 kinds of cheese, all from Britain. It felt like a happy place. I could vaguely hear them cracking jokes in the kitchen; a counterpoint to the baa-ing of the sheep outside. I ate onion soup with a sweet, soft flavour, that was warming and well-made, and was garnished with a subtly spiced onion bhaji.

Of the many gastropubs I visited, one of the most impressive, in a relaxed sort of way, was The Star at Harome, a thatched-roof pub on the North Yorks Moors. It is a hospitable place, with a sense of history. It was created in the 14th century as a hostel for travelling monks; Rievaulx Abbey is nearby. On a November mid-week lunchtime, the bar was full, so we went to the slightly smarter restaurant room where the friendly staff were unfazed by a 16-month-old throwing yoghurt and reaching for the brandy bottle. The chef-owner, Andrew Pern, is particularly good at using local ingredients in dishes that tap into, and develop, native tastes.

To give two examples of puddings: bramble roly-poly he serves with a Granny Smith scrumpy sorbet and apple sauce, while baked ginger parkin comes with rhubarb ripple ice-cream, hot spiced syrup and stewed rhubarb. A game faggot came with a thyme rösti and cranberry sauce, and a risotto had queenie scallops, leeks and Lancashire cheese. The pub-grub old-timer of gammon and pineapple is transformed into a gammon terrine with spiced pineapple pickle and a fried quail's egg. If this sounds a bit fancy, rest assured that his dishes work naturally on the taste buds. The food also shows a real commitment to the surroundings. Andrew has, for example, been instrumental in helping a farmer to diversify into free-range poultry in an operation called, unforgettably, Loose Birds. The Star is here to stay. I thought of the people who would work there, over time, and carry this ethos elsewhere. At my most optimistic, this sort of place feels like the roots of a real revolution.

The striking quality about The Star was that it felt active yet settled. I noticed that good clusters of restaurants are found in places where chefs came to stay for good, where the traditional farming had never gone away and where there was enough affluent custom, both local and visiting, to sustain them. Ludlow in Shropshire, with its own constellation of Michelin stars, is the best example. The town still has shopkeepers and local producers who bother about taste; it still has the seasons and the countryside in its veins. In a quieter way, another such concentration of good food can be seen in the restaurants strung like buoys along the coast of north Norfolk: Morston Hall, Yetman's, the Hoste Arms, Rococo and, further inland, The Ark. These chefs use ingredients such as shrimps from the Wash, mussels from Stiffkey, samphire from the shoreline and crabs that feed to sweetness on the bank that lies off the coast. Traditional farms and the landed Norfolk estates bring grass-fed beef and game to the table. Clive Houlder, a restaurateur-turned-wild-food merchant, is the local mushroom man who finds the local puff-balls, morels, ceps and the orange monster, Chicken of the Woods, as well as buying from the London market. A talented organic grower with a walled garden, Pat Kemp has Italian artichokes and other treats, and there are other small producers who are part of this informal network.

It is worth stressing, again, that this kind of cooking is not purely about the local produce or dishes traditional to England. English food has long borne foreign influences and ingredients – the pineapple that comes with the gammon, for a start. 'Modern British' food contains influences from France to Thailand. In another complicated cross-cultural twist, chefs are also inspired by the ingredient-led purism of Alice Waters at Chez Panisse, a Californian restaurant itself inspired by cooking in France. So you get English restaurants coming back to European ideas about food via the States. Chez Panisse is a place so committed to good ingredients that Waters employs a dedicated forager whose role is to find and build up suppliers as locally as possible.

For all the foreign influences and ingredients, the menus of the best restaurants still bring a greater strength and savour to English cooking by choosing native ingredients and by turning their skills to traditional dishes. It is not always easy to do this. Egon Ronay's words about over-fancy chefs echoed in my ears as I talked to restaurateurs who complained that customers always wanted a twist to their food. They didn't want just a classic dish done well: crème brûlée had to be crème brûlée with lemongrass. In one smart restaurant I ate a dish of "rhubarb and custard". It could have been so good but the chef had felt the need to gel the fruit and denature the ingredients rather than using his art to bring out their character. But many chefs are more successful at updating native tastes, serving excellent fish and chips, cured meats with piccalilli, bread-and-butter pudding, and so on. This is one trend that is bound to survive and grow, because these dishes appeal to established tastes and nourish a desire for the familiar. For all the fast sweep of fashion, there is a part of eating that remains naturally conservative.

In Aldeburgh in Suffolk, Sara Fox and Peter Hill have set up a classic neighbourhood restaurant, The Lighthouse, which is open every day of the week and not afraid to serve well-cooked, straightforward food. They have deliberately kept their prices reasonable so that people can visit often rather than occasionally. The menu is interesting and some of the dishes are also grounded in English traditions. You can get liver, bacon and onions here: calves' liver, Suffolk dry-cure bacon, the gravy made with stock and the onions roasted shallots. Down the road, The Regatta sells sprats off the beach fried in garlic butter and parsley. So what if sprats are humble fare? Lots of locals were ordering them, and with good reason: they were simply fresh and delicious.

The personality of a restaurant matters enormously, too. To give just one example, The Tontine in Staddlebridge, North Yorkshire, is a restaurant with genuine Teeside *craic* – a big fire, laughter, whistling, the owner walking through in braces, with long hair and clicking fingers, old wood, mirrors, candles, blues music, crashing pans, waitresses gossiping, long white aprons running around and a laid-back glamour and energy. In spirit it was like a good French brasserie. The apple and ginger sponge had a lightness but also sticky crumbs, and came with marmalade ice-cream on the side.

You can still get the best sort of English food in which the tastes still come through strong and true. Whenever I enjoyed a more evolved English dish, such as the mutton and caper puddings at The Castle Hotel in Taunton, or the sausages at The Baltic Fleet in Liverpool, I was encouraged. The country has not been over-run by chicken tikka trifles, haggis soufflé garnishes and other idiocies. The restaurant revolution is strengthening our native savours.

A trip to a number of these countryside restaurants takes you to places which feel far from the motorway (even if they are, in fact, quite close). Go along the coast of Kent on the Seasalter-Graveney road and you find yourself in a kind of estuarial hinterland where the defence towers at sea look like giant golf balls on tees, ten green beach huts stand in a row (khaki, emerald, *eau-de-nil*) and pylons stride out to the horizon. The sun drops like a huge neon strawbery into the estuary after dinner. The area is famous for its sunsets: Turner woz 'ere. In this setting, Steve Harris has taken over The Sportsman, a pub far from any sign of a neighbourhood: the sort of place that, in another incarnation, could easily be a bikers' pub. Here he serves the likes of local oysters with chorizo and proper free-range chicken from down the road with tiny, peeled broad beans, spring cabbage and peas picked that day. This is food that brings with it the fresh

*A crab, caught and prepared
by the Frary family who
have a stall by the quayside
of Wells-next-the-Sea,
Norfolk.*

sappiness of early summer to your senses. Some of his dishes are made
entirely from ingredients that come from within two miles of his
stove. I'm not sure I would have stopped and lingered on this stretch
of coast had I not been interested in the restaurant, but the off-beat
charm of this particular corner of England crept up on me with each
good mouthful. I walked by the water after dinner, off the unmarked
roads and on to a footpath, where I slowed down altogether, sat down
and enjoyed the sunset.

The water's edge is the place to space out. In west Dorset, the
Riverside restaurant in West Bay is in what used to be a hut where
local campers got water, tea and chips. It is well known now, but has
not lost its sense of welcome or put on airs and graces. There I ate
joyfully juicy cod in a crisp, dark Guinness batter and peas mushed
with butter and mint and watched seagulls arc through the sky.
In Cornwall, at the Hotel Trestanton, St Mawes, you can sit on the
terrace watching green sea wash over black seaweed and eat suckling
pig from a local breeder who has crossed Tamworth pigs with wild
boar for flavour and succulence, or a fat tranche of turbot roasted and
caramelised, with lemon juice, chilli flakes, capers, and braised chicory
wrapped in Parma ham. Breathing in the ozone blast of the sea air
sharpened the appetite, and the produce seemed to have leapt from
the sea to the pan to the plate without losing its gleam of life. The
owner, Olga Polizzi, is a member of the Forte family; the capers,
mozzarella and olive oil here are part of her own roots that she brings
to this Cornish setting.

Would I go to these places if I weren't in pursuit of food? Would I
spend so much time in them – footling around country towns before
lunch, walking on quaysides under stars and velvety skies after dinner?
La Casa Verde is a simple, Italian-style café in Larch Cottage garden

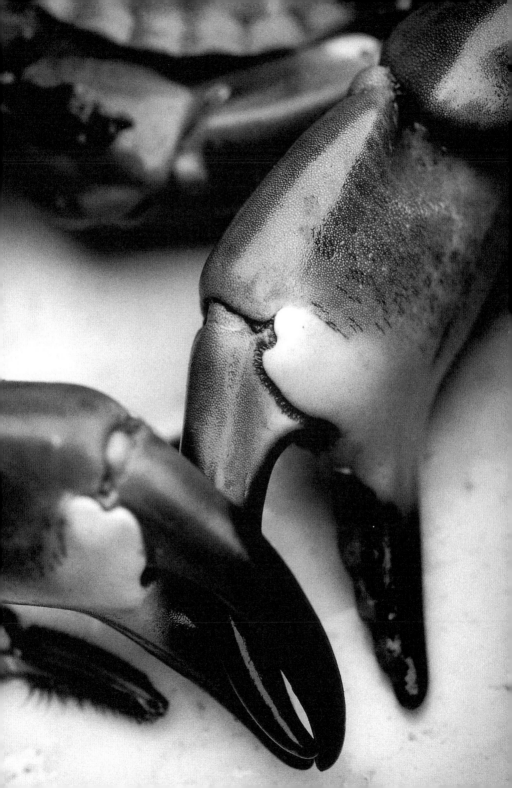

nursery, near Penrith in Cumbria, whose owner has fallen in love with Italy and built a pizza oven. I found myself wandering through pots of herbs and unusual plants with hills in the background, before having an espresso and a cake rich with butter.

In Hereford, I sat in the roof space of a medieval church, eating a potato and smoked Cheddar soup with good bread, followed by brownies, and taking a bird's-eye view of the architecture. This was All Saints Café, in the heart of a working church. The unrepentantly modern 'pod' of the kitchen fits into the old building so well that it was short-listed for a Royal Institute of British Architects award. Old ladies come and shelter from the rain, sitting on the modern rail like birds on a line; others come in to drink a glass of wine and have a salad, or to pray.

Rosamund the Fair is an Oxford restaurant on a canal boat where you can sit outside between courses, moving serenely through the dark landscape. I heard a rumour of a Swiss *pâtissier* in Waterperry Gardens, just outside Oxford, and there, in a plain-looking tearoom, sat some almond croissants that would alone have made the trip worthwhile – even without the beautiful gardens and homemade apple juice pressed from the garden's 14 varieties. Odd corners of England, and always with something good to eat, which is handy.

One of the chefs who best illustrates the idea of ingredient-led cooking is Nick Coiley. He used to be the head chef at a seminal restaurant of this kind, Joyce Molyneaux's Carved Angel in Dartmouth and has now set up solo in Ashburton, a market town off Dartmoor, drawing in ingredients from the moor and the coast in a part of the country that is a cornucopia of good produce. In the summer, there might be ten kinds of tomatoes – yellow beef, tiger-striped – sitting in a bowl to catch the sun through the window. Nick is a mushroom hunter and the restaurant, Agaric, is named after an old term for mushroom. Nick's former second chef at The Carved Angel, Ben Harris, carved the huge sculpted cep in the new restaurant, using a chainsaw and a piece of dead elm, which had itself sprouted wild mushrooms. "I don't want to be Michelin-starred," Nick says. "I want to produce good food." It is quite hard to find a simple, well-done, really fresh crab salad in English restaurants, but you can order one here.

The connection between all these restaurants and their ingredients is crucial to their success. It is also complicated to arrange and sustain. Instead of getting daily orders from contract suppliers, who can be relied on for cheap bulk, these chefs build up complex networks to bring in the quantity and quality they need for every meal. They also have to keep their minds and menus open to catch the best of the season and accommodate windfalls, like the old boy who brings a sea bass to the back door.

The chap who catches the crabs for Nick Coiley's crab salads drops them off at the restaurant on his way from his boat to his home. Frances Atkins cannot buy her sheep directly from the farmers on her doorstep, but must get them from a butcher who steers them through an abattoir. She says this process is surprisingly hard to arrange, considering The Yorke Arms is surrounded by sheep. Nicola and Chris at The Stagg Inn get some of their meat from part-time farmers, the sort of person sometimes referred to as a '21st-century peasant' or a 'hobby farmer'; they notice that the quality of the meat depends on who has raised the animal. Some really stand out.

Peter Robinson at the Hotel Trestanton says that, for ingredients

Nick Coiley at Agaric in Ashburton, Devon, takes delivery of some rhubarb.

he cannot get locally, he has had to set up direct supply lines from London. The wholesalers in his area may have produce that has come from France, then to New Covent Garden Market, then sat around at the Bristol depot before sitting in a local depot. Samuel Gicqueau at The Sandgate Hotel on the Kent Coast would like to buy his lettuces *in* France, not just *from* France. He reckons he would pay up to two-thirds less there, when you take into account all the wastage of wilted leaves between the French grower, the French wholesale market Rungis, New Covent Garden Market and Kent.

The perfect answer, of course, would be enough good local producers to provide all supplies direct or through local wholesalers. Some pioneering chefs, such as Paul Heathcote in Longridge in Lancashire, have been instrumental in supporting local suppliers and encouraging the highest standards. Sara Fox at The Lighthouse in Suffolk works with growers called Beverley and Phil Ling of Rue Herb who have set up in a village called Newborn near Felixstowe. This is one of the 'new' villages set up in the 1930s during the Depression for out-of-work coal miners, to give them greenhouses and smallholdings as an opportunity to start again. Beverley's mother used to grow tomatoes and lettuces here for a co-operative. This finished, and her daughter and son-in-law are now using the land for more interesting growing: different types of cabbages, pumpkins, ruby and yellow chard and great bunches of herbs that are cut in the morning for restaurants. It is a network that offers an alternative to mass production: every time someone else joins in, the whole operation gains in strength.

I would not like to pretend that the picture is simple. Many restaurants source their fruit and vegetables through New Covent Garden Market, where supplies come in from France and elsewhere, and of course it makes sense to buy elsewhere when English produce is not in season. The chefs I met sometimes had to encourage their suppliers rather than pluck from a ready-made Eden. Chris Johnson and Ros Hunter's Ramsons Restaurant in Ramsbottom, Lancashire, is an archetype of the individualistic place that offers character, generosity and food made from good ingredients, at very fair prices. In the summer I first met them, in the late 1990s, Chris was making a hundred-mile trip several times a week to get some sensational strawberries from an old-fashioned grower. They managed to get the bread for their shop fresh from the excellent De Gustibus bakery in Oxfordshire by hitching a lift for the loaves on a lorry that went past the bakery on its way to Lancashire.

Both Ros and Chris have become disillusioned with even English organic produce these days. Along with problems with supplies, they feel the movement has let slip some of its belief in flavour and slow growth in the rush for volume to meet increased demand. Instead, they now import directly from the Milan market, using a supplier who sources from small, family farms where less-intensive methods, the richness of the soil and the warmth of the sun produce vivid flavours. In the Italian-style *enoteca*, or wine bar, below the main restaurant, you can eat pecorino with cherries from a co-operative near Verona, or plump peppers from the Milan market with succulent scraps of anchovy and ripe tomatoes from Sardinia.

To get round some of the problems of irregular or poor-quality supplies, a number of restaurants are now growing their own produce or making direct links with farms. This is the route Chez Panisse has taken in California. Percy's is a restaurant-with-rooms in Virginstow, in a very quiet part of Devon, north of Tavistock. It is set on 130 acres of land, and has vegetable plots outside the bedrooms. Their livestock eye you up as you take your pre-dinner walk. Tina Bricknell-Webb runs a canny kitchen, getting the most of what is best and freshest. She might use tarragon stalks to flavour the water in which she cooks the potatoes, has seven kinds of spuds, stir-fries greens and serves salads of six or more kinds of leaves, picked that day. It is the sort of place where, if you walk around the land, you can watch the wind ripple through the grass. It will be interesting to see if this seasonal approach to cooking throws up new classic combinations in the way that someone discovered gooseberry sauce went with mackerel because both were available at the same time.

Of course, chefs-who-grow are nothing new, but their numbers are growing. I once wandered into the garden of Le Manoir aux Quat' Saisons, a celebrated example of a restaurant that grows some of its own produce, and got talking to the gardener who said they had used "100 tonnes" of manure on the beds in the last year. They pick the vegetables young, on the day they are going to be served. He said Raymond Blanc came into the garden every day which was fine until he started telling him to plant his turnips deeper. The response, I imagine, was a "do-I-tell-you-how-to-use-a-tin-opener" kind of a look.

A chef who has worked with Raymond Blanc, Michael Caines of Gidleigh Park, near Chagford in Devon, made a point of introducing me to his gardener, Keith Mansfield. Caines has set up his own establishment in Exeter, a restaurant and café at the Royal Clarence Hotel, where he has made an effort to source locally, including meat from Piper's Farm for the burgers in the café. His idea is to spread the concept around the country, with each place using what is best on its doorstep. It is an impressive ambition.

On the north coast of Cornwall is England's most famous of these ingredient-inspired restaurants, Rick Stein's Seafood Restaurant in Padstow. It may be 30 per cent more expensive than others in the area, but you pay for a class act.

My theories about chef family trees did not entirely work in Cornwall. I had got very excited by the idea that there would be 'Sons of Stein' setting up all the way to Land's End, serving excellent food at less-elevated prices. Paul Sellars, who used to have a well-reviewed restaurant in St Ives, had moved back to Padstow to teach at the cookery school. Another chef, David Pope, cooked the best fish dish I ate in a week of dining in Cornwall. But he had also come back to Padstow. The best food I had in St Ives was at Al Fresco, whose chef, Grant Nethercott, had worked with Paul Sellars as well as Gary Rhodes when he was at The Castle in Taunton – which gives him an interesting combination of roots. On the menu, the cooking had a mix of foreign influences, but on the plate it was clearly founded on a classical training and local ingredients. Just as I was going, the herbs arrived in a van from Heather Lane Nurseries which is also a workplace that supports people with learning disabilities. They brought in boxes of beautiful rocket and mizuna and the room filled with the smell of basil, mint, rosemary, chives and thyme. I took note that it was not Nethercott's own restaurant. He subsequently left and, at the time of writing, was setting up his own place in St Ives, Alba. It is always worth following chefs like this wherever they may go in an area, and in the end they tend to get their own place and settle, which is good news.

Chef family trees will spread, and it is worth remembering that some of the most inspirational chefs, such as Raymond Blanc and Rick Stein himself, come from outside the system. The same rule applies to chefs as to food producers. Some are from family firms and others are inspired indivduals.

You can feel the spread of Stein's enthusiasm, from the woman serving in the deli, advising customers to use palm sugar in their treacle sponge to the smart attention of the waiting staff in the Seafood Restaurant, who could answer any questions about where the fish had come from. A real philosophy spreads, one way or another. Another chef told me his views on chefs who move too quickly around too many kitchens: "You can stay long enough to pick up recipes but you will not have got the philosophy." I think of a comment Paul Sellars made to me: "Cooking is okay, but there are two other bits: the ingredients and the eating. Those are the best bits. The bit in the middle is hard work." The first time he came to Padstow, Paul was bowled over by the Seafood Restaurant. He ate mussel, leek and saffron soup followed by a ragoût of scallops and brill, realised how good fish could be, went three times – and counted the overdraft later. Talking to him, you can hear the excitement and inspiration he gets from ingredients: very much Stein's attitude to food.

Some of these restaurants were expensive but I was struck by the fact that a truly wonderful meal was really not much more than a standard three-course meal at a pizza chain, and often the same as something mediocre in a pretentious restaurant. Three courses at The Stagg Inn, at the time of writing, cost around £25. The set dinner menu at Shaun Hill's Merchant House in Ludlow was £30, and for that you get wonderful cooking, all done by the man himself. The kitchen is too small for a brigade and the budget is worked out for a

'down-sizing' chef who wanted to cook rather than delegate. All the
money goes on good ingredients rather than legions of staff and
swags of linen. There are just seven tables and the setting is plain,
although there is plenty to look at: the ceramics and paintings are
his and Anja's taste and not off a designer's shopping list. When I ate
there, the mange-tout in one dish was not so much baby as foetal;
about the size of a fingernail with the tender freshness that you only
get from the just-hand-picked. It was certainly one of the best meals
I have had in England.

Individuality can occur anywhere. There was a man who operated
in the car park opposite Hound Tor on Dartmoor, who picked out
the best of the crabs he could find from the south Devon coast and
put them in sandwiches which he sold alongside a rich fruitcake
made to a family recipe. The name of his customised mobile catering
van was The Hound of the Basket Meals. He was planning to retire
when I spoke to him, but perhaps he is still there.

Another of my favourite places in the whole of *Eating England*
was the restored Victorian station buffet on a railway platform at
Stalybridge Station, near Manchester. It is famous for its real ales – 20
guest beers a week – and is a suitable spot for a car-free pub crawl
(there is a leaflet which gives details of the Rail Ale Trail, from
Scarborough to Liverpool). The specials board advertises liver and
onions, pie and peas, bacon and egg on toast, and there are packets of
biscuits on cut- glass cake stands in a polished glass case. The building
is long and narrow, like the carriages of a train, starting with a
conservatory with stained-glass flowers in the windows and ending
with the former first-class ladies' waiting room. Another gurgle of
people comes in every time a train arrives, including, when I was
there, a couple who regularly came out of their way especially to

change trains here. The more convenient station only had wooden benches and they had never managed to find any toilets. Train stations have become increasingly inhospitable, unless you are prepared to pay out for a cardboard cup of chain-store coffee or part with the best of a fiver for some soulless food.

I'm sure there used to be more little places with individuality, 'greasy spoons' where you could get a mug of tea, a fry-up or a bowl of pud. The kind of place with its own quirks: like the sort of caff where the owner may give a Traditional English Welcome (a curt nod) with the Traditional English Fry-Up, all his or her concentration turned to spinning out dishes to hungry workers in minutes. Free-range? No. Organic? No. But is it anonymous? Definitely not. A real caff is an infinitely better place to tuck yourself into for an hour and have a mull over some strong tea. It is so hard to settle in chain cafés that you suspect some clever marketeer has designed them to keep the units moving.

To turn back once more to beer, one example illustrates how economies of scale work for large chains and narrow choice for the consumer. I had tasted some wonderful beer made by a small brewery in Harrogate called Rooster. The owner, Sean Franklin, is fascinated by the aromatic qualities of hops and makes a style of beer that brings their qualities to the fore. I had tried other beers of this style and was struck by how refreshing they were, partly through the fresh quality of the aromatics and the lightness of the beer itself. It is a style of brewing very much suited to wine-drinkers and something that must be set to grow. Were beer-drinkers, seen as traditional types, happy to try this style? I asked Sean. "You couldn't get a more down-to-earth place than Yorkshire," he replied, "And if a pint's not good, you're a very unpopular man. I don't think it is the public that are against interesting tastes. I think it is the brewers who are frightened of the marketing." His brews are sold all over the country; The White Horse in Parson's Green in London and The Fat Cat in Norwich and in Ipswich are three places you can get them down south. That is a lucky gain if you live down south, but the fact that it's available there is also down to the fact that he cannot sell it all in his own area, owing to the huge discounts that some chains may demand. A barrel of one of Rooster's beers normally costs £220 wholesale and a chain may demand as much as a £100 discount per barrel. The small operators just cannot absorb that cut; they must spread themselves around the small independents to reach the customer.

The wholesalers in the background affect what we eat and drink. I came across an interesting operation run by Peter Paprill, the regional foods merchant near Chester mentioned in chapter four, on regional food. Peter has a quiet influence in food, behind the scenes. When the English Tourist Board had a conference, he subbed the celebration dinner so that they got air-dried Cheshire ham, Cornish clotted cream and other real foods from around the country. If the Tourist Board cannot appreciate what there is to offer, how can the enthusiasm be passed on to visitors? He challenges the assumption that Foreign is Best, suggesting chefs try out Yorkshire Blue rather than just always going for Dolcelatte, or Halen Môn sea salt from Anglesey rather than French sea salt. Gradually, he is seeing a visible swing back to regional products.

Peter's operation is called Pendrill, and is named partly after a family who lived in Boscobel House near Telford. There is an oak in the ground descended from the one in which Charles II hid from

Cromwellian troops. When he was hiding, the five Penderel brothers, yeoman farmers, brought food to sustain the fugitive monarch: cheese, bread, beer, meat and so on. When Charles came back from exile, he rewarded the Penderel brothers handsomely.

The story is about how giving someone good food – hospitality, sustenance, pleasure – means so much more than mere matter. The food may disappear, but the experience does not. I think this is why, in the end, I really love the restaurants that bother, and feel so empty about the ones that are merely processing platefuls. There is a lift to the spirit from a good meal. I have some photos of platefuls on tables – some at restaurants, more at homes – and looking at them brings back to me elements of the day, the people, the weather, the conversation, what happened before and odd details of our lives at that time, and far better than if I had taken photos of people around the table. Each plateful happened at a particular time, never to be repeated. When you eat well, the good time resonates and is both heightened and fixed in your mind by the food.

10 home cooking

THE CHARACTER AND
PLEASURE OF ENGLISH
FOOD ARE CLEAREST
WHEN YOU APPRECIATE
EVERYTHING FROM THE
RAW INGREDIENTS TO
THE END PLATEFUL.
THIS FOOD CHAIN, IN
THE END, LEADS BACK
TO ONE PLACE: THE
HOME KITCHEN.

I WRITE FOR THE PLEASURE AND CHARACTER OF ENGLISH FOOD, and against anonymity and bland standardization. Much of this comes from appreciating food from the raw ingredients to the end plateful. And in this food chain there can be a missing link: the home kitchen.

It is the cook who notices when ingredients are fresh or faded – or safe: the pertness of a fresh-laid egg; the sappy spring of a good cabbage; meat that is on the turn or in its prime. To prepare farmers' market or organic vegetables – the opposite of cling-wrapped, ready-to-eat fodder – you may have to be comfortable about dealing with their idiosyncracies. Cooks appreciate the shop that sells good produce and grumble about the second-rate and so help maintain high standards. While it is perfectly possible to enjoy food without spending any time in the kitchen, the more you know, the more you appreciate what is on the plate. The proof of the pudding may be in the eating, but plenty of evidence is gathered along the way.

Cooking is learned gradually, by practice, absorption and the development of taste from what we eat habitually. For all the excitement of restaurant food and the inspiration that comes from travelling and eating, home food matters most of all. The Sunday roast is still, for many, at the heart of our feelings about English food. Yet how long will this last, when roasts are less commonly cooked and eaten at home? You may eat a roast lunch in a restaurant, but part of the full sensual experience is lost: the smell of roasting meat and the wisps of fragrant steam from the vegetable pans that build up the appetite; collapsing into a favourite chair after pudding. The 'roast' potatoes in the restaurant may be steamed and briefly deep-fried to brown them, the joint tired and boring, the vegetables cooked from frozen and reheated hours later in a microwave. Even if the food is well cooked, what about the chance to sneak past the joint, on the pretext of clearing the plates, and steal pickings of the sweet meat nearest the bone? Or lobbying for the bits of steak and kidney pie crust where the gravy has bubbled up from underneath and formed a dark, glossy sheen? What about the childhood task of whipping the cream, or the sight of the sugar-crusted pie cut open to reveal the fruit? Do you ever get that unsettling feeling that certain things – English roasts, cycling to school – may not just be part of your own childhood, but part of the past?

Home food was my fairy godmother. We had fresh produce from the garden and I was allowed to lick bowls and make green drop scones. Let loose in the kitchen, I felt like a wizard in a den. In summer the occasional wild salmon would reach the table, to be served with ceremony and hollandaise sauce. Any trout I caught had to be gutted, an experience that means more to me now; though, at the time, it was intriguingly weird and smelly.

The will to cook may be acquired at any age but the initial taste for fresh food is a precious gift to a child: potatoes with melting butter; fat, sweet carrots rich from the stew; flakes of fish; grilled chicken: the simple tastes you never get from ready-prepared foods or even from most restaurants. If the habit of fresh food and the sense of the daily rhythms of a kitchen are embedded early, you are more likely to bother for yourself later. Then again, I know cooks who have been inspired by the sheer direness of what they ate at home: the watery stew, the lumpy stodge, the general staleness and routine boredom that surrounded food. For me, childhood food was sitting on the grass in the summer holidays, while the radio played pop, eating Zoom lollies (part of the daily food shopping trip), peeling potatoes and putting them in a pan with sprigs of mint picked by the back door.

It is, of course, not just the food but the friendships and relationships that go with it that matter. In a brasserie in Durham, I bit into a chocolate and Drambuie madeleine. It had been a desultory choice: a madeleine does not mean much, apart from echoes of Proust and a *Carved Angel Cookbook* recipe subtitled "honey buns". This chocolate version looked good enough on the plate but I did not swoon at first sight, because it was not part of my memory in the same way as trifle or queen of puddings or apple pie. But the texture of the sponge and the taste was exactly the same as the steamie pudding my grandmother used to make.

My mind reeled off to visiting her flat in London, and the sound of Grannie's voice as we stood at the front door, watching the slow shape of her figure through the glass moving towards us, leaning on her stick, greeting us as she came: "Cooooooo-eeee!" Edible treats were part of our visits, from the sweets kept on top of the highest kitchen cupboard to the layered cake she made with strawberry, chocolate and vanilla sponges jammed together. I stopped in the restaurant with my chocolate madeleines and for a moment they did not exist, nor did the week, nor the year, nor Grannie's death. "Cooooo-eeee!"

Fiona Hamilton-Fairley used to run cookery classes for young professionals. Some came because they had worked their way through all the supermarket ready-meals and were finally bored, some wanted to cook to impress. One student had not even lit the pilot light of his new oven – after two and a half years. Another put a bulb of garlic into a stew rather than a clove. There was a huge shift in confidence when they knew how to make anything; getting over the "I-can't-cook" hurdle was the problem, not the cooking itself. Fiona is now trying to set up a national network of cookery schools and is running a pilot project, The Kids' Cookery School, in Acton, west London, with 40 per cent of the places assisted or free, and places for children with special needs. After five years of experience, it no longer comes as a surprise to her how little children and adults know about food. Some children think that carrots grow on trees. She has seen an anaemic three-year-old and many others who are obese or have food phobias. Some have never sat down at a table with their family to eat together. "We have a big problem," she summarises. "We have lost the thread of family food."

It used to be more normal to cook basic food at home, to peel carrots, if not to make soufflés. All the same, in domestic cooking as in restaurant food, there was no recent Golden Age to tarnish; food writers throughout the 20th century have bemoaned the lack of interest and discrimination, the taste buds trained on tinned foods. The thread of family food was weak enough to break.

Arabella Boxer's *Book of English Food* (1991) is a really interesting cookbook because it describes a more positive part of the past. In her introduction, she describes a "discreet revolution" in simple but refined English food that took place among the middle and upper classes between the wars. It was a reaction to the pomposity of Edwardian cooking and consisted of food with a refreshing elegance and simplicity which, at its best, was about good ingredients, carefully cooked. The cross-fertilisation of cultures included trend-setting Americans, such as Wallis Simpson, who prided herself on the exquisite food she served, and a Frenchman, Marcel Boulestin, who was *Vogue*'s influential food writer until 1928, as well as being a restaurateur, running a cookery school and, in 1937, becoming the first chef to demonstrate here on television. Fashionable puddings included the delectable toffee pudding, made of fingers of white bread soaked in milk, then dipped in toffee sauce and served hot with cream, and our legion of apple puds such as apple hat (recently revived by Simon Hopkinson and Sara Paston-Williams), apple Charlotte and apple snow. What is striking is how many of the flavours in the book – deep-fried parsley, rhubarb sorbet, braised oxtail, game pies, eggs Benedict – feature on the menus of restaurants today, as if contemporary chefs have picked up a lost thread of good English food. The recipes in the book feel familiar enough to try at home without feeling self-conscious about 'heritage' cooking.

Arabella Boxer believed that this "brief flowering" of cooking was undone by the rationing and post-war austerity of the Second World War. It was replaced, after the war, by the worship of foreign foods, partly under the influence of Elizabeth David. Looking at food today, you sometimes sense how the long shadow of the war continues. We still live with the effects of post-war farming policy, which favoured productivity rather than quality, and encouraged our cheap food culture. Quite apart from the paucity of ingredients, the war, in part, institutionalized eating.

English restaurants (state-sponsored providers of cheap, nutritious meals), works canteens and school dinners proliferated. Christina Hardyment's book on the second half of the 20th century, *A Slice of Life*, sets out some statistics: in 1941, 79 million lunches were eaten in factory canteens; in 1944 it was 170 million. Before the war, one in 36 children ate school dinners; in 1945 it was one in three and by 1949, it was over half. This institutional food no doubt improved

A bread stall in London's Borough Market.

basic nutrition for many; a crucial issue still, as far as schools are concerned. But, as Hardyment points out, it also took more people away from eating at home; I wonder if this trend further weakened the thread of family cooking? School dinners certainly gave a pretty basic interpretation of English food. No wonder we all rushed to tarte tatin (which has obvious merits) rather than English apple puddings debased by margarine and meanness. But sponge puddings, liver and beetroot all have managed something of a comeback. Faggots are only just starting to recover. Even butter beans are no longer a swear word.

Flicking through the past, the overwhelming feeling is that the appreciation of real food involves a massive reversal of time and trends. Add to this the absolutely crucial fact that domestic cooking has traditionally been a female world and that women's work patterns have changed dramatically over the last 30 years, and you wonder whether the kitchen will turn into a sterile place for white goods or designer ware rather than tastes, sizzles and smells.

A dream voice within me wonders if, since the time is past when a woman – or anyone – *has* to cook, given take-aways, ready-meals and prepared foods, perhaps this could be the time for deeper change. Maybe the urge to cook could be motivated by pleasure or value, rather than just obligation – bit by bit, perhaps, if people think that it matters to bother we shall reap the rewards. Recognizing that the thread of family food is broken or weak is, in many ways, depressing. But, from another perspective, it means that we should forget about romantic idylls. It makes me feel less impatient for change and more understanding of the fact that change has to come from going back to the basics. It also makes me look for the threads we can pick up, other than Mother's apron strings.

How do the advances made in restaurant food translate to the home kitchen? I have mixed feelings about some - though not all - chef cookbooks. Certainly, they have been a part of my cooking over the last ten years. Chefs' skills have rescued English dishes from school-dinner debasement. The way Anton Mosimann championed bread-and-butter pudding is an early example, cooking it at a gentle heat, in a bain-marie, with a generosity of ingredients and care in execution. Gary Rhodes is another chef who has done much for English dishes. Chefs can raise standards and refine tastes. They can be inspirational and I happily nibble the scraps of experience they throw out mid-recipe or absorb their philosophy, over time, if they have one.

On the other hand, there is a point in many a chef's recipe at which I write, in a screaming frustrated scribble across the page, "TOO BIG FOR MY COOKER", or some such complaint, or find myself looking at the photographs (pure gastroporn) rather than using the instructions. I do not fault their taste or technique. It is simply that chefs develop recipes under different circumstances from the home cook's and with different equipment. If you use a sieve, day in, day out, it will not seem a bother to sieve your sauce or your mash to get that extra little bit of fineness. If you want to get supper on the table quickly, it will. Chefs cook dishes that suit the service of a restaurant, with lots of advance preparation and assembly at the last minute in a red-hot kitchen. The home cook does not need that kind of stress after work or at the weekend when cooking for friends. Then there is the small matter of a team of sous-chefs and some poor soul who must do the washing-up.

So while I enjoy cooking from some of these chef books, recipe books that come from home kitchens are ultimately closer to my heart and my hearth. In her introduction to *English Food*, Jane Grigson traces the English classical tradition to home, with the "domestic virtues of quiet enjoyment and generosity", a description that conjures up dabs of butter and companionship. This is the cookbook that most of all, for me, distils the essence of English savours – gooseberry fool, buttered parsnips, lemon curd, game pie, kedgeree (a classic Anglo-Indian dish) – and gives us a line to hold on to amid the chopping-changing currents of sun-dried tomatoes and other food fashions. It is also one of those books you can read and use. Jane Grigson is a household goddess; Elizabeth David is a glamorous and slightly spiky presence, with wonderful prose and a voice that has the edge of lemon; M F K Fisher, an American, is the first food writer I read who explicitly connected food to life. Jeremy Round, Simon Hopkinson (a chef who has translated to the domestic kitchen as a food writer), Margaret Costa, Philippa Davenport, Anna del Conte... all these writers sit on a shelf where I can pull them down and badger them with questions or simply sit and listen to them talk about tomatoes. Not English purists or even English, but all people who, in their own styles, have a way of inspiring you to cook and enable you to do so.

The recipe books that you find yourself using time and time again are the ones which fit in with your interests and way of living. Jane Grigson has a special place in my personal pantheon, but in my early 20s I cooked more from her daughter Sophie's books, which reflect the way travel and a diversity of ethnic ingredients influenced my generation. At that stage I was using every scrap of money I could get my hands on to travel as far away from England as possible, and the heady scent of garlic and the smell of toasting nuts were part of cooking from her books. Recipes do not exist in a vacuum, but as part of life. Nigella Lawson, in recent years, has brought the day-to-day oxygen of home and life into cooking. One of my favourite cookbooks is the recently re-issued *The Independent Cook*, by the first food writer on *The Independent* newspaper, Jeremy Round. With wit and relish, Round espouses seasonal cooking with recipes that reflect the way life slips into your taste buds and kitchen from various sources. Food and eating arise from a patchwork of influences; recipes and ideas are garnered from every corner; the ones that take hold are the ones that mean the most to you. They might become favourites through excellence (like Raymond Blanc's rhubarb and lemon tart) or through the way they fit into your life (I find Indian dhals nutritious and delicious when I am low on funds, for example, and proper English puds fill the gaps after non-meat dishes – several friends are vegetarian). Or they might be habitual, rooted foods – Mum's mince, cheese soufflé with peas.

Another influence, from the US, has been the scientist Harold McGee, whose clear eye sees through the many old wives' tales about food. McGee can explain why you brown meat (for colour and flavour, not to "seal in the juices") or the chemistry of mayonnaise. To understand what is happening when you cook cuts through insecurity, and means that you can pick up the thread without having had an Italian grandmother imparting kitchen wisdom in your ear throughout youth. Harold McGee's books, *On Food and Cooking* and *The Curious Cook* may not be recipe books, but they have influenced contemporary food writers, and so knowledge filters through. Television programmes can give some of the sensory pleasures of cooking: close-ups which magnify food and 'sound-ups' on a sizzle or a stir. Watching Delia Smith is soothing because her programmes offer an enhanced version of what you do in the kitchen yourself,

Sea bass at Billingsgate market, London

and she does not get in the way of the food. In television food programmes, it helps if the props upstage the presenter. Ultimately, however, any cookery on television feels like having your nose pressed against the window of a sweet shop: temptation and sensory deprivation until you can get your own hands on the ingredients and experience food in real time.

Unless they really do inspire you to cook, when it comes to picking up the thread of real cooking, television programmes are far less useful than cookery courses. A number of chefs in the "Eating Out" chapter (*see chapter nine*), and many other people – including those with pubs and shops – offer cookery courses. Some of them even start with buying the ingredients. The fun of these courses comes partly from the sheer quality and quantity of ingredients you get your hands on: great fronds of dill instead of a small packet, a lovely wild salmon. Then there is the succession of smells and sounds all around, and hearing snippets of food gossip and ideas from other people. These courses guide you through the basic preparation of ingredients and I think this is the heart of their usefulness. You may never fillet a fish again, but to do so on a course, or at home, gives you confidence to ask a fishmonger to do it for you. It makes you happier about buying whole fish of good quality from an independent rather than a dull packaged fillet off the bone.

These courses cost money and often teach you to make dishes that you will not make every day, but the familiarity with ingredients that you gain filters through to day-to-day cooking. What really matters in the end is the knowledge you pick up through your hands, eyes, nose and mouth. One of the most useful bits of kitchen know-how I have acquired, while on a cookery course at Leith's Cookery School in London, was how to joint a chicken. It does not take long and means you buy a proper bird at a butcher and use different parts in different ways, from chunky thighs to silky breasts, and end up with magical, shimmering stock. There is something *bonne femme* about the whole process: deeply satisfying. You could always get a butcher to do the work or buy ready-jointed, free-range, organic chickens. But by getting your hands on a bird you gain a different level of knowledge and appreciation of what you are eating, as well as saving money. The muscles of a free-range bird are very different to those of factory-farmed, semi-automated matter. You can get tell this from the taste and texture, but you learn even more through touch and sight on the chopping board. People complain that real food is expensive but cooking fresh ingredients yourself is less expensive, quite apart from being more delicious, when you compare it to bought-in, ready-prepared food.

Fresh home cooking is a matter of health as well as pleasure. How do restaurants and ready-meal manufacturers make their food appealing? The quickest route is by adding fat, sugar and salt. And when it comes to paying attention to healthy eating, how can you be aware of what goes into food unless you cook it yourself?

This is not a book about food policy, but there is one way in which public policy touches on home cooking, or could do. Home Economics was a rather dry term for the way food was taught in schools; nonetheless, it was a time in which the basics could be learned. Food is now part of Design and Technology, and pupils design pizzas on paper and work out how to market them for profit. If only there were some way of getting the basics over instead. It need not be rock buns, but perhaps how to use onions, potatoes, carrots and cabbages; how to make a stew, a soup, roast a chicken, make a crumble, make a pizza or an economical stir-fry, how to use some ingredients in season. How to bake and roast in an oven and use a fridge to store food safely. How food relates to farming and the countryside, or how to get a handle on whatever food scare is in the news. If home economics still existed, it would be a chance for all these subjects to be explored. There are many reasons, when you walk around a town or city in England, that there is a particular processed-food pallor in the faces that you see. To deny a basic food education to schoolchildren is to throw away a valuable lifeline.

Cooking matters, at whatever age. For whenever politicians posture and headlines scream, all the talk about food has to come back, in the end, to one grounded, practical, individual, personal place, if it is to mean anything at all: the kitchen.

guide introduction

THE LAST PART OF THE BOOK gives some answers to the crucial
question: where do you go to find good food and drink? The one
fundamental rule is to find the people who take the trouble to do
things properly, as a matter of course. Find the people who bother
and you have a far better chance of eating well. They will also be able
to give other tips on who else is good in the area.

   This section is a personal attempt to bring together just some of
the talented chefs, food producers and sellers around England. I am
writing for the visitor, and so have selected 20 parts of the country
that are particularly interesting to explore. Other excellent guides give
more comprehensive entries on particular strands of food and drink
or areas (the bibliography lists some of the most useful). This guide
section of *Eating England* brings together brief tastes of several types
of place: the gastro-pub and the old-fashioned boozer; the restaurant
– posh or plain – where the chef is always inspired to find the best,
freshest ingredients and treats them with joy and respect; the deli,
farm shop and market that showcases local, regional and national
excellence. Some of these are in the centres of major cities, others
 are reached by minor roads that take you off the obvious and into
the glorious. My main aim was to find places with real character
 and genuinely high standards, which offer value for money at
whatever price.

Cornwall

ON THE NORTH COAST, Rick Stein's **Seafood Restaurant** in Padstow is one of the best places to eat fish in England. Expensive for Cornwall, but worth it. (*See also chapter nine.*) Stein's deli has upmarket fish and chips, fish curry and so on, and the **Padstow Seafood School** runs throughout the year. The Stein empire also includes **Rick Stein's Café** and **St Petroc's** bistro.

Dennis Knight's shop, in an old pilchard shed, is a good place to buy fresh fish and shellfish, in the harbour village of Port Isaac. Park at the top of the village rather than driving in. He also sells in Rock.

Helsett Farm's ice-cream in Lesnewth is carefully made, by Sarah Talbot-Ponsonby and Eila Allen, with good ingredients, including their own clotted cream and homemade fruit purées. Specialities include white coffee bean, and honey and lavender. They sell from the farm and at shops, including Di's Dairy in Rock and Trudgeons in Probus, near Truro. Further up the coast, **Sue Proudfoot** in Marhamchurch near Bude uses milk from her own cows to make the semi-hard Trelawny and Miss Muffet, and the soft cheese, Cornish Herbert. She sells from the farm, in shops in the area and in cheese shops further afield. (*See also chapter seven.*)

As you come into Cornwall on the A30 or A38, the National Trust's **Lanhydrock House**, near Bodmin, has a fascinating Victorian kitchen with a scullery, a bakehouse, a dry-goods store, a fish larder, a meat larder, a dairy scullery (with a clotted-cream range) and a dairy. The tearoom has Cornish splits - soft white buns - instead of scones with the clotted cream teas.

Lostwithiel Farmers' Market, run by the Cornish Guild of Smallholders, was the first of its kind in Cornwall; it runs fortnightly on Fridays, from 10am-2pm and has 22-26 stallholders from within a 35-mile radius, including Sue Proudfoot and Helsett Farm.

Seafood Restaurant,
Padstow Seafood
School, St Petroc's and
Rick Stein's Café
01841 532700
Padstow
www.rickstein.com
bedrooms
Dennis Knight
01208 880498
1 Fore Street
Port Isaac
and
01208 862422
1 Azime Court
Rock Road
Rock
Helsett Farm
01840 261207
Lesnewth
Boscastle
(ring in advance)
Sue Proudfoot
01288 361317
Whalesborough Farm
Marhamchurch
Bude (ring in advance in winter)
Lanhydrock House
01208 73320
Lanhydrock
near Bodmin
**Lostwithiel
Farmers' Market**
Joy Cheeseman
01840 250586
Community Centre
Lostwithiel
www.cgos.co.uk

Cornish Smoked
Fish Company
01726 72356
Charlestown
St Austell
www.cornishsmoked
fish.co.uk

Pine Cottage
01872 501385
Portloe
www.pinecottage.net
bedrooms

Hotel Tresanton
01326 270055
Lower Castle Road
St Mawes
www.tresanton.com
bedrooms

Pandora
01326 372678
Restronguet Passage
Mylor Bridge

Trengilly Wartha
01326 340332
Nancenoy
near Constantine
bedrooms

Duchy of Cornwall
Oyster Farm
01326 340210
Porth Navas

On the south coast, Martin Pumphrey at the **Cornish Smoked Fish Company** in Charlestown, near St Austell, has perfected a method of cold-smoking mackerel, and sells this and other products by mail order, in shops and at the smokehouse.

Portloe is a very small, tucked-away, Cornish fishing village, with the coastal path taking you up into the wildflowers on the clifftops. Clare Holdsworth used to run the award-winning Tregain restaurant in the village post office and has now moved into a B&B, **Pine Cottage**, where she does dinner for residents using fresh, local produce, including lobster to order, weather permitting.

Further down the coast at St Mawes is the stylish **Hotel Tresanton**, with sea views from the dining room and terrace. The chef, Peter Robinson, inspired by Alice Waters and Chez Panisse, uses his art to let the flavours of the ingredients come out and takes trouble to source locally, going, for example, to Lostwithiel Farmers' Market on the trail of good marmalade-makers. (*See also chapter nine.*)

Pandora at Restronguet Passage near Mylor Bridge is a thatched pub on the water's edge, with flagstones and a warren of rooms. It gets particularly busy in summer. You can walk along the coast from here and watch the sail-powered oyster-fishing fleet, from October to March. (*See also chapter four.*)

Trengilly Wartha at Nancenoy, near Constantine, is an exceptional gastro-pub tucked away within walking distance of an unspoiled wooded creek of the Helford River (the name means "the house high in the woods"). The seafood is very fresh and even the cheese biscuits are homemade. One of the owners, Nigel Logan, runs a wine business.

The **Duchy of Cornwall Oyster Farm** at Porth Navas sells native oysters relaid from the Fal Estuary, and Pacific oysters and mussels, and is a peaceful spot for a picnic.

Huw Jones of **Merrivale Farmhouse** in Gweek makes charcuterie, including his unique Cornish salami made with black pepper, garlic and rum. He sells this and other products by mailorder, through shops and in restaurants as well as from the door.

Near here, you can buy cheese at **Menallack Farm,** near Treverva, from John and Caryl Minson. They sell 24 Cornish cheeses including their own 12, the cow's cheese, Menallack, the best known. Seeing the long grass here, as glossy as a model's hair, made me realize why dairy produce is so good in this area.

Heading down to the southeastern part of the Lizard, **Roskilly's**, near St Keverne is an excellent place to go with children (or without) to see a working Jersey dairy herd and to eat luscious ice-cream at the farm's Croust House Tea Rooms. Clotted cream, vanilla, raspberry, a tangy lemon, cardamom, orange mascarpone and gooseberry are just some of the flavours you have to get licked. The ice-cream and fudge are also sold in shops around Cornwall.

At the end of the Lizard, at **Lizard**, a sign on the main road into the village leads you to the **Lizard Pasty Shop**. These have crisper pastry than others and come in cheese as well as the traditional beef. Ann Müller also does specials, including a Popeye pasty with spinach, watercress, parsley and egg which she eats every day to give her energy when she rows during the Cornish Pilot Gig season (gigs are the fast, narrow boats that were once used to guide ships).

The **Halzephron Inn** at Gunwalloe has good food and is a snug space out of the wind. Along from here, **Halzephron Herb Farm** is full of surprises, including parrots. Their herbal range covers everything from marinades to cordials.

John Strike's **Quayside Fish** is a high-quality, friendly, modern fishmonger's, with a smokehouse, in Porthleven, a Victorian harbour

Merrivale Farmhouse
01326 221506
Gweek
www.cornishsalami.
co.uk
Menallack Farm
01326 340333
Treverva
Penryn
campsite
Roskilly's
01326 280479
Tregellast Barton Farm
St Keverne
self-catering cottages
Lizard Pasty Shop
01326 290889
Sunny Corners
The Lizard
www.connexions.
co.uk/lizardpasty
Halzephron Inn
01326 240406
Gunwalloe
bedrooms
Halzephron Herb Farm
01326 240652
Gunwalloe
www.halzherb.com

Quayside Fish
01326 562008
Harbourside, Porthleven
www.quaysidefish.co.uk
Guinevere
01326 565911
Harbourside, Porthleven
The Ship Inn
01326 564204
Porthleven
Pilchard Works
01736 332112
Newlyn
www.pilchardworks.co.uk
www.cornishfish.com
The Tate
01736 796226
Porthmeor Beach
**Matthew Stevens
and Son**
01736 799392
Back Road East, St Ives
www.mstevensandson.
com
Heather Lane Nurseries
01736 740198
Canonstown, Nr Hale
closed at weekends
The Market Garden
07801 926814
Bread Street Penzance
Old Chapel
01736 798307
Zennor
hostel
Tinners Arms
01736 796927
**Wayside Folk
Museum**
01736 796945

town where the sea booms against the granite walls. He also sells fish by overnight delivery. *(See also chapter eight).* Just along the quayside from here is **Guinevere**, a restaurant with style and genuine warmth, run by Carl and Rachel Grove. Carl used to be front-of-house at Pont de la Tour and Blake's in London. They have plans for a hotel in Sithney, nearby. Further on, right over the waves and built into the cliff, is an old fishermans' pub, **The Ship Inn**.

An exceptional place to visit, unlikely as this might sound, is the **Pilchard Works** at Newlyn. It gives you a window onto the social and natural history of the area. They also sell salted pilchards packed in oil, delicious salt cod and fresh fish by courier. *(See also chapter four.)*

St Ives has taken off as a place to visit for art and food by the sea. Barbara Hepworth's studio and garden are particularly interesting, and the café in the **Tate** has great views. There is a lot going on in the St Ives restaurant scene. Grant Nethercott, a good chef based here, was, at the time of writing, setting up his own restaurant, Alba, plus a deli and bistro, in the old lifeboat house. *(See also chapter nine.)* The two beachside cafés at Porthminster and Porthmeor beaches are in prime positions. **Matthew Stevens**, who supplies fish to restaurants in the area, has a retail shop and sells by mailorder. Grant Nethercott gets beautiful fresh herbs and salads from **Heather Lane Nurseries** in Cannonstown, to the south of St Ives, which is a project for adults with learning disabilities. Heather Lane also sells from its shop in Cannonstown, in the **Market Garden** in Penzance and to many restaurants in the area, including the Seafood Restaurant.

In the charismatic village of Zennor, the **Old Chapel** hostel is a useful place for walkers. **The Tinners Arms** is an atmospheric pub. **The Wayside Folk Museum** is full of yarns and the church has a celebrated carved mermaid.

devon

Exeter and East Devon Starting east of the M5, the 15th-century **Drewe Arms** in Broadhembury serves mostly fish, beautifully cooked. One of the owners, Kerstin Burge, is Swedish, and gravadlax and pickled herrings are on the menu. Their beers are from the nearby **Otter Brewery**, which is based in Luppitt and has tours, by arrangement, in the summer. The brewery's local, the Luppitt Inn, is one of those utterly unchanged country pubs: the side room of a farmhouse with just a couple of tables.

Magdalen Road in Exeter is a street of good independents, including an exceptional butcher, **Piper's Farm** and a fishmonger, **Gibson's Plaice**. Piper's also sells from the farm, near Clyst Hydon, northeast of Exeter. (*See also chapter eight.*)

Exeter's cathedral close is blessed with **Michael Caines at the Royal Clarence** hotel. Caines, otherwise the chef at Gidleigh Park, a top country-house hotel on Dartmoor, is a passionate advocate of regional produce. The Royal Clarence has an imaginative, well-priced menu. (*See also chapter nine.*)

South of Exeter, Topsham has an organic farm shop on its outskirts, **Highfield Harvest**, and in the town, another branch of the excellent **Country Cheeses**, based in Tavistock (*see below*). South of Topsham, the riverside **Bridge** pub has been in the same family for four generations and serves up to ten real ales and straightforward food made with good ingredients, such as Stilton-and-cider soup and smoked salmon sandwiches. A gem.

Dartmoor and West Devon Heading west from Exeter, on the A30, **The Drewe Arms** at Drewsteignton is a fine old thatched pub which commemorates the late landlady, Mabel Mudge, who presided over proceedings here for 76 years.

The Drewe Arms
01404 841267
Broadhembury
Otter Brewery
01404 891285
Mathayes
Luppitt
Piper's Farm
01392 881380
27 Magdalen Road
Exeter
and near Clyst Hydon
Gibson's Plaice
01392 495344
38 Magdalen Road
Exeter
Michael Caines at the Royal Clarence
01392 310031
Cathedral Yard
Exeter
www.michaelcaines.com
bedrooms
Highfield Harvest
01392 876388
Highfield Farm
Clyst Road
Topsham
Bridge
01392 873862
A376 to Exmouth
on Bridge Hill
Topsham
www.cheffers.co.uk
Country Cheeses
01392 877746
26 Fore Street
Topsham
The Drewe Arms
01647 281224
Drewsteignton
bedrooms

James Bowden
and Sons
01647 433271
Chagford
Webber and Sons
01647 432213
Chagford
Moorland Dairy
01647 432479
Black's Deli
01647 433545
22 Mill Street
Chagford
01647 432244
bedrooms
Gidleigh Park
01647 432367
near Chagford
www.gidleigh.com
bedrooms
Wild Beef
01647 433433
Hillhead Farm
Chagford
Nobody Inn
01647 252394
Doddiscombsleigh
bedrooms
Rugglestone Inn
01364 621327
Widecombe-in-
the-Moor
Warren House Inn
01822 880208
B3212 NE of Postbridge

Chagford has two classic hardware shops, next door to each other on the village square. **Bowden's** has a mini-museum at the back, and is an amazing warren of useful thingummies and whatchamacallits; **Webber's** has more cookware and also makes for entertaining rummaging. **Moorland Dairy** has local clotted cream, from a pedigree Guernsey herd, and Devon honey. Local fruit and veg are sold in the nearby Market House, a building known locally as 'the pepper-pot' because of its shape. **Black's Deli** has a good range. **22 Mill Street**'s chef-proprietor, Duncan Walker, used to cook at Gidleigh Park; it's stylish and good value.

For a premier league blow-out, Paul and Kay Henderson's **Gidleigh Park** is a vision that ends a magical drive down Devon lanes near Chagford. The set-price meals are full of art and fine ingredients, including produce fresh from their garden, where Michael Caines works closely with the gardener. There is an exceptional wine list and, more simply, the spring water tastes as pure as the air.

Michael Caines gets some of his beef from Richard Vines, at **Wild Beef**, who grazes his South Devon and Welsh Black cattle on the moors and on unimproved permanent pasture with deep-rooted plants that bring up the minerals from the soil. The meat is hung for at least three or four weeks. He sells by mail order, at farmers' markets in the southwest and Borough Market, London.

Just off the A38 south of Exeter, The **Nobody Inn** at Doddiscombsleigh is well known for its food, wines, whiskies and cheeses, including a choice of 50 from the southwest.

The **Rugglestone Inn** at Widecombe-in-the-Moor is a granite-floored local near Hound Tor and Haytor and the **Warren House Inn** near Postbridge is a walkers' pub with views across the moor. Alan Smith is a gent who I found selling fresh crab sandwiches (crusts removed on request), good fruitcake and a choice of 17 teas, from a customized mobile catering can called 'Hound of the Basket Meals' in the car park at Hound Tor. He always used to be there every day from Good Friday to the end of September and then at weekends, but there has been talk of retirement.

To the east of Dartmoor, at Tavistock, **Country Cheeses** has an exceptional range of cheeses from the south-west. (*See also chapter eight.*) North of here, near Virginstow, Tina and Tony Bricknell-Webb at **Percy's at Coombeshead** take the principle of freshness to a logical and delightful conclusion by growing their own ingredients, including raising some livestock, and offer a short menu using ingredients at their peak. The restaurant is set in 130 acres of peaceful countryside. (*See also chapter nine.*)

South Devon Joyce Molyneux's **Carved Angel** in Dartmouth has been one of the most celebrated ingredient-led restaurants in England. I have not been able to try out the restaurant under the new management, but the former head chef, Nick Coiley, has set up his own place, **Agaric**, in the unspoiled market town of Ashburton and this certainly continues the principles of freshness, local suppliers and clear flavours. A relaxed, informal place with excellent food. (*See also chapter nine.*)

South of here, near Dartington Hall, the **Riverford Farm Shop** at Staverton is a big place with a wide choice, including meat, sourced if possible from local and organic producers. They can let you know about farm walks.

In Totnes, **Grey's Dining Room** is a teashop/café with cakes in the window and local free-range eggs in the omelettes. **Ticklemore Cheese** shop is run by Sarie Cooper, who is the partner of Robin

Country Cheeses
01822 615035
Market Road
Tavistock
(in Pannier Market)
Percy's at
Coombeshead
01409 211236
near Virginstow
(follow brown signs
off A388)
www.percys.co.uk
bedrooms
Agaric
01364654478
30 North Street
Ashburton
Riverford Farm Shop
01803 762523
Riverford
Staverton
Grey's Dining Room
01803 866369
96 High Street
The Narrows
Totnes
Ticklemore Cheese
01803 865926
1 Ticklemore Street
Totnes

Rocombe Farm

inquiries: 01626 834545

shop: 01803 293996

123 Union Street

Castle Circus

Torquay

www.rocombefarm.

co.uk

Sharpham

01803 732203

Ashprington

Dittisham post office

01803 722214

Fingals

01803 722398

Dittisham

www.fingals.co.uk

bedrooms

Wardroom

01548 842620

19 Fore Street

Salcombe

Burgh Island Hotel

01548 810514

Burgh Island

near Bigbury-on-Sea

bedrooms

Congdon, one of the best cheesemakers in England, known for his ewes' milk cheese Beenleigh Blue, goats' milk Harbourne Blue, cow's milk Devon Blue, hard goats' cheese Ticklemore and ewes' milk Ticorino.

Rocombe Farm organic ice-creams, sorbets and frozen yoghurts are available countrywide and they have a shop in Torquay.

The **Sharpham** estate is in a beautiful position overlooking the River Dart near Ashprington, south of Totnes; it is well worth a trip to buy the wines and to walk on the lovely promontory by the vines and the water. I tried the Madeleine Angevine 1998, which had a natural spritz and a light, fresh, breezy, elegant taste – the essence of the place – and they have managed to make a praised red, Beenleigh Red. Debbie Mumford makes cheeses from the milk of the Jersey herd on the estate: an unpasteurised Brie-style cheese, Sharpham; a triple-cream cheese, Elmhirst and Rustic, a semi-soft cheese. You see them in good cheese shops, in Devon and elsewhere.

Dittisham is known for its plums, which are in their short and juicy prime in August. They are sold from **Dittisham post office** and by one or two people in boxes around the village. They may be used, along with other good ingredients by Richard Johnston at **Fingals**, a convivial place which feels more like a household than a hotel, and where everyone eats good food together at dinner.

Heading to the south coast, the **Wardroom** in Salcombe has crab salads and tables overlooking the harbour.

Burgh Island near Bigbury-on-Sea was a holiday spot for Agatha Christie and Noël Coward in the cocktail-swigging 1930s. The restored hotel, reached by foot or in an eccentric sea-tractor, over a nice beach, serves lunch and dinner to non-residents and cocktails and tea in its Palm Court.

North Devon Treloar's deli in Crediton was set up by Guy Garrett, who ran Food for Thought vegetarian restaurant in Covent Garden in the 1980s. Homemade pâtés, desserts and other products are made by Jane Vigurs, who cooks at the back of the shop. Cheeses from Britain and Europe are sourced with care. It's an excellent shop.

I have never managed to get into **Pophams** in Winkleigh. It is so small – just ten seats – that you need to be lucky, or very well-organised, to get a booking. The Michelin inspectors managed to get in: they have given Melvyn Popham a star. It is open Wednesday to Friday, lunchtime only. The 12th-century **Duke of York** in Iddesleigh, west of Winkleigh, is a quintessential village pub, with great real ales, warmth and freshly made food, served all day.

Some of the farmhouse B&Bs in the West Country serve the sort of simple, well-flavoured food that is hard get in a restaurant. *A Taste of the West* guidebook took me to the friendly **Newhouse Farm**, near Oakford, and another that has been recommended is **Kerscott Farm**, Ashmill, where they have their own pigs, Devon Red Ruby cattle, free-range eggs and homemade preserves. **Bawdens**, the baker in Bampton, is part of the world that might have been observed by the photographer James Ravilious. They bake old-fashioned loaves and have butterfly cakes for 16p. North of here, you can buy **Vulscombe** goats' cheese directly from Jo and Graham Townsends' farm, by mail-order or in local shops. Phone for directions.

I enjoyed the Pannier Market at **South Molton,** held on Thursdays and Saturdays and the health-food shop, **Griffin Wholefoods.**Barnstaple market is also worth visiting and has a permanent row of shops including **Marshford Organics**. Marshford's own farm shop in Northam, near Bideford, is worth a wander, amid the birdsong. They do local deliveries.

Treloar's
01363 772332
38 High Street
Crediton

Pophams
01837 83767
Castle Street
Winkleigh

Duke of York
01837 810253
Iddesleigh
bedrooms

Newhouse Farm
01398 351347
Oakford
B&B

Kerscott Farm
01769 550262
Ashmill
B&B

Bawdens
Brook Street, Bampton

Vulscombe
01884 252505
Higher Vulscombe
Cruwys Morchard
(phone for directions)

South Molton market
Pannier Hall
Broad Street
South Molton

Griffin Wholefoods
01769 572372
120 East Street
South Molton

Marshford Organics
01237 477160
Northam, Bideford
and
01271 322855
14 Butchers Row
Barnstaple

dorset

Long Crichel Bakery
01258 830852
Long Crichel

The Butchers Shop
01747 811229
Iwerne Minster

Cann Mills
01747 852475
Cann

Trehane Nursery
01202 873490
Stapehill Road
Hampreston

THIS SECTION CONCENTRATES mostly on west Dorset, a special and unspoiled part of England, where you still find networks of good producers and shops in the midst of beautiful countryside.

To start in the east of the county, east of Blandford, **Long Crichel Bakery** is in an 18th-century stable block that has been converted into a state-of-the-artisan bakery with a wood-fired brick oven, built by Paul Merry and run by the baker Tom Hitchmough. The owners, Rose and Jamie, have been influenced by French baking and the bread is sold in local shops and farmers' markets in Dorset, Somerset and Hampshire, and at Borough Market in London. The range includes sourdough loaves and currant buns that spice the air with cinnamon. (*See also chapter seven.*)

North of Blandford, **The Butchers Shop** at Iwerne Minster is worth a detour for the impeccable meat and 40 unpasteurised cheeses. Simon Harvell sells meat from traditionally farmed native breeds such as organic White Park cattle, Gloucester Old Spot pigs and Dorset Horn sheep. Beef is hung for three weeks to a month.

Further north, on the A350, and a mile and a quarter south of Shaftsbury, **Cann Mills** is a watermill in Cann where Stoate's stone-ground flour, including organic, is made and sold. The business has been run by the Stoate family since 1832 and is currently in the hands of Michael Stoate, the fifth generation.

Going south, off the A31 between Wimborne and Bournemouth at Hampreston, **Trehane Nursery** is an unusual pick-your-own farm that is part of a larger operation specialising in blueberries, which suit the sandy heathland soil. The fruit is ready to pick from July to September. The owner, Jeremy Trehane, pays great attention to variety, quality and flavour. Among his varieties, which succeed each other as the season progresses, is the Herbert, with perfumed, juicy flesh.

It can also be found, labelled by variety, in Marks & Spencer.

High up on the south side of the Isle of Purbeck, **The Square & Compass** at Worth Matravers is a classic freehold pub, which has been in the same family for more than 90 years. In a side room you find an amazing collection of fossils and seashore finds, and outside, the landlord Charlie Newman has chickens running around and sculptures made during stone-carving courses.

The B3157 west of Weymouth rides the dips and heights of this lovely stretch of coastline. **Joy and Michael Michaud** grow interesting vegetables and run a business selling chilli peppers by post at West Bexington. They do not sell from the door, but you can buy their produce and some plants from the Washingpool Farm shop (*see below*), and they have an open day with other small farms, generally on the third weekend in August. Phone to check. Further along the coast is Burton Bradstock and between here and Litton Cheyney is **Modbury Farm**'s shop, where they sell organic Jersey cream, green-top milk, and pork and bacon from pigs fed on the skim of the milk.

Michael and Joy Michaud also supply the **Riverside Restaurant** in West Bay, which started life long ago as a hot-water hut for local campers and is now a well-known fish restaurant run by Arthur and Jan Watson. Outside, it looks not unlike a larger, smarter version of the chip sheds opposite. Inside, it is full of paintings and seaside light from the water around the building. Nobody is going to rush you off your table as you drink good coffee and watch the seagulls after your meal. My cod, in a crisp, dark, Guinness batter, was joyfully juicy and the mushy peas were cooked with mint and butter.

Bridport and **Poundbury**, on the outskirts of Dorchester, have farmers' markets worth checking out for local producers. Near Bridport, **Washingpool Farm**'s shop, run by the Holland family, has

The Square & Compass
01929 439229
Worth Matravers
Peppers by Post/Joy and Michael Michaud
01308 897892
Modbury Farm
01308 897193
near Burton Bradstock on the B3157
The Riverside Restaurant
01308 422011
West Bay
Bridport/ Dorchester-Poundbury Farmers' Markets
and
Dorset Local Food Links
01305 848107
Amanda Crocker
Washingpool Farm
01308 459549
North Allington
Dottery Road, Bridport

Bridfish Smokery
01308 456306
1, The Old Laundry
Trading Estate
Sea Road North
Bridport
Leakers
01308 423296
29 East Street
Bridport
Denhay Farms
01308 422770
Broadoak
www.denhay.co.uk
Down to Earth
01305 268325
18 Princes Street
Dorchester
Manor Farm Dairy
Manor Farm
Godmanstone
www.manor-farm-
organic.co.uk
**Longmeadow
Organic Vegetables**
01300 341779
Godmanstone
WE House
01300 320265
73 Dorchester Road
Maiden Newton
Summer Lodge
01935 83424
www.sumerlodge
hotel.com
Evershot
bedrooms

an emphasis on local produce, including their own. **Bridfish Smokery** sells award-winning kippers and other smoked fish, including smoked eel and cold- and hot-smoked mackerel. **Leakers** bakery makes organic loaves using local flour from Cann Mills near Shaftsbury.

West of Bridport, in Broadoak, **Denhay Farms** is a successful operation making Cheddar and feeding the whey to their pigs, from which they make dry-cured bacon, sausages and an air-dried ham. (The same connection between cheese and ham is made between the Parmesan and Parma ham-makers in Italy.) You can buy at the farm shop, open Monday and Thursday, by mail-order or from shops around the country. **Down to Earth** in Dorchester is a well-established health-food shop with bread from Long Crichel and Manor Farm organic milk and cream.

North of Dorchester, in Godmanstone you find **Manor Farm Dairy** itself; they do farm-gate sales of organic milk, cream and, ordered in advance, lamb prepared for the freezer. (*See also chapter six.*) Opposite Manor Farm is a shed with the vegetables grown by Hugh and Patsy Chapman of **Longmeadow Organic Vegetables**. The Chapmans also sell at Dorchester Farmers' Market.

Going northwest of Dorchester, Maiden Newton has an authentic village shop, **WE House**, with a turn-of-the-century oven in which they make lardy cake, Dorset apple cake and shortbread.

The picturesque village of Evershot was a film location for Ang Lee's *Sense and Sensibility*. Here you find **Summer Lodge**, the posh restaurant of the area. I liked the food here but you will have to check out its present form in the *Good Food Guide* as the chef, Tim Ford, has since moved on to run his own place, Little Barwick House, just over the border in Somerset (*see Somerset section*).

The Fox Inn at Corscombe is an atmospheric pub with an interesting collection of sporting prints, stuffed birds and huge curling ram's horns above the large fireplace. Supplies are local and used in such dishes as a warm salad of pheasant breast and bacon, leek and celeriac soup, rack of Dorset lamb and cod steaks with anchovies, garlic and olive oil. Behind the bar are homemade elderflower cordial, damson gin and real ales.

The countryside north of the A35 between Dorchseter and Bridport has a number of pubs with good food and views. Among these, it may be worth trying **The Spyway** at Askerwell and the **Marquis of Lorne** at Nettlecombe. **The Three Horseshoes** at Powerstock came under new management at the time of writing, but is in a glorious position. You can also drive up to the top of Eggardon Hill and walk around the Iron Age fortifications to see right across to Devon and the sea. **The Brace Of Pheasants** at Plush has a good reputation.

Frampton & Sons of Beaminster sells good meat, including meat from rare and minority breeds, and a selection of other foods.

In the special, quiet countryside to the west of Bridport, Coneys Castle and Lamberts Castle are neighbouring hill-forts that can be covered in one short, steep walk. At the foot of Lamberts Castle, **The Bottle Inn** at Marshwood is very much a local, with darts and skittles. The surprise is that it also has a good range of organic and vegetarian food. The landlady, Chloe, used to work with Manor Farm Dairy and has good contacts with small growers and farmers. The puddings include Rocombe Farm's organic ice-cream from Devon in flavours like brandy-vanilla clotted cream. There is an organic guest ale every month, among the other real ales, and a field and outside tap for camping.

The Fox Inn
01935 891330
Corscombe
www.fox-inn.co.uk
The Spyway
01308 485250
Askerwell
bedrooms
Marquis of Lorne
01308 485236
Nettlecombe
Three Horseshoes
01308 485328
Powerstock
bedrooms
Brace Of
Pheasants
01300 348357
Plush
Frampton & Sons
01308 862253
19 The Square
Beaminster
The Bottle Inn
01297 678254
Marshwood
field for camping

north wiltshire

The Tollgate Inn
01225 782326
Ham Green
Holt
The Pear Tree
01225 709131
Whitley
near Corsham
The Quarryman's
Arms
01225 743569
Box Hill
Box

NOT EVERY GASTRO-PUB owner bothers with beers, but **The Tollgate** in Holt, near Bradford-on-Avon, has a choice of four or five real ales, changing weekly. Alexander Venables, who used to be head chef at Lucknam Park restaurant in Colerne, cooks delicious, well-priced food, including a good-value Sunday roast and ignored classics such as omlette Arnold Bennett. The bar room has sofas and comfy chairs. The puddings here are too good to resist: caramelized banana pancakes with a toffee sauce, steamed lemon pudding with a lemon-and-lime butter sauce and bread-and-butter pudding made with marmalade. They do summer seafood barbeques, weather permitting, on Friday evenings from June.

Gastro-pubs can breathe new life into old buildings. When Martin and Debbie Still took over **The Pear Tree** in Whitley, near Corsham, an 18th-century farmhouse, they pulled up the sticky carpet to discover handsome flagstones and knocked through some boarding to open up a lovely old fireplace. The menu goes from sausages to traditional comfort foods with a twist, to more eclectic dishes, including a good range for vegetarians.

For straightforward pub food, **The Quarryman's Arms** near Box is a freehouse pub with wonderful views across the valley. They always have Butcombe bitter from near Bristol, other guest beers and generous platefuls of freshly cooked food at reasonable prices. I was given three pheasant breasts in a mushroom, celery and wine sauce and plenty of vegetables for £6.50. "If I get a good deal, I pass it on," said the landlord, John Arundel. It is an untarted-up locals' pub whose character and heart come through. Long may such places survive against bland pub chains.

North Wiltshire, historically, is pig country. Calne became a bacon centre because it was a stop-off point for the pigs being walked from

Ireland to the London markets in the days before railways. **Sandridge Farmhouse Bacon**, Bromham, is an exceptional set-up. Here the Keen family make Wiltshire cure and smoked bacons and five traditional hams, including the delicious Brumham, with its notes of juniper and molasses, and the Devyses which is made with a cure including Wadworth's 6X Ale. Some of the recipes come from old *Farmers Weeklies* from the 1920s and 1930s. The pork scratchings are wicked. There are pigs for children to see and, up on the wall, articles on bacon-making and its connections to this area. (*See also chapter four.*) While you are in the area, go to **V and P Collins** on the junction of the Bromham and Calne roads (A3102 and A342), a down-to-earth, excellent fruit-and-vegetable farm shop where you get the likes of pink fir apple potatoes, sprout sticks and tiny carrots: lots of flavour and good prices. They also sell at most of the Wiltshire and Bath farmers' markets, as do the Keens.

V and P Collins supply **The George and Dragon** at Rowde. This well-known pub, run by Tim and Helen Withers, serves food using good ingredients, priced accordingly. It takes admirable nerve, and art, to let food speak for itself. My turbot came with hollandaise sauce and simple, fresh veg: what could be better? It was perfect. Less than perfection feels expensive, though. The building has retained the form of an old pub, including outside loos.

For good meat from humanely reared animals, **Michael Richards** in Calne and his son Alan, who now runs the shop, are affiliated to the Wiltshire-based **Real Meat Company**, which also sells by mail order and through 26 shops around the country. To go with your meat, **Wiltshire Tracklements** makes top-class mustards, a horseradish so hot it makes your nose tingle, and other good sauces, made in small batches to keep up the quality. They are available at

Sandridge Farmhouse
Bacon
01380 850304
Bromham

V and P Collins
01380 850228/186
nr Bromham

The George and
Dragon
01380 723053
Rowde

Michael Richards
01249 812362
21 London Road
Calne

Real Meat Company
01985 840562
www.realmeat.co.uk

Wiltshire
Tracklements
01666 840851
Sherston
www.tracklements.co.uk

Skidmore's Butchers
01666 840268
Sherston

Polly Tearooms
01672 512146
26 High Street
Marlborough

Mackintosh's
01672 514069
42 High Street
Marlborough

Marlborough Farmers'
Market
01672 513950
Jo Ripley

Berkeley Farm Dairy
01793 812228
Wroughton

Harrow Inn
01672 870871
Little Bedwyn
www.harrowinn.
co.uk

Eastbrook Farms
Organic Meat
01793 791460
www.helenbrowning
organics.co.uk

Michael Richards, at **Skidmore's Butchers** in Sherston, where Wiltshire Tracklements is based, and in other food shops around the country.

In Marlborough, The **Polly Tearooms** is a classic blow-out, from scones to Jamaican Sun ice-cream sundaes. **Mackintosh's** is a good deli with traditional cheeses (about half from Britain), organic apple juice from Pewsey, Baxter's potted shrimps (when available) and food made in their own kitchens. Marlborough also has a farmers' market with plenty of local and organic produce, held generally in the Town Hall on the second Saturday of the month, from 9 am to 1 pm. They have organic trout from Tony Free of Purly Organic; organic veg from Purton House; Sheep Drove organic meat and Ventours and Edwards sausages from near Burbage.

North of Marlborough, **Berkeley Farm Dairy** at Wroughton has Guernsey milk. Christine Gosling sells the butter, as well as milk and cream, at the farm, and also through Michael Richards in Calne, Mackintosh's in Marlborough and Marlborough Farmers' Market.

East of Marlborough, the **Harrow Inn** at Little Bedwyn is a restaurant rather than a pub, in a nice village near the Kennet and Avon canal. They sell plenty of fish and game in season and source ingredients with great care. Even the specific beef herd is listed on the menu. They have interesting wines.

Eastbrook Farm, run by Helen Browning on the Wiltshire/ Oxfordshire border, heads a strong brand of organic meat. Helen farms 120 Saddleback pigs on the Wiltshire Downs, and other livestock including sheep and veal calves, and gets meat from 15 other organic farmers. The meat is sold by home delivery and through supermarkets.

bristol, bath and somerset

Bristol I was very impressed by the food at **Markwick's**, in Corn Street. Squid stewed in red wine with fennel, orange and chilli, and duck with a honey glaze, peas and Sauternes sauce were both perfectly judged and made with the evolved good taste of a chef who loves and understands food. Stephen Markwick learned to cook with George Perry-Smith and later with Joyce Molyneaux at The Carved Angel in Dartmouth and continues their line of following the seasons and sourcing ingredients with diligence. He has helped establish a nursery that grows specifically for a couple of the best Bristol chefs, so they can get freshly picked vegetables, grown with care. Around 30 to 60 per cent of the veg at Markwick's come from here. Also in Corn Street you find the city's farmers' market, which is so successful that it runs weekly, on Wednesdays. It includes Anthony Lyman-Dixon of Arne Herbs (*see below*), and other producers such as the cheesemaker Mary Holbrook and Common Loaf, bakers from Devon.

Up the hill, on Whiteladies Road, **Quartier Vert**, formerly Rocinantes, is run by Barny Haughton, who has had a commitment to organic, local, high-quality produce, since the place opened in 1988. As well as a restaurant, there is a bar, café and cookery school here.

The former chef at Rocinantes, Christopher Wicks, has his own place, **Bell's Diner**, in the funky, slightly unravelled district of Montpelier. The interior is partly decked out in old shop fittings, the shelves well-stocked with liqueurs, antique bottles and jars of preserved lemons. The food is full of flavours, but unfussy. I also liked the refreshing citron *pressé*: the secret, apparently, is a pinch of salt. In Montpelier, Christopher recommends the Italian deli, **Licata**, which has been run by the Licata family since they arrived from Sicily in 1958. Around the corner, **Herbert's** bakery is a family business that

Markwick's
0117 9262658
43 Corn Street
Bristol
Bristol Farmers'
Market
0117 9224016
Corn Street
Bristol
weekly on Wednesdays
9.30 am - 2.30 pm
Quartier Vert
0117 9734482
85 Whiteladies Road
Bristol
www.quartiervert.
co.uk
Bell's Diner
0117 9240357
1-3 York Streeet
Montpelier
Bristol
Licata
0117 9247725
36 Picton Street
Bristol
Herbert's
0117 9247713
12 York Road
Bristol

still makes old-fashioned, tasty bread and does specials at weekends.

Riverstation is a restaurant with a modern glamour, in a great position on the river. Here, you can go for a plateful, the works or something to take away from the deli. **Chandos Deli** has branches on Whiteladies Road and in Clifton and stocks a full range of cheeses and other foods, including the good Hobbs House bread, made in Chipping Sodbury, north of Bristol.

Bath The **Green Street Seafood Café** in Bath shows off fish and fish cookery. In the shop downstairs, they sell fresh fish, supplied mostly by Wing of St Mawes in Cornwall. Fish is served upstairs, in a colourful, relaxed café. **The Old Green Tree**, just across the road, is a classic pub with wood-panelled rooms.

The Fine Cheese Company in Walcot Street sells about 150 cheeses, about 100 of which are British, and the vast majority unpasteurised. As well as selling high-quality sandwiches using Hobbs House bread, they also serve plates of cheese, bruschetta, *mezze* and other tapas-like platefuls to eat in the shop.

Bath pioneered farmers' markets and has one twice a month (on the first and third Saturdays). The permanent **Guildhall Market** includes **Gillards** tea and coffee shop with its own special hard-water blend for the local water, and other house mixes.

Somerset An unchanged pub with three small rooms, **Tucker's Grave** in Faulkland, south of Bath, was built on the grave of a suicide in 1747 (suicides were buried on crossroads, apparently). They serve Butcombe bitter and Cheddar Valley cider on draft.

If you are driving through Somerset on the A303, you can stop off at North Cadbury, where one of the finest unpasteurised

Riverstation
0117 9144434
The Grove
Bristol
www.riverstation.co.uk
Chandos Deli
0117 9743275
6 Princess Victoria Street, Bristol
0117 9706565
121 Whiteladies Road
Bristol
www.chandosdeli.com
Green Street Seafood Café and shop
01225 448707
6 Green Street
Bath
The Old Green Tree
12 Green Street
Bath
The Fine Cheese Company
01225 483407
29 Walcot Street
Bath
mail order:
01225 448748
www.finecheese.co.uk
Bath Farmers' Market
Laura Lockston
01761 470098
Green Park Station
Bath
Gillards
01225 463430
55 Guild Hall Market
Bath
Tuckers Grave
01373 834230
east of Faulkland
on A366

Cheddars, Montgomery's, is made. Buy some at a good price in **North Cadbury's Post Office and Stores**. Some of the cows graze near Cadbury Castle, which may or may not have been one of King Arthur's vantage points across the land. It is certainly worth climbing up for the views.

South of Yeovil, on the Dorset border, **Little Barwick House** in Barwick is a comfortable and welcoming restaurant with rooms, serving good, classically cooked food. Chef/owner Tim Ford used to be head chef at Summer Lodge in Evershot, Dorset.

North of the A303, on the Somerset Levels, **Brown & Forrest** has a smokery-restaurant and shop at Hambridge. This watery setting is appropriate to their most famous product: hot-smoked eels. In the restaurant, the eel comes with rye bread, horseradish sauce (either home-picked and homemade, or from Wiltshire Tracklements - *see page 237*) and a beetroot salad. This is a great example of a place where good produce speaks for itself. The likes of smoked food, salads, soups and great cakes (buttery, dark-sugar-crunchy American apple cake) are served simply, in comfortable surroundings. (*See also chapter three.*) The owner, Michael Brown, likes the **Halfway House** at Pitney, as a pub near here. Another classic old-time Somerset pub is the **Rose & Crown,** always known as Eli's, in Huish Episcopi. The farm-workers used to cook their kippers and other food on the fire in the back room to go with their cider. The pub has been owned by the same family for more than 130 years.

Near Hambridge, the **Somerset Cider Brandy Company** sells from an old barn at Burrow Hill, near Kingsbury Episcopi. As well as cider brandy, they make still and sparkling cider and a delicious cider aperitif, Kingston Black. Further north, **Roger Wilkins'** cider shed in Mudgeley, near Wedmore, is an authentic farm cider experience.

North Cadbury Post
Office and Stores
01963 440201
Little Barwick House
01935 423902
Barwick
bedrooms
Brown & Forrest
01458 250875
Hambridge
The Halfway House
01458 252513
Pitney
The Rose & Crown
(Eli's)
01458 250494
Huish Episcopi,
on A372
Somerset Cider Brandy
Company
01460 240782
Burrow Hill
nr Kingsbury Episcopi
Roger Wilkins
01934 712385
Land's End Farm
Mudgeley
nr Wedmore

Arne Herbs
01275 333399
Limeburn Hill
Chew Magna
www.arneherbs.co.uk
Phil Bowditch
01823 253500
7 Bath Place
Taunton
The Castle Hotel
01823 272671
Castle Green
Taunton
www.the-castle-
hotel.com
Swaddles Organics
01460 234387
www.swaddles.co.uk
**Somerset
Farm Direct**
01398 371387
www.somersetfarm
direct.co.uk
**Bay Tree Food
Company**
01749 831300
www.thebaytree.co.uk
**Exmoor Blue Cheese
Company**
01984 667328

South of Bristol, in Chew Magna, **Arne Herbs** has a range of 720 culinary and medicinal herbs. You can get a catalogue for £2 (refundable on first purchase) or see the list for free on the internet. Visitors should phone Arne Herbs to place their orders in advance. They sell their salad leaves to good restaurants, including Markwick's in Bristol, and at Bristol Farmers' Market and Glastonbury Farmers' Market (held on the fourth Saturday each month).

In Taunton, **Phil Bowditch** has a spruce fish shop down an interesting alley, where you also find the Women's Institute's shop. Kit Chapman at the **Castle Hotel** has long investigated the traditions and flavours of British food with his chefs (most notably Gary Rhodes and Phil Vickery). I would happily work my way through his menus for this reason alone. The quality of the ingredients is high and the restaurant's suppliers are listed on the menu. My steamed mutton and caper pudding was absolutely delicious. Some may find the French service a touch formal and some of the food too 'fine'.

Swaddles Organics get farms in Somerset and Dorset to produce high-quality, organic meat to its specification, which they sell by mail order, a London delivery van and in shops such as Fresh and Wild in Notting Hill Gate, London. As well as selling fresh meat, bacon and other products, Bill and Charlotte Reynolds have developed organic ready-meals, including a range for children.

Somerset Farm Direct is run by the Wood family, who farm traditionally on the edge of Exmoor and have set up an informal co-operative of local famers to sell properly hung lamb, mutton, free-range poultry, game and other meat directly to the public, delivering anywhere in the country. Look out for the high-quality preserves made by the **Bay Tree Food Company**, and for the cheeses made by **Exmoor Blue Cheese Company**.

kent

WHITSTABLE IS A GOOD PLACE to wander by the sea and window-browse in a town that has avoided the anonymity of modern chain stores. It is a working harbour town, less chi-chi than smarter seaside resorts and more lively than those left stranded as holiday-makers went off to warmer climes. **The Royal Native Oyster Stores**, run by The Whitstable Oyster Fishery Company, is a stripped-down restaurant and a cinema in a Victorian warehouse, where you can eat fresh, simply cooked seafood while watching the sun plop into the sea beyond the shingle beach. The company also owns the art deco **Hotel Continental** on the other side of the harbour, which has a roomy dining room full of bleached-out sea-light.

Wheelers Oyster Bar was opened in 1856 by a relative of the Wheelers' chain, and is quintessential Whitstable, with its seafood bar at the front and small Victorian parlour at the back. It gets booked up weeks in advance for weekend dining and is a real gem.

Whitstable has an exceptional deli, **Williams & Brown**, run by an ex-head chef of the Oyster Stores, Chris Williams, and another chef, David Brown. The shop has a plain look which frames their well-selected food finds, including Italian products such as wild boar and olive oils bought directly from the farm. On the high street, there are a number of old-fashioned food shops, including Hubbard's bakery, where they still give their bread a proper, slow rise.

Another good place to eat is just outside Whitstable: an unadorned pub, on the road towards Graveney, called **The Sportsman**. The chef/proprietor Steve Harris believes in "seasonal ingredients, as fresh as possible, cooked as well as possible". Here I found salt-marsh lamb, just-picked greens and tiny broad beans, juicy Monkshill Farm chicken, oysters and other seafood served in a hinterland landscape of estuarial England. (*See also chapter nine.*)

Royal Native Oyster Stores
01227 276856
The Horsebridge
Whitstable
www.oysterfishery.co.uk

Hotel Continental
01227 280280
29 Beach Walk
Whitstable
bedrooms

Wheelers Oyster Bar
01227 273311
8 High Street

Williams & Brown
01227 274507
28A Harbour Street

The Sportsman
01227 273370
Faversham Road
Seasalter
Whitstable

Brogdale Horticultural Trust near Faversham has the national fruit collection, and is an exceptional place to visit. Between April and November they run guided tours that weave social history, horticulture and anecdote with a walk around the orchards, where there are around 2,500 apple varieties, alongside other orchard and soft fruits. September and October are the months when the apples are at their full glory, but it is worth visiting at any time of year, and the spring blossom is beautiful. The well-stocked shop includes Brogdale's own apple juices. (*See also chapter six.*)

Just on the outskirts of Faversham (a mile from junction 7 off the M2, turn left into Selling Road, opposite a Shell garage), the **Macknade farm shop** grows and sells around 30 varieties of apple alongside other fruits and just-picked vegetables, and has a huge selection of food and drink.

Another excellent farm shop, **Perry Court**, can be found on the A28 at Bilting, near Wye. In season, Heidi Fermor sells around a hundred varieties of apples, nine types of plum and ten types of pear, and sells her own apple juices and plenty of other produce.

On the south coast of Kent, Samuel and Zara Gicqueau run an excellent French restaurant at the **Sandgate Hotel**, a seaside hotel in Sandgate, near Folkestone. Follow them if they were ever to move from here, for here is a chef with great taste and skill with ingredients. (*See also chapters two and nine.*)

Griggs of Hythe has a shop selling seafood right on the beach; you can wander onto the shingle and see the boats that land here.

Romney Marsh is one of the most charismatic parts of Kent: a place apart, with a strange charm that grows on you. **The Red Lion** in Snargate is a classic, genuine old pub that has been in the same family since 1911. It has bare floors, outside loos and a marble-top

Brogdale Horticultural Trust
01795 535286/535462
Brogdale Road,
Faversham
Macknade Farm Shop
01795 534497
Selling Road
Faversham
Perry Court
01233 812 408
Perry Court
Bilting
Sandgate Hotel
01303 220444
The Esplanade
Sandgate
Folkestone
bedrooms
Griggs of Hythe
01303 266410
Fisherman's Landing
Beach
Hythe
(ask for directions)
The Red Lion
01797 344648
Snargate
on B2080

counter. They have good beers and no food, but there is a nice garden for a picnic. Their annual beer festival is held in June, on the weekend nearest mid-summer. (*See also chapter one.*) The shingle at Dungeness has beautiful flowers, particularly in the first half of summer. Look out for local honeys in the shops, including those of JA Finn. In a hut near Derek Jarman's wonderful garden, Jim Lydd, a former fisherman, sells fresh fish and products from his own smokehouse, including bloaters and smoked haddock. (*See also chapter three.*)

In the Weald, **The Three Chimneys**, Biddenden (near the gardens at Sissinghurst) and in West Kent the **The Harrow Inn**, Igtham Common, are two gastro-pubs with real ales and decent food.

The **Organic Gardens at Yalding**, part of the Henry Doubleday Research Association, are an excellent series of gardens ranging from a 13th-century apothecary's garden to an early 19th-century cottager's garden to a post-Second World War allotment. I also enjoyed the **Museum of Kent Life**, signposted from junction 6 of the M20, which has exhibits on the hop and fruit growing of the area.

Kent is a hop-growing county, if less so than it once was. Of the local beers, Shepherd Neame in Faversham is the main regional brewery, and look out for beers by Goacher's, made in Maidstone; Swale, made in Sittingbourne; and Larkins made in Chiddingstone.

On the fruit side, Duskin's single-variety apple juices, made in Kingston, near Canterbury, are well worth exploring to find your favourites. Alongside apples, you will see summertime cherries in Kent and, from the end of August to October, cobnuts, a type of hazelnut, generally eaten fresh rather than dried. For information, send a sae to the **Kentish Cobnuts Association**.

The Three Chimneys
01580 291472
Biddenden on A262
1 mile W of village

The Harrow Inn
01732 885912
Igtham Common

Yalding Organic Gardens
01622 814650
Benover Road, Yalding

Museum of Kent Life
01622 763936
Sandling
near Maidstone

Kentish Cobnuts Association
Clakker House
Crouch
Sevenoaks
Kent TN15 8PY

brighton and east sussex

TO START WITH THE RESTAURANTS in Brighton, Steve Funnell at the **Black Chapati** uses Eastern influences, picked up from his extensive travels, to make stylish dishes fusing Eastern ingredients and Western cooking. Nearby is the Duke of York's cinema, where they have proper cakes, samosas and a small bar, as well as showing good films. **One Paston Place** is the smartest restaurant in the city and **La Fouchette**, heading towards Hove, is for less-expensive, high-quality French food. Both are run by chef/proprietors, as is **Gingerman**, owned by a former chef at One Paston Place, Ben McKellar. **Saucy**, in Hove, is fun. **The Mock Turtle** is a great, individualistic tearoom near the bus station, with homemade cakes and so forth. The Royal Pavilion has a magnificent historic kitchen.

Of Brighton's many charismatic pubs, **The Evening Star**, near the train station, brews good beers and sells other real ales. In Kemptown, **The Hand-in-Hand** also has a micro-brewery and is a small, dark nest of a pub. Further east, **Fish at the Square** is run by an ex-fisherman who knows what's what. As well as fresh fish, they sell fish pie and so on. Further along, **Egg and Spoon** is a modern kitchen shop with good designs. **The Cheese Shop** in the funky North Laine area has a great selection, including English classics. **Infinity Foods** is a big health-food shop, with organic vegetables and good breads. On the sea front, **Alan and Carol Hayes** do not buy fish from a wholesale market, they just sell whatever a couple of boats have just caught that day. There will be a limited choice – or nothing at all – but it should be fresh.

Heading eastwards, **The Jolly Sportsman** in the small, quiet village of East Chiltington, and the 15th-century **Griffin** at Fletching are both particularly good pubs for food.

In the fine county town of Lewes there is good shopping in the

Cliffe area, including the excellent **Say Cheese** in the Riverside building on the River Ouse. It is run with care and enthusiasm by David and Eleanor Robins, who stock a range of 20 or more Sussex cheeses, including Flower Marie and Golden Cross from Blunts at Greenacres Farm. Also in the Riverside Building, try the café upstairs for coffee, tea cakes and homemade soup. On Cliffe High Street, Bill's Produce Store (number 56), a modern greengrocer/deli with a café, and Harvey's wine and beer shop (number 6) are both good; the John Harvey Armes near the Brewery has simple lunches. The Gardeners Arms (number 46) has interesting real ales.

Off the High Street, up the hill from Cliffe, **The Lewes Arms** is a nice place for a pint of Harvey's hoppy bitter, and the **Brewers Arms** further up the high street has a bigger range of real ales. Near here, **Adamczewski's** has an exceptional selection of fine houseware, sourced from Britain and elsewhere; it is worth a detour if you are into functional quality. South of Lewes, nestled in the Downs, and reached by a farm track, **Breaky Bottom** Vineyard near Rodmell is in a beautiful spot. Owner Peter Hall welcomes visitors, but phone ahead. **Rolfs** in Seaford has good fish.

Off the A27, which runs along the foot of the Downs, the well-known **Ram** at Firle has a garden and sells Breaky Bottom wine. Between Firle and Selmeston, **Middle Farm Shop** has a wide range of food and drink, and the **English Farm Cider Centre** has an amazing selection of 140 bottled and draft ciders. Gospel Green is a high-quality local one. **Rose Cottage** in Alciston is another unspoiled old pub at the foot of the Downs, and **The Cricketers** in Berwick has a lovely atmosphere and good Harvey's. The **English Wine Centre**, near Alfrison, has an exhibition and wines to taste and buy.

Say Cheese
01273 487871
Riverside, Lewes

Lewes Arms
01273 473152
Mount Place, Lewes

Brewers Arms
01273 479475
91 High Street, Lewes

Adamczewski's
01273 470105
88 High Street, Lewes

Breaky Bottom
01273 476427
Rodmell
www.breakybottom.
co.uk

Rolfs
01323 892197
37 High Street
Seaford

The Ram
01273 858222
Firle

**Middle Farm Shop/
English Farm Cider
Centre**
01323 811411/811324
Firle/Selmeston

Rose Cottage
01323 870377
Alciston

The Cricketers
01323 870469
Berwick

English Wine Centre
01323 870164
Alfriston
www.englishwine.
co.uk

Hungry Monk
01323 482178
Jevington

The Food Rooms
01424 775537
The Chapel
53-55 Battle High St
www.foodrooms.
co.uk
Scragoak Farm
01424 838454
Brightling Road
Nr Robertsbridge
The Weald Smokery
01580 879601
Hawkhurst Road
Flimwell
J Wickens
01797 226287
Castle Street
Winchelsea
Landgate Bistro
01797 222829
5-6 Landgate
Rye
Ypres Castle
01797 223248
Gun Garden
(below the Ypres tower)
Ann Lingard
01797 223486
Rope Walk Antiques
18-22 Rope Walk
Rye
Market Fisheries
01797 225175
near Fish Market Road
Rye
Inkerman Arms
01797 222464
Harbour Road
Rye Harbour

The Hungry Monk in Jevington, famous for inventing banoffee pie, is a comfortable restaurant with sitting rooms where you can curl up on a sofa with your coffee after dinner.

Battle has a modern, stylish food shop and café, **The Food Rooms**, where the owners make a great effort to source and promote local foods. North of here, off the Brightling road near Robertsbridge, **Scragoak Farm** is a good organic shop, delightfully off the beaten track. **The Weald Smokery** at Flimwell is an excellent deli and smokehouse, smoking over local oak.

Heading east along the coast, **Jamie Wickens** in Winchelsea is a good independent butcher, with Romney Marsh lamb and beef from Sussex cattle. Toni Ferguson-Lees, the chef of the **Landgate Bistro** in Rye buys meat from Wickens, including Gloucester Old Spot pork and the odd young wild boar – and they really are wild round here, after some escaped from a farm in Kent. Toni particularly likes the cod which comes ultra-fresh from the local boats, and the scallops, brill, turbot and bass that are landed here. The Landgate is a relaxed place that has been going for 16 years, and they focus on flavour rather than formalities.

Ypres Castle (pronounced locally, as "wipers" in WWI fashion) hangs on a slope below the Ypres tower and is only accessible by foot. It changed hands shortly before this went to press, but the new owners were planning to keep the same good suppliers and the jazz and blues evenings. **Ann Lingard**, near the marketplace, has an interesting selection of old cookware, often used by stylists in magazines. Bill Drew, who runs the fish auction, also sells from a shed, **Market Fisheries**, on the river. He owns **The Inkerman Arms** in Rye Harbour, a down-to-earth pub with real ales and fresh fish.

a london selection

West **Oliver's Wholefood Shop** near Kew train and tube station is a useful place to pick up a picnic to take to Kew Gardens, one of the leafy treats of London. Chiswick High Road has an excellent deli, **Mortimer & Bennett**, which is stuffed with good things wherever you look. Along here, you will also find Covent Garden fishmongers, run by Phil Diamond, M&C greengrocers, Macken Bros' butchers and Theobroma Cacao, an exclusive chocolate shop.

South of the river, in Barnes, the northern Italian **Riva** manages to be both celebrated and a genuine neighbourhood restaurant. Some of the most straightforward-sounding dishes on the menu can be the most delicious.

The **Anglesea Arms**, off the Goldhawk Road, is one of London's best gastro-pubs. In Hammersmith, Rose Gray and Ruthie Rogers at the **River Café** focus on delicious Italian-inspired simplicity, by using fine ingredients (priced accordingly) and cooking them in such a way as to leave their freshness and flavours intact. **The White Horse** near Parsons Green tube station has interesting beers, holds regular beer festivals and has a good food menu.

Rococo on the King's Road in Chelsea was set up by Chantal Coady in 1983 and is an exquisite treat of a chocolate shop. It has a Victorian frontage and inside are layers of Rococo's own interesting chocolate bars and chocolates. Across the road, **Bluebird** food store is a Conran-owned shop with a large selection.

Across the Albert Bridge, in Battersea, **Ransome's Dock** is a good restaurant on an inlet of the Thames. It is well-run by Martin and Vanessa Lam and has a menu that shows off British produce such as potted shrimps and Norfolk smoked eel. The interesting and reasonably priced wine list makes it a favourite destination for wine-lovers.

Oliver's Wholefood Shop
020 89483990
5 Station Approach, Kew

Mortimer & Bennett
020 89954145
33 Turnham Green Terrace

Riva
020 87480434
169 Church Road
Barnes

Anglesea Arms
020 8749 1291
35 Wingate Road
Goldhawk Road

River Café
020 7381 8824
Thames Wharf Studios,
Rainville Road
Hammersmith
www.rivercafe.co.uk

The White Horse
020 77362115
1 Parsons Green
www.whitehorses
w6.com

Rococo
020 7352 5857
321 King's Road
Chelsea

Bluebird
020 7559 1153
350 King's Road
Chelsea

Ransome's Dock
020 7223 1611
35-37 Parkgate Road
Battersea
www.ransomesdock.
co.uk

Centre The Star Tavern, a mews pub in Belgravia, is one of the increasingly rare real pubs in London. It has beer from Fuller's, one of London's two main independent breweries, the other being Young's. Elizabeth Street, near Victoria Station, has some delicious treats amid the smart boutiques: **The Chocolate Society**, **Jeroboams**, **Chatsworth Farm Shop** and a London branch of the famous Parisian bakery **Poilâne**, with its crispy little apple tarts and big, round sourdough loaves. Their delicious breads keep well.

There is another run of high-quality shops in Holland Park. **David Lidgate** is a master butcher who believes that breed, feed, slaughtering, butchering and hanging all go towards making meat good to eat. His products prove that care, at every stage, means quality. **Michanicou**, just off Holland Park Avenue, is another place that is too busy to be grand. Whether you want a single peach to eat on the street, a picnic to take to Holland Park or a special salad, it is worth going places as good as these two once in a while, at least, to see what food can taste like at its best.

Going on towards Notting Hill Gate, **Chalmers & Gray** has a large, iced slab that is full of fish worth crossing the road to inspect. The metropolitan and busy Kensington Place, run by Rowley Leigh, has a menu that roams around the best British ingredients. He has a glamorous fish shop next door – tall, narrow and glass-fronted, like a fish tank – where you can gaze at a single, beautiful Dover sole on ice or buy a slice of fish terrine. **Clarke's** is a relaxing restaurant, partly because of its set dinner menu: no bother, just a balanced menu of delicious food turning up at your table. It is one of those restaurants where you can have a proper conversation. Next door is the shop, with breads, truffles, Californian wines and Neal's Yard cheeses.

Off Portobello Road, **Books For Cooks**, has the best range of

The Star Tavern
020 7235 3019
Belgrave Mews West
off Chesham Place
Belgravia
The Chocolate Society
020 7259 9222
36 Elizabeth Street
Belgravia
Jeroboams
020 7823 5623
51 Elizabeth Street
Chatsworth Farm Shop
020 7730 3033
54 Elizabeth Street
Poilâne
020 7808 4910
46 Elizabeth Street
C Lidgate
020 7727 8243
110 Holland Park Avenue
Michanicou
020 7727 5191
2 Clarendon Road
Holland Park
Chalmers & Gray
020 7221 6177
67 Notting Hill Gate
Kensington Place
020 7727 3184
201 Kensington Church Street
Clarke's
020 7221 9225
124 Kensington Church Street
www.sallyclarke.com
Books For Cooks
020 7221 1992
4 Blenheim Crescent
www.booksforcooks.com

food books in London, as well as a kitchen and a couple of tables at the back where you can eat. Go at less busy times and you may overhear delicious morsels of foodie conversation (this was at its most entertaining when Clarissa Dixon-Wright presided). Across the road, Birgid Erath at **The Spice Shop** has a great, wide-ranging selection, with a refreshing lack of fancy packaging. The market is fun, and at its best for food on Fridays and Saturdays.

Going along Westbourne Grove, **Fresh and Wild** gathers together an impressive array of food, with the emphasis on fresh, natural ingredients. Further along, **Planet Organic** stocks everything from snacks to steaks and is unusual in having dedicated meat and fish counters. **Alwaha** is a good Lebanese restaurant with lots of fresh flavours in dishes such as stuffed vine leaves, grilled chicken or quail with a sauce hot with garlic, and the carefully made hummous. The chef/co-owner Mohammed Bader-Alden honed his dishes partly by taking them back home to get his mother's comments. In Queensway, the **Mandarin Kitchen** is a Chinese restaurant famed for its seafood. As you eat, you can study how the experts deal with lobsters using chopsticks. The Edgware Road takes you through Middle Eastern London and offers plenty of great, inexpensive eating and fresh juices, at **Al Dah**, for example, to name just one. **Green Valley** has the largest range of foods to buy, including lots of olives and little, sticky cakes.

Villandry in Marylebone has the likes of wonderful honeys imported from France and many other such treats on its shelves. You can also eat here and buy dishes to take away. In Mayfair, **Mirabelle** has glamour and classically-based cooking. The Japanese/Peruvian **Nobu** has exquisite food and a strange atmosphere: everyone keeps looking up to spot celebrities.

The Spice Shop
020 7221 4448
1 Blenheim Crescent
Notting Hill
Fresh and Wild
020 7229 1063
210 Westbourne Grove
Planet Organic
020 7221 7171
42 Westbourne Grove
Alwaha
0207 2290806
75 Westbourne Grove
Mandarin Kitchen
020 7727 9012
14-16 Queensway
Al Dah
020 7402 2541
61 Edgware Road
Green Valley
020 7402 7385
36 Upper Berkeley
Street
Villandry
020 7631 3131
170 Great Portland
Street
Mirabelle
020 7499 4636
56 Curzon Street
Mayfair
www.whitestarline.
org.uk
Nobu
020 7447 4747
Metropolitan Hotel
19 Old Park Lane
Mayfair

HR Higgins
020 7629 3913
79 Duke Street
Selfridges
020 7629 1234
400 Oxford Street
Paxton & Whitfield
020 7930 0259
93 Jermyn Street
St James's
Red Lion
020 7930 2030
Duke of York Street
St James's
Berry Bros & Rudd
020 7396 9600
3 St James's Street
Lindsay House
020 7439 0450
21 Romilly Street, Soho
**French House
Dining Room**
020 7437 2477
49 Dean Street
A Angelucci
020 7437 5889
23B Frith Street
I Camisa
020 7437 7610
61 Old Compton Street
Soho
Lina Stores
020 7437 6482
18 Brewer Street
J Sheekey
020 7240 2565
28-32 St Martin's Court
off Charing Cross Road
**Monmouth Coffee
House**
020 7379 3516
Monmouth Street
Covent Garden

Near Grosvenor Square, **H R Higgins** has the calm steadiness of a quality coffee and tea merchants, and you can drink a cup downstairs. North of here, in Oxford Street, **Selfridges'** bright food halls are worth a detour. **Paxton & Whitfield** in St James's is a beautiful shop, where you want to spend time looking at the cheeses. **The Red Lion** is a Victorian gem, worth visiting at quieter times as it is small. **Berry Bros & Rudd,** the august wine merchants, now into the eighth generation of family ownership, is a world apart. You can step into the shop just to buy a single bottle and take advantage of the personal service. The wines are fetched for you from a cellar, rather than being on view. They also sell on the Internet.

In Soho, Richard Corrigan's cooking at **Lindsay House** is one of the best examples in the country of how a chef can show off the fineness of culinary art without denaturing the essential character and quality of the ingredients. His food is adventurous but grounded in pure flavours. Around the corner, I also love the gutsy simplicity of the food at the **French House Dining Room**, run by Margot Henderson above an old-time Soho pub. Here you can have the likes of crab and mayonnaise, pot roast Gloucester Old Spot pork belly and apple crumble. Soho generally stirs your senses, from Chinatown, with its smells and vigour – and prices that make other food shops look a bit chi-chi – to the Italian shops, such as **A Angelucci** with its coffees, and the classic **I. Camisa** and **Lina Stores**.

J Sheekey, the revitalised 1890s fish restaurant in St Martin's Court near Leicester Square, has intimacy, an old-fashioned glamour, lovely seafood and puddings such as rice pudding with prunes in Armagnac with a brûleé top. The mirrored bar makes you feel you are a Hollywood star in a black-and-white movie, even though the decor is in fact new.

The **Monmouth Coffee House** in Covent Garden combines expertise with friendliness and has little booths at the top where you can sit and drink. It is a small shop, so best to go at off-peak times. **Neal's Yard Dairy** is one of the very best food shops in London. Randolph Hodgson has long championed farmhouse British cheeses, and his shop is exceptional for the sourcing and maturing of the cheeses. The shop itself is a long, narrow room, with truckles on shelves, crates of apples named by variety, loaves of bread and cheeses on the counter with their makers flagged up on labels. The dairy-fresh smell is one of the ultimate forms of food aromatherapy. As well as classic cheeses such as Montgomery's cheddar, look out for their own cheeses and other dairy products, made in Herefordshire. In Holborn, near Holborn tube station, the **Princess Louise** is a magnificent Victorian pub with etched mirrors, colourful tiles and Sam Smith's beers behind the bar.

City and North Another pub notable for its interior is the Arts and Crafts **Black Friar** near Blackfriars station. Further along Queen Victoria Street, near Mansion House tube station, **Sweetings** opened in 1889 and still serves seafood and old-fashioned puddings and savouries at mahogany-topped counters The walls in the back room are lined with old photographs and cartoons. Prawns and crabs arrive fresh each day to be cooked here. It is open weekday lunches only.

    Spitalfields Market has an organic market on Sundays and other shops and stalls open during the week and on Saturdays. It is one of those places that adds to the character of the city. Let's hope it will escape the pressures of redevelopment.

    Going up from Smithfield, Fergus Henderson's restaurant, **St John**, is one of the best restaurants in the country for plain-dealing,

Neal's Yard Dairy
020 7645 3550
17 Short's Gardens
Covent Garden

Princess Louise
020 7405 8816
208 High Holborn

Black Friar
020 7236 5650
174 Queen Victoria
Street, Blackfriars

Sweetings
020 7248 3062
39 Queen Victoria
Street, Mansion House

Spitalfields Market
Commercial Street,
near Brushfield Street

St John
020 7251 0848
26 St John Street
Smithfield
www.stjohn
restaurant.co.uk

delicious English food, with a modern setting. The St John bakery also sells good bread here and at Barnes farmers' market. The compact **Jerusalem Tavern** in Britton Street has the atmosphere of an old coffee house, and beers from the St Peter's Brewery in Suffolk. Of the Italian delis in Farringdon, **L Terroni & Sons** in Clerkenwell Road is the oldest and has a tempting selection of wines, with tasting notes on the shelves to guide you through. My favourite is the friendly **Gazzano & Sons** in Farringdon Road, with its sausages and old drawers full of pasta. Across the road, the **Quality Chop House**, run by chef/proprietor Charles Fontaine, has wooden-benched booths and a plain-speaking menu offering food that is full of flavour – and toffee cheesecake to finish. Yet another great place to eat around here is **Moro**, which has Moorish/Spanish inspired food – and it is inspired, with the care and taste buds of chef/proprietors Sam and Sam Clark. The Spanish specialists, **Brindisa**, are next door. **O'Hanlons**, up Rosebery Avenue, is an Irish pub, with excellent stout and other beers.

To the east of Islington, The **Wenlock Arms** has a good selection of beers and is too far off the beaten track to be spoiled. Islington has a **farmers' market** on Sundays from 10am-2pm opposite the Green on the Essex Road. Further up, there is a run of shops including a notable fishmonger, **Steve Hatt**, and an old-fashioned butcher, **James Elliott**, who also sells cheese. The best place to buy cheese in north London is Patricia Michelson's **La Fromagerie** north of Highbury Fields. It is worth going at off-peak times so you can really look at the cheeses and ask questions. Across the road, **Frank Godfrey** is another decent butcher.

The Turkish Food Centre at the end of the vibrant scrum of the Ridley Road market in Dalston has breads, groceries and piles of

Jerusalem Tavern
020 7490 4281
55 Britton Street
Clerkenwell

L Terroni & Sons
020 7837 1712
138-140 Clerkenwell Rd

Gazzano & Sons
020 7837 1586
167 Farringdon Road

Quality Chop House
020 7837 5093
94 Farringdon Road

Moro
020 7833 8336
34-36 Exmouth market
www.moro-restaurant.com

Brindisa
020 8772 1600
(main number)
32 Exmouth Market

O'Hanlons
020 7278 7630
8 Tysoe Street

Wenlock Arms
020 7608 3406
26 Wenlock Road

farmers' markets
020 7704 9659
www.londonfarmersmarkets.com

Steve Hatt
020 7226 3963
88-90 Essex Road

James Elliott
020 7226 3658
96 Essex Road

La Fromagerie
020 7359 7440
30 Highbury Park

Frank Godfrey
020 7226 9904

quinces. **Yasar Halim** on Green Lanes is another place to buy big bunches of herbs and browse your way through breads and cakes. The **Mahavir Sweet Mart**'s bigger branch is at 136 Ballards Lane (Finchley Central tube). I fell for the unshowy original, in East Finchley, where the Hindu God Mahavir sits on a shelf next to tins of mango pulp. They make their own not-too-sweet sweets, as well as crisps such as chilli and lemon flavour, and Indian snacks, from samosas to stuffed chillies.

Southeast **Borough Market** sizzles with good food and the buzz of excited shoppers going between stalls from Brindisa's Spanish specialities to Herdwick lamb to Dartmoor beef to Neal's Yard Dairy cheeses to proper breads to Booth's mushroom and asparagus stall to sappy organic fruit and vegetables. It is one of the best places to shop in London, and without the chill of 'boutique' food shopping. *Fish!* is a restaurant that sets out its principle of sourcing fish sustainably, and serves it well. **The George Inn** is a 17th century coaching inn, with galleries overlooking a courtyard, bare boards inside and real ales.

Baldwins, a ten-minute walk down the Walworth Road from Elephant & Castle, is a large herbalist with an authentic interior, where they serve glasses of sarsaparilla.

There is another run of good shops on Northcote Road, near Clapham Junction station. **Doves** has frozen, high-quality pies and is otherwise a proper butcher that has been going since 1889. **Hamish Johnston** is a deli with a good range of cheese. Nearby, **Kelly's Organic Foods** has a wide selection, all organic, plus a link-up with Rococo for chocolate. **The Hive Honey Shop** specialises in honeys and has bees kept behind glass, where you can watch them going about their business.

Turkish Food Centre
020 7254 6754
89 Ridley Road
Yasar Halim
020 8340 8090
493-495 Green Lanes
Mahavir Sweet Mart
020 8883 4595
127 High Road
East Finchley
Borough Market
020 7407 1002
www.borough
market.org.uk
Fish!
020 7234 3333
Cathedral Street
Borough
The George Inn
020 7407 2056
off 77 Borough High
Street
Baldwins
020 7703 5550
171 Walworth Road
Doves
020 7223 5191
71 Northcote Road
Clapham
Hamish Johnston
020 7738 0741
48 Northcote Road
Clapham
Kelly's Organic Foods
020 7207 3967
46 Northcote Road
Clapham
The Hive Honey Shop
020 7924 6233
93 Northcote Road
Clapham

suffolk

SOUTHWEST OF BURY ST EDMUNDS, **The Star Inn** at Lidgate is a 500-year old gastro-pub with a Catalan landlady and Spanish influences in the wines and food. (*See also chapter two.*) Northwest of Bury St Edmunds, Matthew and Louise Unwin run an organic farm shop at **Longwood Farm**, Tuddenham. (*See also chapter six.*)

North of Sudbury, at Long Melford, **Kentwell Hall** has an annual living construction of Tudor life for three weeks in June and July. At weekends and bank holidays, you can visit and watch the volunteers in action, including cooking, baking and working in the dairy.

Eight miles northeast of Bury St Edmunds, the **Leaping Hare Vineyard Restaurant** at Wyken Vineyards, Stanton, is in a lofty 400-year-old barn and run with more than a dash of American informality and verve from the proprietor Carla Carlisle, who has been influenced by her time working at the ground-breaking California restaurant, Chez Panisse. Fresh, good-quality local ingredients are the basis of the food. The wines and cider are well worth trying and you can walk around the lovely sculpture garden and woodland. They have a farmers' market on Saturday mornings.

In **The Angel** in Lavenham, I ate a good beef pie and drank beer from the **Nethergate Brewery** in Clare whose original brewer, Dr Ian Hornsey, sought out old recipes for such brews as the refreshing and subtly aromatic Umbel Ale, made using coriander seeds. Near Lavenham, **The Cock** at Brent Eligh is a well-run, unspoiled pub with a great drinking poem on the wall. Down the road, **The Swan** at Monks Eligh is a friendly pub with nice food that is excellent value for money. Nigel Ramsbottom, who owns the pub with his wife Carol, cooked at the Walnut Tree Inn in Wales for five years and believes in buying locally, in season. I ate pork rillettes and proper piccalilli followed by roast teal, with nuggets of dark, gamey meat.

Joan and Nick Hardingham at the exceptional **Alder Carr farm shop** at Creeting St Mary sell their own high-quality fruit and vegetables as well as other good produce. Their delicious ice-creams include gooseberry and elderflower. There is also a restaurant, crafts on sale and a farmers' market on the third Saturday of the month. (*See also chapter eight.*)

Driving east from here, **The Moon and Mushroom** in Swilland is a popular, friendly pub with fires, their own casseroles and a fine range of Suffolk and Norfolk beers.

Going onto the coast, starting south of Ipswich, **The Butt & Oyster** at Pinmill is a classic pub right on the River Orwell, with old wooden settles, tiled floors and a long bar in the main room. The menu had bacon, leek and potato soup, cullen skink (smoked haddock soup) and minced beef roly-poly with vegetables.

On the coast, Orford has a good smokehouse, **Richardsons**, in an old barn round the corner from the **Butley Orford Oysterage**, with sausages, game, ham hocks, eel and other smoked fish, including bloaters. Ruth and David Watson and chef Brendan Ansbro, previously at the Fox and Goose and Hintlesham Hall, have set up in **Trinity at the Crown and Castle**. The food is fresh and modern, and includes the likes of lemon curd brûlée.

The Lighthouse in Aldeburgh is an excellent restaurant which is not afraid of doing familiar dishes such as fish and chips and liver and onions, well-cooked and with good ingredients. Open all week, it is a place you could go to regularly (prices are reasonable) or for a special treat. (*See also chapter nine.*) Sara Fox also runs the **Aldeburgh Cookery School** with the food writer and broadcaster Thane Prince. **Regatta**, down the road, is a colourful, friendly restaurant. You can buy fish in sheds on the sea front, getting whatever the boats have

Alder Carr
Farm Shop
01449 720820
Creeting St Mary
www.aldercarrfarm.
co.uk
The Moon and
Mushroom
01473 785320
High Road, Swilland
The Butt & Oyster
01473 780764
Pinmill
near Chelmondiston
(signposted off B1456)
Richardsons
Smokehouse
01394 450103
just off Market Hill
Orford
Butley Orford
Oysterage
01394 450277
Market Hill
Orford
Trinity at the Crown
and Castle
01394 450205
Orford
www.crownand
castlehotel.co.uk
bedrooms
The Lighthouse
01728 453377
77 High Street
Aldeburgh
Aldeburgh Cookery
School
01728 454039
84 High Street
Regatta
01728 452011
171-173 High Street

Aldeburgh Food Halls
01728 454535
183 High Street
Ye Olde Wine Shoppe
01728 452298
116-118 High Street
Aldeburgh Fish and
Chip Shop
226 High Street
J R Creasey
01728 660219
Peasenhall
Emmett's Stores
01728 660250
Peasenhall
The Ship Inn
01728 648219
St James Street
Dunwich
Flora Tea Rooms
01728 648433
(closed Dec - Feb)
Adnams brewery
01502 727200
- brewery and The Cellar
and Kitchen store
East Green
01502 722138
-wine shop
Pinkneys Lane
www.adnams.co.uk
Crown Hotel
01502 722275
High Street
Southwold
bedrooms
Kings Head
(Low House)
01986 798395
Gorams Mill Lane
Laxfield
(off B1117, below
churchyard)

brought in. The high street has good shops, old-fashioned and new, such as the **Aldeburgh Food Halls**, and the tiny **Ye Olde Wine Shoppe** with an exceptional selection of 2,000 wines and Adnams' beers on draft. **The Aldeburgh Fish and Chip Shop** is fab. On the A1094, near the golf course, Grange Farm has excellent asparagus, as well as strawberries and new potatoes.

In Peasenhall, **J R Creasey** sell proper meat alongside their delicious bacons and hams, including a Suffolk sweet cure. **Emmett's** is an old-fashioned village shop, now under the ownership of Mark Thomas and with more of a deli influence. The shop still stocks everything from detergent to sea lavender honey, and is famous for its tarry smokeholes, where they make smoked bacon and ham, including a strong, sweet-pickle cure, using Guinness.

There is a shed on the beach at Dunwich which is famous for its reasonably priced Dover soles. **The Ship Inn** is a classic old pub and the Flora tearooms has fish and chips.

Southwold has **Adnams brewery** puffing away in the centre. They also run a high-quality wine business and have a wine shop in the town, and another shop which has kitchenware alongside the range of drinks. **The Crown Hotel** is Adnam's flagship pub, with 20 wines available by the glass, changing monthly. They also run regular wine tastings, in Suffolk and London. (*See also chapter four.*)

The Low House, officially called **The King's Head**, is behind the church in Laxfield and is a thatched, 15th-century house with a charmingly old-fashioned atmosphere, small rooms with old settles, and a tap room.

the north norfolk coast

A NUMBER OF RESTAURANT CHEF-PROPRIETORS have settled on this beautiful stretch of coast, and know how to make the most of the best local ingredients. Look out for crab, lobsters, plump mussels, vegetables from old walled gardens, wild mushrooms from the woods, plentiful game from the big Norfolk farms and estates, pots of sea-lavender honey from the purple flowers on the marshland and the salty, tender marsh samphire – 'sea asparagus' – which partners fish in the restaurants in summer.

Towards the north coast, Burnham Market is an upmarket small town with a classic gastro-pub, **The Hoste Arms**, a good deli, **Humble Pie**, and **Gurney's Fish Shop**, which has the famous local shellfish: lobsters, crab, shrimps and mussels. Mike Gurney also has a place at Brancaster, **The Hole In The Wall**. Others also recommend **The Fish Shed** in Brancaster Staithe nearby. The mussels are particularly good in the colder waters of October to February.

Just inland, **The Lord Nelson** in Burnham Thorpe is an unspoiled pub with a tap room. Nelson was, in fact, a local and drank here. Nearby, **Clive Houlder** in North Creake supplies wild mushrooms to the chefs in the area and does some sales from the door, given notice.

Heading east along the A149 coast road, you get to wide, sandy, pine-fringed Holkham Beach: a dreamscape, a good family beach and a place for a picnic or a walk. The beach huts can be hired by the day. **Holkham Hall Nursery** sells herbs, as well as many other plants, in a six-acre walled garden.

A couple of miles on, back on the coast, Wells-next-the-Sea is a busy, unpretentious but atmospheric town. Nick Anderson has moved his Michelin-starred restaurant **Rococo** from King's Lynn to set up a restaurant with rooms in The Crown Hotel. His well-judged

The Hoste Arms
01328 738777
The Green
Burnham Market
www.hostearms.co.uk
bedrooms
Humble Pie
01328 738581
The Market Place
Burnham Market
Gurney's Fish Shop
01328 738967
Market Place
Burnham Market
The Hole In The Wall
01485 210079
Main Road
Brancaster Staithe
The Fish Shed
01485 210532
Main Road
Brancaster Staithe
Lord Nelson
01328 738241
Walsingham Road
Burnham Thorpe
Clive Houlder
01328 738610
North Creake
Holkham Hall Nursery
01328 711636
entrance at the back of
Holkham park
near Wells
**Rococo at The
Crown/The Jewel**
01328 710209
The Crown
Buttlands,
Wells-next-the-Sea
bedrooms

Country Garden
01328 710846
43-45 Staithe Street
Wells-next-the-Sea
The Wells Deli
01328 711171
15 Quayside
Wells-next-the-Sea
www.wellsdeli.co.uk
Stuart Oetzmann/
Hand Made Food
Company
01603 731133
The Three Horseshores
01328 710547
Warham All Saints
B&B in old post office
The Red Lion
01328 830552
Stiffkey, on A149
Morston Hall
01263 741041
in Morston, on A149
bedrooms
www.morstonhall.
com

cooking uses local ingredients in a menu that might include Norfolk brown shrimps in a beurre blanc or pigeon in a salad with quince crisps and chutney. There is also a brasserie/bar **The Jewel**.

For food shopping, walk down Staithe Street, where you will find an exceptional greengrocer, **Country Garden**, with produce picked up personally from farms in the Fens and such exotica as romanesco, with its funky conical spirals. Along the quayside, **The Wells Deli** epitomises how a shop can draw in well-made produce from the area and further afield, to champion character and flavour over anonymity. They also make their own produce, to high standards. Look out, here and in other Norfolk delis, for the Gloucester Old Spot pork pies made by **Stuart Oetzmann** of the **Hand Made Food Company**. Nearby, on the quayside at Wells, is a stall belonging to the Frary family, who catch, cook and sell local crab. They also sell a useful little cookbook, *Crabs from the Quayside* (by Carla Phillips, who used to run the famous Moorings restaurant and makes Carla's spicy nuts which are on sale in The Wells Deli).

A mile inland from Wells, **The Three Horseshores** at Warham has hearty home-cooked food, including admirably old-fashioned puddings like spotted dick and Bakewell tart. Back on the coast road, **The Red Lion** at Stiffkey gets excellent ingredients from the sea, including mussels, whitebait, crab and sea-trout in early summer. They also serve the Norfolk award-winning beer, Woodforde's Wherry.

The menu at **Morston Hall** in Morston changes daily to adapt to what is best on the day. The chef, Galton Blakiston, spent his childhood summers on a house stranded on nearby Blakeney Spit, collecting mussels and shrimping. Now he turns such ingredients into well-flavoured, well-presented Modern British cooking. There is a set menu at one sitting, but it's balanced so you don't feel capsized by rich food. Delia dines here (and Galton is a Norwich City supporter).

Galton recommends the old-world walled garden at **Wiverton Hall** between Blakeney and Cley-next-the-Sea for seasonal treats such as soft fruit, asparagus and globe artichokes. In Cley itself, go to **Cley Smokehouse** for kippers, bloaters and pots of taramasalata. Down the high street, **The George and Dragon** has a bird watchers' 'bible' on a brass lectern with all the latest sightings and drawings of sightings. **Picnic Fayre** is the village's deli, with a good range of produce from the area, including Hand Made Food Company pies and bread made from Letheringsett Watermill flour (*see below*). They also make their own spice pastes.

Coming inland from Cley, the quirky **Glandford Shell Museum** has an incredible 12-foot piece of embroidery done by a former fisherman, John Caske. It is full of weather, human detail and landscape: seagulls flying off cliffs, the textures of ship rigging, a resting fisherman and people bicycling up hills (there are some inclines in this part of Norfolk). It makes you look again at the coast. On from Glandford, and three miles inland from Cley, **Letheringsett Watermill** in Letheringsett has excellent flours: fans include the much-respected London chef Pierre Koffman. You can walk around the historical display, half-mesmerised by the grind of the millstones.

One of my favourite restaurants in this part of the world is **Yetman's**, a mile on from Letheringsett, in the small town of Holt. The restaurant is New World in its colourful, fresh stylishness and informality. My cod came perfectly grilled and framed by a pink sauce made from blood oranges and Seville oranges; turbot came in a

Wiveton Hall
signs in season off the A149 between Blakeney and Cley

Cley Smokehouse
01263 740282
High Street
Cley-next-the-Sea

George and Dragon
01263 740652
High Street
Cley-next-the Sea
bedrooms

Picnic Fayre
01263 740587
The Old Forge
Cley-next-the-Sea
www.picnic-fayre.co.uk

Shell Museum
01263 740081
Glandford
Open March-October

Letheringsett Watermill
01263 713153
Riverside Road
Letheringsett
off A148

Yetman's
01263 713320
37 Norwich Road
Holt

The North Norfolk Fish Company
01263 711913
8 Old Stable Yard
off the High Street
Holt

Margaret's Tearooms
01263 577614
Chestnut Farmhouse
The Street
Baconsthorpe
(open Easter - end
October and winter
weekends)

Rutlands
01263 860562
13 Briston Road
Melton Constable

Tavern Tasty Meats
01692 405444
Swafield
near North Walsham

The Earle Arms
01263 587376
Heydon

The Ark
01263 761535
The Street
Erpingham
bedrooms

well-judged Champagne and potted shrimp sauce. Peter and Alison Yetman take New World wines away on their holidays to test them out, and the sense of pleasure comes through on the wine menu. Holt has no fewer than four fishsellers. **The North Norfolk Fish Company** also has ready-to-eat food for deli-dinners and picnics.

Margaret's Tearooms is in Baconsthorpe, a village with a ruined castle near Holt. Margaret gets up at 5am every morning to make the breads and then the cakes, breads, soups and so on. She gets flour from Letheringsett Watermill.

Going a couple of miles inland, Melton Constable has a good family butcher, **Rutlands**, where they have sold beef and lamb from the same family farm, with its own abbatoir, for 30 years. The venison comes from the nearby Melton Park estate, where Losey filmed *The Go-Between*. **Tavern Tasty Meats** near North Walsham is a farm shop with rare breeds meat. They provide the pork for the hand made food company's pies.

Deeper into this quiet part of Norfolk, off the B1149 between Holt and Norwich, is the estate village of Heydon, where they still had the sign up for Best Village of 1967 and 1968. The uncluttered **Earle Arms** has Woodfords and Adnams beers and, outside, hollyhocks and a water bowl for dogs.

Also in this area, and about a half hour's drive from Norwich, is **The Ark** at Erpingham, a warm, relaxing, generous, small restaurant with rooms run by Sheila and Mike Kidd. The cooking is inspired by Elizabeth David and European trips, and the produce they use is fresh, tip-top English. Think wild salmon gravadlax, roast leg of lamb with anchovy, garlic and rosemary, British cheeses from Neal's Yard, apricot-honey-almond tart and summer pudding.

oxford and east oxfordshire

Oxford The romantic **Rosamund the Fair** is a restaurant literally on the water, in a canal boat run by a couple. Tim Matthews and Sophia Goodford take turns to cook in the 6´ x 9´ galley kitchen, using good ingredients for their set-price lunches and dinners. The meals take three hours as you cruise along the Thames and the Oxford canal. You can sit outside on the front deck between courses: it is magical to move serenely through the dark landscape at night. Advance bookings only.

Near to where Rosamund is moored in Jericho, Raymond Blanc's **Le Petit Blanc** is a busy, modern place, with classically based cooking. Across the road, **Gluttons** deli has been going for 20 years and has a good range, including organic and local produce. It is a useful place to buy a picnic to take to Port Meadow, where you can go for a walk alongside the Thames. The curious will also appreciate the atmospheric graveyard near Gluttons. The **Loch Fyne** company has one of its seafood restaurants in Walton Street. In Walton Crescent, **Al-Shami** is a long-standing, good Lebanese restaurant, with reasonably priced accommodation.

In the city centre, the café at the **Ashmolean** Museum of Art and Archaeology is a calm space to rest your mind and feet and have a cup of coffee or hot milk and honey on one of those damp Oxford days. They make their own food, from cakes to fishcakes.

The Covered Market, just off the High Street, is an excellent place to shop. There is **Hayman's Fisheries** for seafood and two butchers, **Hedges**', and **Fellers**', who focus on organic meat and game. **The Oxford Cheese Company** stocks around 180 cheeses.

An Encyclopaedia of Oxford Pubs, Inn and Taverns, written by Derek Honey (Oakwood Press), covers everything from historic brawls to satellite screens.

Rosamund the Fair
01865 553370
Castlemill Boatyard
Jericho, Oxford
www.rosamundthe
fair.co.uk

Le Petit Blanc
01865 510999
71-72 Walton Street
Oxford
www.petit-blanc.com

Gluttons
01865 553748
110 Walton Street
Oxford

Loch Fyne Restaurant
01865 292510
55 Walton Street
www.lochfyne.com

Al-Shami
01865 310066
25 Walton Crescent
Oxford
bedrooms

Ashmolean Museum café
01865 288183
Beaumont Street
Oxford

Hayman's Fisheries
01865 242827
21, Avenue 1 Covered Market, Oxford

Hedges'
01865 242318
61-62 Covered Market

M. Feller
01865 251164
54-55 Covered Market

The Oxford Cheese Company
01865 721420
17 Covered Market

Waterperry Gardens
01844 339254
nr Wheatley
Jcn 8 or 8a off M40
Le Manoir aux
Quat' Saisons
01844 278881
Great Milton
www.manoir.co.uk
bedrooms
Dorchester Abbey
Tearoom
Margot Metcalfe
01865 340054
Dorchester-on-Thames
The Black Horse
01491 680418
Checkendon

South-east Oxfordshire

Waterperry Gardens, (junction 8 or 8a off the M40, and follow the brown tourist signs from Wheatley), are gardens and nurseries near Oxford. They used to have a wonderful Swiss *pâtissier* in the tearoom who made superb almond crossiants. He has now retired, but they still make everything fresh and serve their own single-variety apple juices. These are also sold in the shop, alongside 14 or so kinds of apple, in season. These include Blenheim Orange, a variety which was discovered around 1740, growing against the boundary wall of Blenheim Park. It became a celebrated dessert apple, praised by the connoisseur Edward Bunyard for its warm, nutty aroma and "mellow austerity": "An apple of the Augustan age," he called it. Waterperry also sells honey. Once the bees have pollinated the fruit trees in the orchards, they are moved on to the gardens, which include a long herbaceous border.

Le Manoir aux Quat' Saisons in Great Milton, Raymond Blanc's famous restaurant, uses produce from the garden and other ingredients that are carefully sourced and sauced. This is high-class food, charged accordingly.

South of here, on the Thames, the **Dorchester Abbey Tearoom** in Dorchester-on-Thames is one of those charming places with homemade jams and cakes, such as Dorset gooseberry cake, all made by people in the village. It is open between Easter Saturday and the end of September on Saturdays, Sundays and bank holidays, and on Wednesdays and Thursdays from mid-May.

Fans of old-fashioned pubs may want to take the trouble to search out the **Black Horse** on the outskirts of Checkendon. The pub has been in the same family for four generations. Their beers include Brakspears and West Berkshire's Good Ole Boy. If you come through Checkendon from the south, off the A4074, the village green will be on your right. Half a mile further on, going towards Stoke Row, in a dip in the road, turn left and follow the long track to the Black Horse.

Mapledurham Watermill, near Reading, is a delightful place to visit. Built originally in 1423, and extended twice after that, it fell out of use in the 1930s and was restored in the 1970s, using money earned when the estate was used as a location in the film *The Eagle Has Landed*. The miller, Mildred Cookson, stone-grinds locally grown English wheat and sells from here and in shops in the area. It is open on weekends and bank holidays from Easter to the end of September.

I particularly liked **The Goose** at Britwell Salome which is small, informal and unfussily classy. The shortness of the menu – three choices for each course – makes you trust the quality and focus of the kitchen. Chef/proprietor Chris Barber cooked for Prince Charles for 12 years, and the food is full of care at every stage, using the best ingredients, local when possible, and following the seasons. Saddle of lamb may be from the locally reared Jacob breed and comes with fondant potato and a gratin of spinach. There will be good meat, too, in the shepherd's pie which may appear on the set-lunch menu. The free-range pork comes from the farm next door, and some of the summer fruits and vegetables are grown in the walled garden of a big house down the road. It is also handy for London, off Junction 6 of the M40.

The Granary at Watlington has long had a fine choice of cheeses – around 90, predominantly British – and other well-made products. It has changed ownership. The new owners say they are planning to continue in the same style.

Mapledurham
Watermill
01189 723350
Mapledurham
near Reading
The Goose
01491 612304
Britwell Salome
Jcn 6 off M40
The Granary
01491 613585
Watlington

herefordshire

CAFÉ ALL SAINTS in Hereford is a non-puritanical and modern vegetarian café in the heart of a working medieval church. (*See also chapter nine.*) Herefordshire is famous for its cider, hops, orchard fruits and beef. There is an interesting **Cider Museum** in the city, and the county's celebrated breed of beef cattle, the Hereford, is sold by **Richard Moxley**, a butcher who buys prize animals. There are two branches, one to the east of the city, in Tupsley, the other to the west, in Westfields. **The Mousetrap** cheese shop has branches in Hereford and Leominster and a café-shop attached to the cheesemaking dairy where the owner, Mark Hindle, makes unpasteurised cheeses at **Monkland**, on the A44 west of Leominster.

Three miles west of Hereford, on the A438, and a mile down Breinton Lane, **Breinton Fruit Farm** has pick-your-own apples, pears and plums for about six weeks from mid-September, and sells the picked fruit from from mid-September to March. They have 25 varieties of apple, and a tasting table in the shop. **The Big Apple** is a harvest-time celebration of apples and cider held at the end of October in the Much Marcle area.

South of Hereford, the **Cottage of Content** in Carey is a pretty, cottagey pub in a quiet spot. They have good food and take trouble over their wines.

Barry Clark at **English Natural Food** at Wormbridge bred the Trelough duck, much favoured by chefs, and he sells his poultry and other produce, including pork from Gloucester Old Spot pigs, at the door and by carrier service.

Going west towards the Black Mountains, **The Bulls Head** at Craswall is a stone drovers' inn with flagstones and a friendly atmosphere. Neal's Yard Creamery is based in the Golden Valley, and make delicious cheeses, including the little Perroche cow's milk cheeses and the goats' milk Ragstone, as well as crème fraîche, yoghurt and other products. These are sold in the Neal's Yard Dairy shops in London, by good cheesemongers around the country, in The Mousetrap cheese shops in Herefordshire, and in Dorstone and Peterchurch local post offices.

Pru Lloyd at **The Dairy House** in Weobley makes organic yoghurts, fromage frais and soft cheeses, and other non-organic dairy products, including delicious butter which they mould using the traditional wooden 'Scotch hands'. Also in the town is **Jule's Restaurant**, with a characterful owner and good-value food.

Heading west, **September Organic Dairy**, four-and-a-half miles west of Kington on the A411, has a small farm shop selling its own ice-cream in flavours such as elderflower, and blackberry and apple crumble. They also sell their own meat, and cordials and preserves.

North of Kington, the Michelin-starred **Stagg Inn** at Titley is one of the best pubs in the country for food. The chef, Steve Reynolds, sources his ingredients carefully from the area and uses his art to bring out their flavours. (*See also chapter nine.*) Before setting up his own place, Chris was at the **Riverside Inn** at Aymestrey where they also have high standards and a real belief in local produce. East of Kington, **Dunkertons** makes grown-up cider and sells it from a shop and in a restaurant in a 400-year-old barn, signposted from Pembridge. I enjoyed the pear-and-blackberry combination of their perry with *crème de mûre*.

Six-and-a-half miles north of Hereford, on the A49 at Dinmore, Sheila and David Jenkins run an organic farm shop, **Green Acres**, where they have a colourful range, including 16 kinds of squash during the autumn and other produce including meat, butter, cheese and ice-cream.

Bulls Head
01981 510616
Craswall
bedrooms
The Dairy House
01544 318815
Whitehill Park
Weobley
Jule's Restaurant
01544 318206
Weobley
September Organic Dairy
01544 327561
Almeley
nr Kington
The Stagg Inn
01544 230221
Titley
www.kc3.co.uk/stagg
bedrooms
Riverside Inn
01568 708440
Aymestrey
bedrooms
Dunkertons
01544 388653
Luntley
Pembridge
Green Acres
01568 797045
Dinmore

shropshire

Merchant House
01584 875438
Lower Corve Street
Ludlow
Hibiscus
01584 872325
17 Corve Street
Ludlow
Mr Underhill's
01584 874431
Dinham Weir
Ludlow
bedrooms
D W Wall & Son
01584 872060
14 High Street
Ludlow
A H Griffiths
01584 872141
11 The Bullring
Ludlow
Carter's
01584 874665
6 King Street
Ludlow
Reg Martin & Sons
01584 872008
1 Market Street
Ludlow Local Produce
Market
Elizabeth Bunney
01584 890243
Local Food Directory
01584 878398

THE LOVELY MARKET TOWN OF Ludlow has no fewer than three Michelin- starred, good-value restaurants. One of England's first-rate chefs, Shaun Hill, moved here from the country house hotel Gidleigh Park in Devon to run his own place, **The Merchant House**. Here he simply serves great food, cooked by him: all the money goes on the ingredients rather than fancy linen, a battalion of sous-chefs and flutters of waiters. There are only seven tables and a set-price menu. It is great value if you love food. (*See also chapter nine.*)

Also, top-notch Claude Bosi at **Hibiscus** has an inventive and successful style of cooking which distils the purity of flavours. His burnt-milk ice-cream with chestnut soufflé was sophisticated, delicate and delicious.

Mr Underhill's has a set menu, until the puddings, and is a relaxing place in a glorious position, right on the River Corve. Like the other two restaurants, its success lies in the skill of the chef-proprietor, the quality of the produce and the fact they are on such a small, personal scale yet within a three-hour drive from many big cities. Ludlow is an attractive place to visit, with its castle, St Laurence's church, views of hills at the ends of the streets, timber-framed houses and beautiful, varied and peaceful countryside all around.

Ludlow still has no fewer than six butchers. Shaun Hill recommends **Wall's**, which has rare-breeds meat, and **Griffiths'**, which has its own abbatoir and gets animals from local farms. **Carter's** is known for its sausages and other pork butchery, and **Reg Martin & Sons** is another good place to buy sausages and bacon to take home. As well as a regular market on Mondays, Fridays and Saturdays, and Wednesdays from April to September and the first three weeks of December, the town also has a **local produce market** on the second Thursday of the month and a food festival held over the second weekend of September.

Going towards the Welsh border and Bishop's Castle, with its off-beat Victorian charm, **The Three Tuns** is a pub with a grade II listed tower brewery and an exhibition on beer; it serves food such as a game terrine with a red onion marmalade, soups, crispy duck with walnut stuffing with port and redcurrant gravy, and brownies with ice-cream. **The Six Bells** also has its own brewery and is very much part of the distinctive atmosphere of this town: it is a place that runs to its own clock. **The Castle Hotel** is a friendly old coaching inn.

Ruth Lawrence makes delicious cheeses using her own goats' milk, on **Womerton Farm**, on the Long Mynd, near All Stretton. Ruth is best known for the hard-pressed Womerton cheese and also makes Long Mynd and St Francis cheeses, which you can buy from their farm shop or from other cheese specialists.

Going northeast of Ludlow, about five miles south-west of Much Wenlock on the B4371, the **Wenlock Edge Inn** at Hilltop is a friendly, family-run pub that is both cheerful and mellow. The food is reasonably priced and homely, including such dishes as Shrewsbury lamb, with the meat cooked in a gravy flavoured with redcurrant jelly.

Country Friends restaurant in Dorrington has a comfortably old-fashioned feel, eastern touches to the menu, and local ingredients, for instance a summer pudding with ice-cream made with elderflowers from the garden, and venison with damson sauce.

T O Williams in Wem is a deli now run by the third generation of the family who has owned it since 1935. It is a great place to buy cheeses, such as well-priced Appleby's Cheshire, the delicious cloth-bound, unpasteurised cheese that is made in the north of Shropshire. There are branches in Shawbury, Shrewsbury and Whitchurch.

The Three Tuns
01588 638797
Salop Street
Bishop's Castle
bedrooms

Six Bells
01588 630144
Church Street
Bishop's Castle

The Castle Hotel
01588 638403
Market Square
Bishops' Castle
bedrooms

Womerton Farm
01694 751260
near All Stretton
www.womerton-farm.co.uk

Wenlock Edge Inn
01746 785678
Hilltop
bedrooms

Country Friends
01743 718707
Dorrington
1 bedroom

T O Williams
01939 232552
17 High Street
Wem
www.williamsof
wem.co.uk

liverpool, chester and cheshire

60 Hope Street
0151 7076060
60 Hope Street
Liverpool

Number Seven
0151 709 9633
7-15 Faulkner Street
(off Hope Street)
Liverpool

Ye Cracke
0151 709 4171
13 Rice Street
(off Hope Street)
Liverpool

Philharmonic Dining Rooms
0151 707 2837
36 Hope Street
Liverpool

Everyman Theatre
0151 709 4776
5-9 Hope Street
Liverpool

Cain's Brewery
0151 709 8734
www.breworld.com/cains

The Brewery Tap
0151 709 2129
Stanhope Street
Liverpool

Dr Duncan's
0151 709 5100
St John's House
St John's Lane
Liverpool

The Dispensary
0151 709 2160
87 Renshaw Street
Liverpool

Liverpool The deep-fried jam sandwich with Carnation milk ice-cream at **60 Hope Street**, a stylish, modern restaurant, had to be tried. It turned out to be a huge affair, not unlike a doughnut, with fresh strawberries in the middle instead of jam. Hope Street has plenty to do between the Catholic and Anglican cathedrals at either end. Off the north side of the road, **Number Seven** is a good deli and café. Around the corner from 60 Hope Street, **Ye Cracke** in Rice Street is an old boozer with lots of rooms, so you can quietly read your paper in one while another roomful gets more raucous. Good beers. Back on Hope Street, the **Philharmonic Dining Rooms** is one of the most spectacular pubs in England, fitted out by the craftsmen who worked on Liverpool's famous cruiseliners. Further down the street, the bistro at the famous **Everyman Theatre** is like a canteen with well-priced food. The bar has real ales.

Robert Cain's built a majestic brick brewery on the edge of Toxteth in the late 19th century. In its hey-day, Cain's kitted out the Philharmonic, and also The Vines, another sumptuously decked-out pub (by the Adelphi hotel in the city centre, and worth a peek). The company and the pubs were sold and, eventually, brewing stopped altogether in the building in the 1990s. But the name of **Cain's** has since risen from the ashes under a new company run by Steve Holt, who has brought regional brewing back to the city. True to tradition, he looks after the style of the new estate of pubs, using old fittings while avoiding fake nostalgic themery.

The Brewery Tap, at the side of the brewery, won a Camra and English Heritage award in 1994 for its refurbishment. **Dr Duncan's**, in a listed building which was formerly an insurance office in the city centre, near Lime Street station, has a great tiled room. **The Dispensary**, which uses the trappings of an old pharmacy, was voted

pub of the year in 2000 by the Merseyside branch of Camra.
My favourite Liverpool pub is **The Baltic Fleet**, not far from
the excellent museums and the Tate in Albert Dock. As you
drive along the dockside road, it is next to a bright-yellow sculpture
known as The Superlamb Banana. Simon Holt stocks good beers,
including those from the interesting Passageway Brewery, and serves
straightforward, quality food, including Hereford beef and
Doddington unpasteurised cheese. (*See also chapter four.*)

Chester and Cheshire The Cheese Shop in Chester, run by Carole
Faulkner, is worth a detour. A farmer's daughter, she is critical of
agri-business and supports traditional farmers and buying British.
The shop has about 200 cheeses, 80 per cent of them made in Britain
and Ireland, and including the three unpasteurised Cheshires:
Bournes', Appleby's and Mollington Grange. She also runs a restaurant
around the corner, **Elliots**, which adheres to the same principles.

Peter Paprill is a regional foods merchant whose company
Pendrill operates from Mollington Grange, near Chester. Peter has
come up with the splendid idea of creating weekend boxes,
containing hams, oils, cheeses, wines and other foods sourced from
high-quality small producers. These are delivered to customers, ready
for when they finish work on a Friday night. (*See also chapter nine.*)

Sandra and Michael Allwood at **Ravens Oak Dairy** have a good
organic shop at Burland and make cow's, sheeps', goat's and buffalo's
milk cheeses. The most established is the sweet Burland Green, made
using their own organic cow's milk. **The Cheshire Smokehouse**
is a top-notch smokery with a very popular restaurant attached, in
Morley Green, near Wilmslow. It is a family business, run by John
Ward, who has high standards and a big range.

The Baltic Fleet
0151 7093116
33A Wapping
Liverpool
The Cheese Shop
01244 346240
116 Northgate
Chester
Elliots
01244 329932
2 Abbey Green
Chester
bedrooms
Pendrill
01244 851600
Mollington Grange
Chester
www.pendrill.co.uk
Ravens Oak Dairy
01270 524624
Burland
(on A534)
Cheshire Smokehouse
01625 548499
Vost Farm
Morley Green
nr Wilmslow

manchester and lancashire

Rhodes & Co
0161 868 1900
Waters Reach
Trafford Park
Manchester
Yang Sing
0161 236 2200
34 Princess Street
Manchester
The Circus Tavern
0161 236 5818
86 Portland Street
Manchester
The Grey Horse
0161 236 1874
46 Shudehill
Manchester
The Smithfield
0161 839 4424
37 Swan Street
Manchester
The Hare and Hounds
0161 832 4737
46 Shudehill
near A664 and
A665 junction
Manchester
The Beer House
0161 839 7019
6 Angel Street
off Rochdale Road
(A664)
Manchester
The Pot of Beer
0161 834 8579
36 New Mount Street
off Rochdale Road
(A664)
Manchester
The Marble Arch
0161 832 5914
73 Rochdale Road
Manchester

RHODES & CO, ONE OF GARY RHODES' brasseries, is to the southwest of Manchester, right by Old Trafford football stadium, and handy for the Lowry Museum on Salford Quays. It is a brisk place, with well-executed dishes that play on English classics: smoked haddock rarebit, steak and kidney sausages, marmalade and orange sponge pudding.

Yang Sing in the city centre is an energetic, well-established Chinese restaurant on two floors. Here you see businessmen celebrating deals with Champagne and big parties out on the town alongside serious Chinese students and foodies getting down to work. The waiters can help give you recommendations to build up a personal banquet. Just around the corner are two old-time Manchester pubs, the plain **Circus Tavern**, with its tiny bar right by the entrance and the small, friendly **Grey Horse**, with Hyde's beers. Beer prices are notably low in Manchester, especially Holt's, which can be as low as £1 to £1.20 a pint.

The Northern Quarter is an interesting part of town, with fine old boozers, independent shops and buildings that have escaped the developers. It is worth a wander: a bit rough around the edges but full of life. On the edge of this area, a fine pub crawl might start at **The Smithfield** at the top of Swan Street (the A665 just south of the A664 junction), which is a downhome pub with a good range of real ales. The nearby **Hare and Hounds** is an old-timers' pub with Holt's beer. **The Beer House**, just off the north side of the Rochdale Road, is very much a real ale pub with a big selection of beers. Near here, **The Pot of Beer** is one of those pubs with a tardis-like quality: a closed face on the outside, but full of warmth and life inside, including the surprise of Polish food. Continuing down the Rochdale Road, on the north side, **The Marble Arch** has a lovely tiled interior, sofas and a micro-brewery.

Go to Rusholme in southeast Manchester for the 'Curry Mile' (*see also chapter two*) which is a great sight, quite apart from the food. A 15 minute train ride from Manchester takes you to the fabulous **Stalybridge Station Victorian Buffet**, with an exceptional range of real ales, little fires and friendly atmosphere. (*See also chapter nine.*) If you want a dose of 'ethnic English' have a wander around Bury Market, and queue up for black puddings at Chadwick's stall: one counter is tripe, the other just loops of black puddings, which you can have hot or cold and fatty or lean.

North of Manchester, I recommend **Ramsons Restaurant and Café Bar** in Ramsbottom. It is run with passion by Chris Johnson and Ros Hunter, who import produce from the Milan for food that is vivid with flavour. The downstairs café-bar is modelled on an Italian *enoteca*, or wine bar, and there is a restaurant on the ground floor. (*See also chapter nine*).

If you like old shops, make a special detour to go to **Herbal Health**, a temperance bar and herbalist in Rawtenstall. There are 140 jars of herbs on the old shelves and a marble-topped bar with a splendid, gleaming copper heater for hot drinks in the winter. People drop by for black beer and raisin cordial and sarsaparilla ice-lollies. It is a rarity that is used in an everyday way.

On the A59, **Northcote Manor** at Langho is a smart hotel and restaurant with excellent food using English flavours. The plate of Lancashire starters includes potted shrimps and brawn and, as a spin on the classic combination of an apple and a hunk of cheese, you may get Lancashire ice-cream with an apple crumble soufflé. It works.

North of here, the Forest of Bowland has remained an unspoiled corner of England. One of the best places to stay is **The Inn at Whitewell**, which is a quintessential country inn, subtly notched up

Stalybridge Station Buffet
0161 303 0007
Rassbottom Street
Stalybridge

Ramsons Restaurant and Café Bar
01706 825070
16-18 Market Place
Ramsbottom

Herbal Health
01706 211152
5 Bank Street
Rawtenstall

Northcote Manor
01254 240555
Langho
A59, 8.5 miles east of Jcn 31 off M6
www.ncotemanor.demon.co.uk

The Inn at Whitewell
01200 448222
Whitewell

The Hark to Bounty
01200 446246
Slaidburn
The Mulberry Tree
01257 451400
Wrightington Bar
on B5250 off
jcn 27, M6
Booths
Head Office:
01772 251701
James Baxter & Son
01524 410910
Thornton Road
Morecambe
Maritime Museum
01524 64637
St George's Quay
Lancaster

to make it even more special. There are great views and good food, Victorian hip-baths, deep beds, big fires and total peace and quiet. Some of the bedrooms have their own fires. It is a romantic and comfortable place, set by a river and amid hills. Also in the Forest, **The Hark to Bounty** is an old pub in the charming village of Slaidburn. They serve admirably old-fashioned food such as steak and kidney pie and proper puddings.

Going to the west of the county, **The Mulberry Tree** at Wrightington Bar has a chef/proprietor, Mark Prescott, who used to cook at the Roux brothers' White Horse at Nayland. Here he has set up a good-value place with high-quality British food such as meat-and-potato pie with a parsley crust and Lancashire cheese and top-notch fish and chips, alongside Modern British dishes.

I was impressed by **Booths** supermarket, where they flag up local produce on the shelves and have a big range of high-quality foods. It is based in Preston with branches all over the northwest. All over Lancashire, look out for Morecambe Bay potted shrimps **Baxter's** is a good brand run by Bob Baxter in Morecambe. They do mail order. **The Maritime Museum** in Lancaster tells the story of the trade more generally. Also look out for Lancashire cheese in the markets, shops and restaurants, especially Sandham's, Kirkham's and Shorrock's. (*See also chapter four.*)

cumbria

Centre Starting in Kendal, **Farrer's** is in a 17th century building which became a coffee house in 1819, and is now a tea and coffee shop with an espresso bar and café. They use bread from **The Staff of Life**, an interesting bakery run by Simon Thomas, who makes continental-style breads, in flavours such as rye bread with preserved orange peel and fennel. Simon's shop is down a passageway, reached by Hadwins electrical shop on Finkle Street. Next door is a good independent wine merchant, **Frank Stainton**. At the farmers' market, look out for **Diane Halliday**'s cake stall. She also sells from her bakery at home near Kirkby Stephen. In Keswick, the **Museum of Lakeland Life** is an excellent introduction to the history of the people and traditions of the area, including farming, crafts and cooking.

The Lake District has many real ale pubs, with fires, food and accommodation. One of the best for its choice of beers, **The Watermill** at Ings, is east of Windermere. North of Windermere, **The Queen's Head** in Troutbeck is one of the classic old pubs of the region, in a beautiful spot, and with a bar made out of a carved wooden Elizabethan four-poster bed.

Ambleside has three premises run by Lucy Nicholson, who used to promote bands in London before going to live in the Lakes. She has made a tape of her meetings with food producers in the area, called *Lakeland on the Table* and her deli, **Lucy's Specialist Grocers**, is stuffed with regional produce. She also has a café next door, Lucy on a Plate, and a wine bar, Lucy Four. People recommend **The Glass House** restaurant in a converted mill, next to the owner's glass studio and workshop. **The Armitt** is an interesting museum and displays Beatrix Potter's scientific watercolours, including fungi. **Sarah Nelson's Grasmere Gingerbread Shop** is in an old

Farrer's
01539 731707
13 Strickland Gate
Kendal
www.farrers.com
The Staff of Life
01539 738606
2 Berry's Yard, Kendal
Frank Stainton
01539 731886
3 Berry's Yard, Stainton
Farmers' Markets
Sarah Plummer
01539 732736
Diane Halliday
017683 72519
Dalefoot, Mallerstang
Museum of Lakeland Life
01539 722464
Abbot Hall, Keswick
Watermill
01539 821309
Ings, just off A591
The Queen's Head
015394 32174
Troutbeck
bedrooms
Lucy's
015394 32223 - shop
015394 31191 - café
Church Street, Ambleside
015394 34666-wine bar
St Mary's Lane, Ambleside
The Glass House
015394 32137
Rydal Road
Ambleside
The Armitt
015394 31212
Rydal Road
Ambleside
www.armitt.com

Sarah Nelson's
Grasmere Gingerbread
Shop
015394 35428
Grasmere
Jumble Room
015394 35188
Langdale Road
Grasmere
Britannia Inn
015394 37210
Elterwater; bedrooms
Eric & Sue Taylforth
015394 37364
Millbeck Farm
Great Langdale
B&B and self-catering
The Old
Dungeon Ghyll
015394 37272
Great Langdale
bedrooms
The Drunken Duck
015394 36347
Barngates
Hawkshead
The Black Bull
015394 41335
Yewdale Road
Coniston (A593)
bedrooms
The Barn Shop
01539 560426
Low Sizergh Farm
Sizergh
(just off A591)
Punch Bowl Inn
015395 68237
Crosthwaite
www.punchbowl.
fsnet.co.uk
bedrooms

schoolhouse in Grasmere. They still make the chewy, thin slabs to the Victorian recipe. Try them combined with another Lakes' speciality, rum butter. **The Jumble Room** is a colourful, friendly café. **The Britannia Inn** at Elterwater is one of the nicest pubs in the Lakes, with a relaxed atmosphere, real ales and Herdwick lamb on the menu. This is supplied by **Eric and Sue Taylforth**, who sell from their farm in Great Langdale and do mailorder. Sue can also serve lamb for supper, if you are staying with them as B&B guests. (*See also chapter six.*) There is a popular walkers' pub further down the dale, **The Old Dungeon Ghyll**, which opens for breakfast.

    The Drunken Duck at Barngates, near Hawkshead, is a characterful pub with excellent food, a micro-brewery and amazing views. One of the best small breweries in the area is the Coniston Brewing Company, behind the **Black Bull** in Coniston. The Bluebird Bitter has won the Champion Beer of Britain award and is commonly sold by real ale pubs in the Lakes.

South The **Barn Shop** at Sizergh near the A591, south of Kendal, is an exceptional farm shop which gathers together good local produce. West of Kendal is a top gastro-pub, **The Punch Bowl Inn** at Crosthwaite. The chef-proprietor, Steven Doherty, trained at Le Gavroche. His cooking combines fine techniques and local produce, and the prices are very fair. (*See also chapter two.*) The pub's setting is the beautiful and unspoiled Lyth Valley, which is famous for its damsons. Peter Cartmell has set up a **Westmoreland Damson Association** to encourage the revival of the fruit; there is an enjoyable Damson Day in the spring, usually the second Saturday of April, when the blossom is at its best. Produce sold includes jams, chocolates, wine and damson gin. **Lyth Valley Farm Shop** sells home-grown fruit and vegetables, including the damsons from mid-September for about three weeks. **The Mason's Arms** at Strawberry Bank near Cartmel Fell, a couple miles south of Windermere, has its own damson beer alongside 150 bottled beers and draft real ales.

Going right down south, **Cartmel Village Shop** is a charming place where they sell their own sticky toffee pudding. **Ainsworth's** in Grange-over-Sands is a useful deli. Mid-way between Grange and Newby Bridge, **Airey's farmshop** at Ayside, in the same family since 1853, is a butcher/farm/abbatoir which specialises in native breeds meat, such as Gloucester Old Spot and Saddleback pork, Herdwick lamb, and Dexter and Shorthorn beef.

West Past the huge Glaxo factory, **The Bay Horse** near Ulverston has real ales, high-quality food and views across Morecambe Bay. You will see **Demels** Chutneys in Cumbria and beyond. Made by a Sri Lankan lady, Mrs Trepte, to family recipes, they are excellent. She also sells by mail-order and at the door. **The Manor Arms** in Broughton-in-Furness is a 16th century inn with six well-kept beers, a big fire and a down-to-earth, welcoming atmosphere.

Out west, **Woodall's** post office/village shop in Waberthwaite has hams hanging from the ceiling, some with gold foil on the shank end. They make matured Cumberland hams and two air-dried hams. The Cumbria Mature Royal has beer and treacle in the cure. They also make dry-cured bacon and Cumberland sausages. Although Woodalls' goods are widley available, it is still worth making a detour – a long one, from the rest of the Lakes – to go to the shop itself.

This is an unspoiled part of Cumbria. If you want an extra-long detour, drive on past the mesmerising Wast Water with its reflections

Westmoreland Damson Association
015395 68246
www.lythdamsons.org.uk
Lyth Valley
Farm Shop
01539 568248
Dawson Fold (on A5074)
The Mason's Arms
015395 68486
Strawberry Bank
Cartmel Fell
self-catering
Cartmel Village Shop
01539 536201
The Square, Cartmel
Ainsworth's
01539 532946
Kents Bank Road
Grange-over-Sands
Airey's Farm Shop
01539 531237
Ayside
Nr Grange-over-Sands
The Bay Horse
01229 583972
near Ulverston
signposted off A590
bedrooms
Demels
01229 861012
The Barn
Arrad Foot
near Ulverston
The Manor Arms
01229 716286
The Square,
Broughton-in-Furness
bedrooms
Woodall's
01229 717237
Lane End, Waberthwaite
www.richardwoodall.co.uk

Wasdale Head Inn
019467 26229
Wasdale Head
bedrooms

Toffee Shop
01768 862008
7 Brunswick Road
Penrith

Graham's
01768 862281
Market Square, Penrith
www.cumbria.com/
grahams

MacKays
01768 863374
35 Great Dochray
Penrith

Sharrow Bay
017684 86301
Ullswater
www.sharrow-bay.com

Rampsbeck Hotel
017684 86442
Watermillock
www.rampsbeck.fsnet.
co.uk

The Old Crown
016974 78288
Hesket Newmarket
B&B next door

Hesket Newmarket
Brewery
016974 78066
Hesket Newmarket

The Water Mill
016974 78267
Church Terrace
Caldbeck

of slopes, and end up in the **Wasdale Head Inn** in Wasdale at the head of the valley, where they serve Herdwick lamb.

North The charming **Toffee Shop** in Penrith sells only its own delicious toffee and fudge. (*See also chapter seven.*) **Graham's** in the market square in Penrith is a period piece of a shop, with antlers on the walls and stained glass in the windows. They stock many of the best Cumbrian foods. Food historian Ivan Day recommends **Mackays** as a good butcher's selling local meat and their own bacon.

Many of the restaurants in the Lakes are old-fashioned blow-outs in country-house hotels. Two notable ones are on either side of Ullswater, one of the most beautiful of the lakes. **Sharrow Bay**, two miles from Pooley Bridge on the east side of the lake, opened in 1948. It has picture-postcard views of mountains tumbling down to the water and the well-oiled smoothness of a Victorian household stuffed with servants. Dinner is a set menu, with starters served on the dot of eight o'clock. You can also come here for tea.

Less well-known, the **Rampsbeck Hotel** at Watermillock is an unstuffy place in a glorious position. The chef, Andrew McGeorge, is from the area and has been here since 1989, staying in the Lakes when chefs at other restaurants have tired of sheep and rain and run off back to London. Going northwest of Penrith, **The Old Crown** in Hesket Newmarket has a brewery behind it owned by a co-operative of the village and other regulars. The brewery was set up by a former maths lecturer, Jim Fernley, who also carefully tested and amassed recipes for curries, which are served in the pub. The beers bear names like "Doris' 90th Birthday Ale", created to celebrate Jim's mother-in-law's birthday. The Priest's Mill at Caldbeck has been carefully restored and converted into a nice café, **The Water Mill**, above the rushing water. It also has a shop selling local foods.

Just off the A595 Carlisle to Cockermouth road, in the former outbuildings of an old hall near Thursby, Carolyn Fairbairn at **Thornby Moor Dairy** makes cow's and goat's milk cheeses, which you can try and buy in the shop. She also does cheesemaking courses by arrangement. Fans of local museums must go to the one in **Keswick** which has, among much else, a Victorian seven-octave xylophone made out of Skiddaw slate. **Hodgson's** butcher tries to source all its meat from within a five-mile radius of the shop and sells the delicious meat from the fellside Herdwick sheep.

In one of the most dramatically beautiful parts of the lakes, Borrowdale, I can thoroughly recommend the unfrilly **Flock-in Tearoom** at Yew Tree Farm, run by Hazel Relph at Rossthwaite. She serves the likes of pints of tea, scones, tea-bread and 'Herdiburgers' made from their own Herdwick sheep. They also sell to Hodgson's in Keswick. (*See also chapter six.*)

If you drive west from Keswick on the A66, **The Pheasant** at Bassenthwaite Lake is a comfortably old-fashioned hotel with a relaxing bar room and a restaurant using local produce. It is a place to stay if you want peace and quiet. **The Bitter End** in Cockermouth makes its own beers and has Cumberland sausage sarnies. Jennings, a regional brewery, is in the town. If you like pottering round old-fashioned hardware shops, or are just generally curious, **J B Banks and son**, established in 1836, is worth a visit.

Northeast An excellent example of how the independent can offer more quality and character than the average chain can be found at **Westmorland Service Station** at Tebay, off junction 38 of the M6.

Thornby Moor Dairy
01697 345555
Crofton Hall
Thursby

Keswick Museum
01768773757
Fitzpark
Station Road
Keswick

Hodgson's
01768772525
3 Blencathra Street

Flock-in Tearoom
01768777675
Yew Tree Farm
Rossthwaite
bedrooms

The Pheasant
01768776234
Bassenthwaite Lake
bedrooms

The Bitter End
01900 826626
15 Kirkgate
Cockermouth

JB Banks & Son
01900 822281
Market Place

Westmorland
Service Station
015396 24511
Tebay

Slack's
01539 624667
www.edirectory.co.uk/
slacks
TM Ewbank
017683 51462
Appleby-in-
Westmorland
The Old Smokehouse
01768 867772
Brougham Hall
La Casa Verde/
Larch Cottage
Nurseries
01931 712404
Melkinthorpe
Little Salkeld
Watermill
01768 881523
Little Salkeld
Dukes Head
016974 72226
Armathwaite
Shepherds
01768 881217
Melmerby
The Village Bakery
01768 881515
Melmerby
Angus Quality Meats
01768 885384
www.countryfarms.
co.uk

It has old-fashioned English food, proper curries, cakes and relaxing surroundings. Northeast of here, **Slack's** makes dry-cured bacon and sausages from free-range or whey-fed pigs. It sells by mail order and in shops in the north and elsewhere.

A quality old-fashioned butcher, **T M Ewbank** in Appleby-in-Westmorland, rears and butcher its own cattle and also sells pork, lamb and mutton. The legs of lamb come wrapped in caul fat to keep them moist while cooking. Well worth visiting. (*See also chapter eight.*) Going back towards Penrith, **The Old Smokehouse** at Brougham Hall has truffles and smoked produce, including char, a freshwater fish which is a delicacy of the Lakes. Rona Newsome has retired but has passed her recipes and techniques on to the new owners. Fingers crossed they keep up the quality.

South of here, in Melkinthorpe, **La Casa Verde** is an Italian-influenced café at **Larch Cottage Nurseries** which sells unusual plants. The owner, Peter Stott, built the wood-fired pizza oven himself and the crisp-crusted pizzas and rich cakes are delicious. It is a short drive off the M6, junction 40.

Northeast of Penrith, in the Eden Valley, **Little Salkeld Watermill** has a craft shop, great flours and interesting booklets explaining organic flour, baking and milling. If you head on north in this pretty and unspoiled part of Cumbria, **The Duke's Head** at Armathwaite is a village pub with real ale, and the menu includes Morecambe Bay potted shrimps.

Melmerby has a popular pub with hearty food, **The Shepherds**. **Village Bakery** is a pioneering bakery with a restaurant and shop, which sells organic groceries, baking equipment and books. **Angus Quality Meats**, based in Calthwaite, sells Herdick lamb by mail order.

leeds and the yorkshire dales

Leeds is a good city to visit: there is a lot going on, it doesn't take long to walk across the centre, and you can get your bearings from magnificent Victorian buildings like the Town Hall. Coming out of the station and bearing right, if you walk along Boar Lane you see the oval 1860s Corn Exchange. Inside are layers of small, funky shops. Near here, Call Lane has a number of independent café-bars, from the modish Norman to the mellow **Art's**, my favourite. One of the many fine Victorian pubs in Leeds, **The Adelphi**, by Tetley's Brewery, is near Call Lane.

Beyond Call Lane, further up the River Aire, **42 The Calls** is a modern and stylish hotel in a mill conversion. There are two good restaurants in the same building but with different entrances. **Pool Court at 42** feels like a boat, with curving walls, portholes and the feeling of being above water. The menu is luxurious and refined. The kitchen also provides the well-presented, good-value food in **Brasserie Forty Four**. If you walk further along the river, the **Royal Armouries Museum** explores arms and fighting, from the rituals of medieval tournaments to media coverage of modern warfare. I urge you to go, even if you think the subject a total turn-off: it is a fascinating, state-of-the-art musuem.

Heading north from the Corn Exchange, up Vicar Lane, the indoor Victorian Kirkgate Market is on the right and worth a visit for the building alone. There are 620 stalls, including a butchers' row of 22 shops, and it is full of Leeds characters and scraps of chat. The Victoria Quarter is the smart place to shop, with its beautiful restored arcades of shops selling French pâtisserie, Italian shoes, buttons and so forth. **Harvey Nichols** is here, with a café-restaurant on the fourth floor. Amid the shopping area west of Briggate, tucked away in a yard near Debenhams and Littlewoods, is the classic Leeds

Art's
0113 245 6377
42 Call Lane
Leeds

The Adelphi
0113 245 6377
1-5 Hunslet Road
Leeds

42 The Calls
0113 244 0099
42 The Calls
Leeds
www.42thecalls.co.uk

Pool Court at 42
0113 244 4242
44 The Calls
Leeds

Brasserie Forty Four
0113 2353232
44 The Calls
Leeds

Royal Armouries Museum
0113 220 1999
Armouries Drive
Leeds
www.armouries.org.uk

Harvey Nichols
0113 204 8000
107 Briggate
Leeds

Whitelocks
0113 245 3950
Turks Head Yard,
off Briggate
Leeds
Pasta Romagna
0113 245 1569
26 Albion Place
Leeds
Mojo
0113 244 6387
18 Merrion Street
Leeds
Hansa's
0113 244 4408
72 North Street
Leeds
The Victoria
0113 245 1386
28 Great George Street
Leeds
Gueller's
0113 245 9922
3 York Place
Leeds
www.guellers.com
Brett's
0113 289 9322
12-14 North Lane
Headingley
Leeds

pub, **Whitelocks**, which is long and narrow, with old advertisments and stained glass. Also off Briggate, in Albion Place, **Pasta Romagna** is run, *con brio*, by Gildea Porcelli, a southern Italian. You will know you are nearby from the opera which she both sings and plays. It is a place for a stop-off and a lift-up.

Heading north of Briggate, **Mojo** is an independent bar known for its cocktails. In North Street, **Hansa's** is a good-value Indian restaurant gently imbued with the personality of its owner, Hansa Dabhi. She serves delicious Gujarati vegetarian food cooked in an all-female kitchen. *(See also chapter two.)*

Back towards the city centre, on Great George Street, **The Victoria** is another good Victorian pub. It is behind the magnificent Town Hall, with its columns, sweep of steps and stand-up display of Victorian civic pride. Leeds City Art Gallery is next door.

South of here, heading back towards the station to the financial district, Simon Gueller, the chef who made Rascasse restaurant (also in Leeds) so well known, has set up his own restaurant, **Gueller's** in York Place. The décor is cool, the divisions between the tables make for intimacy, and the cooking is precise and stylish. He uses local produce when possible, including asparagus and soft fruit picked from the fields near to his home, local game and the catch landed at Whitby. The diver-caught scallops might be used in a dish with creamed celeriac and a truffle vinaigrette.

There are a number of chippies worth visiting in Leeds: you can tell the best by the briskly moving queues. Ask for 'scraps', the little bits of deep-fried batter, as an extra to your fish and chips. For a sit down fish-and-chips meal, it would be hard to beat **Brett's** in Headingley, north Leeds, which opened in 1919 and has wooden panelling on the dining room walls. As is the Yorkshire custom (and done elsewhere, also) they fry in beef dripping, for flavour, though vegetarians can have their chips cooked in oil. The take-away is at the side. **Bryan's** is another celebrated place to eat fish and chips in Headingley. An example of a fast-moving, quality local, is **Midgley's**, near the Original Oak pub. It gets very busy, especially on rugby league match days, but you never seem to have to wait long to get served. They also fry in beef dripping. **Oakwood Fisheries**, a chippie in Oakwood has a modernist frontage and chrome details.

The Dales Heading on up towards the Dales from Leeds, Ilkley has the famous **Box Tree** with fine food and an entertaining clutter of collectables to look at. **Bettys** displays what you might call the Austrian side of Yorkshire: fine baking, spruce service, gleaming décor. Here, I once saw a fellow customer use a lorgnette to peruse the tea list. This Ilkley branch (there are also Bettys in York, Harrogate and Northallerton) has a remarkable, large piece of marquetry depicting a hunting scene. The front shop and café sell teas and coffees from all over the world (courtesy of Bettys' partner company, Taylors), chocolates, cakes and all sorts of goodies, including the classics of Yorkshire baking: curd tarts, pikelets, parkin and so on. A good place for lunch or tea.

From Ilkley, you can go north to Bolton Abbey, or head into the Dales through Skipton. **David Humphreys** has moved here from Ilkley, to a café-shop and bakery, where he will continue to make chocolates in front of the customers, with the air perfumed by fountains of melted chocolate falling into churning vats. Although making a quality product, Mr Humphreys, like all good Yorkshiremen, keeps an eye on the price. "I've seen what they charge in London and it's robbery without the violence," he says. Also in the

Bryan's
0113 278 5679
6 Weetwood Lane
Leeds

Midgley's
01132 7427427
St Michael's Lane,
Headingley
Leeds

Oakwood Fisheries
0113 240 0872 492
Roundhay Road

Box Tree
01943 608484
37 Church Street
Ilkley
www.theboxtree.co.uk

Bettys
01943 608029
32-34 The Grove
Ilkley
www.bettysandtaylors.
co.uk

Humphreys at Walkers
01756 791494
4 Water Street
Skipton
www.exclusive-
chocolates.co.uk

Stanforth's
01756 793477
9, Mill Bridge
Skipton
Bizzie Lizzie's
01756 793189
36 Swadford Street
Skipton
The Angel
01756 730263
Hetton
The George
01756 760223
Hubberholme
bedrooms
Wensleydale Creamery
01969 667664
Gayle Lane
Hawes
www.wensleydale.
co.uk
Humble Pie
01969 650671
Market Place
Askrigg
The Sun Inn
015396 25208
Dent
bedrooms
Coniston Hall Lodge
01756 748136
Coniston Cold
www.conistonhall.co.uk
bedrooms
The Marton Arms
015242 41281
Thornton in Lonsdale
bedrooms

town, **Stanforth's** sells pork pies warm from the oven, as can be testified by the pavement outside, which is stained with gravy: the unset jelly spurts out as customers tuck in by the shop. **Bizzie Lizzie's** is a good chippie where you can eat in or take away.

Driving up into the Dales, **The Angel** in Hetton is a classic gastro-pub with a well-established reputation for brasserie-style food. It is a short drive from here to the famous limestone scenery of Malham Cove. Going north on the B6160, **The George** at Hubberholme, a mile from Buckden, is an unspoiled inn where J B Priestley used to drink. You can then take the high road northwest over to Hawes, where the **Wensleydale Creamery** has a visitor centre, which tells the history of the cheese, and a café and shop. I have not managed to go here, but a trusted food-lover recommends **Humble Pie** in Askrigg, if you find yourself in the northeast Dales, near the falls at Aysgarth. Here, Elizabeth Guy makes home-cooked food – cakes, pies, etc – which you can take away in single portions.

West of Hawes, in the remote, starkly beautiful countryside of the western Dales, Dent is a great base for walking. **The Sun Inn** is a snug pub with a micro-brewery. It takes a good day's trip to walk up Whernside from Dent. You can also approach The Three Peaks of Yorkshire – Ingleborough, Whernside and Pen-y-Ghent – from the A65, going west from Skipton. On the way, and also useful for Malham Cove, **Coniston Hall Lodge** at Coniston Cold opens at 7am for breakfast. The restaurant's chef, Stephanie Moon, uses game from the estate in dishes such as wild duck with honey-roast parsnips and sloe-gin sauce.

A more down-to-earth venue, and a top real-ale pub, **The Marton Arms** in Thornton in Lonsdale has curries and other pub food, and good-value accommodation.

East of the Dales The original **Bettys** in Harrogate is the place to eat cakes before reclining in the Harrogate Turkish baths. **Taylors** tea and coffee merchants sell here, as they do in Ilkley, and also by mail order. **Rooster** is an interesting small brewery based in Harrogate. The owner, Sean Franklin, is fascinated by hops, and brews beers with the emphasis on their aromatic qualities: these are beers that wine-drinkers will appreciate. In Harrogate, you may find Rooster brews as guest beers at The Old Bell Tavern and The Tap and Spile, neither of which I know. Otherwise, you can find his beer in The Maltings, a beer-house in York and in good real ale pubs in the south. (*See also chapter nine.*)

The **Farm Dairy** in Knaresborough has a good selection of cheeses from the north and other craft foods. Just north of Knaresborough, **The General Tarleton** in Ferrensby is an 18th-century coaching inn with good food, owned by John Topham, co-owner of The Angel in Hetton.

If you head northwest of Knaresborough and go back into the hills, north of Pateley Bridge into Nidderdale, **The Yorke Arms** in Ramsgill is a superb example of a restaurant which uses the produce of the surrounding countryside. (*See also chapter nine.*) Middlesmoor is a special village at the head of the dale, huddled up high against the elements. **Dovenor House** is a bed and breakfast with a good tearoom. Here they sell the excellent preserves made by Elspeth Biltoft at **Rosebud Preserves**. Elspeth makes these in Healey, and sells by mail order, at the farmers' markets in Ripon, Knaresborough, Harrogate, and in good food shops.

Driving north-west of here, on the A6108, beyond Jervaulx, the **Blue Lion**, in East Witton is a civilised pub with a handsome front room and good food.

Bettys and Taylors
01423 565191
1 Parliament Street
Harrogate
www.bettysand
taylors.co.uk
Rooster brewery
01423 561861
Harrogate
www.roosters.co.uk
Farm Dairy
01423 865027
3 Market Square
Knaresborough
The General Tarleton
01423 340284
Ferrensby
bedrooms
Yorke Arms
01423 755243
Ramsgill
www.yorke-arms.co.uk;
bedrooms
Dovenor House
01423 755697
by the church
Middlesmoor
bedrooms
Rosebud Preserves
01765 689174
Rosebud Farm
Healey
www.farm
connection.co.uk
The Blue Lion
01969 624273
East Witton
bedrooms

Black Sheep Brewery
01765 680101
Masham
Joneva's
01765 689323
Market Place
Masham
Shepherd's Purse
01845 587220
Leachfield Grange
Newsham
www.shepherds
purse.co.uk
York Beer and
Wine Shop
01904 647136
28 Sandringham Street
Fishergate
York
www.yorkbeerand
wineshop.co.uk
Betty's
01904 659142
6-8 St Helen's Square
The Maltings
01904 655387
Tanners Moat/
Wellington Row
below Lendal Bridge
The White Horse
01482 861973
Hengate
Beverley
Womersley Crafts and
Herbs
01977 620294
Womersley Hall
Womersley
Near Doncaster

Back down southeast on the A6108, Masham is a market town where the **Black Sheep Brewery** has a visitor centre and good-value café with fish in beer batter, beef and beer casserole, scones with Rosebud preserves and so on. Just off the market square is a deli, Reay's, and Beavers' butcher, famous for its sausages. On the square is an excellent sweet shop and deli, **Joneva's**, with bars of '*grand cru*' chocolate and other craft produce, sweet and savoury, including the Richard III Wensleydale, made by Suzanne Stirke. Elspeth Biltoft recommends The Mad Hatter, just off the square, for good lunches and homemade cakes.

Judy Bell at **Shepherd's Purse** in Newsham is another good local cheesemaker, known for her cow's milk Yorkshire Blue, ewes' milk Mrs Bell's and Yorkshire feta. She sells by mail order and in shops around the country.

East of Leeds The **York Beer and Wine Shop** has a huge selection of beers, including Timothy Taylor's Landlord on draught, up to 40 ciders, wines and up to 60 cheeses, including unpasteurised ones. Three quarters of the cheeses are British and Irish. The shop's co-owner, Jim Helsby, makes great tours of the country buying directly from small producers, some of them very much off the beaten track. **Bettys** has a branch in York with wood panelling and art deco stained glass. **The Maltings** is a renowned real ale beer-house in the city.

The White Horse, near the bus station in Beverley, is an old pub, still with gaslight, fires and a warren of rooms. Southeast of Leeds in Womersley, Martin and Aline Parsons, at **Womersley Crafts and Herbs**, make superb vinegars and preserves from their own herbs. You can find their products in good delis around the country. They also sell a huge selection of herbs as plants for the garden.

west yorkshire

Mumtaz
01274 571861
Great Horton Road
Bradford
Bombay Stores
01274 729993
Bombay Buildings
Shearbridge Road
Bradford
Kolos Bakery
01274 729958
128-132 Parkside Road
Bradford
**Asa Nicholson
& Sons**
01274 833149
Oats Royd Bakery
Denholme
near Bradford
Salt's Diner
01274 530533
Saltaire
The Boltmakers
01535 661936
117 East Parade
Keighley

ALTHOUGH IT IS LESS CELEBRATED than the Dales and the Moors, the industrial heritage and the wild moors of west Yorkshire make it an interesting area to visit. Bradford has an engaging mixture of Asian culture, magnificent Victorian buildings like the Wool Exchange and good musuems. **Mumtaz** is a well-run restaurant up Great Horton Road, and ten mintues' walk away, **Bombay Stores** is an Asian department store with 30,000 square feet stuffed with saris, fabrics and other goods, plus a café. Around the city, you see the bread made by the Ukranian **Kolos Bakery**, including the celebrated rye bread, and you can buy from the bakery itself in south Bradford and see trayfuls of beautiful loaves.

Just outside Bradford, at Denholme, **Asa Nicholson & Sons** family bakery and tea shop still sells a modern version of a Yorkshire oatcake; they also have an authentic traditional oatcake-throwing machine, though it was not in use at the time of writing. *(See also chapter four.)*

Saltaire, northwest of Bradford, was built by the Victorian industrialist, Titus Salt, to take his production and workers out of the furnace and the mire of 19th century Bradford. In the 20th century, the vast Salt's Mill was bought and revitalised by a modern-day enterepeneur, the late Jonathan Silver, who turned part of the building into galleries displaying the works of David Hockney. The cheery **Salt's Diner** is a good place to eat, and the whole place makes a good half-day outing, with plenty of quality shopping, the galleries and the village itself, which is fascinating.

Keighley is home to one of the best breweries of the north, Timothy Taylor. Look out for their beers, particularly the award-winning Landlord. **The Boltmakers** is a small Taylor's pub, near the train station, with a fire and malt whiskies, near the train station.

Keighley & Worth
Valley Railway
01535 645214
01535 647777
- timetable
Keighley to Oxenhope
Weavers Restaurant
01535 643822
13-17 West Lane
Haworth
bedrooms
The Fleece
01535 642172
Main Street
The Hare and Hounds
01422 842671
Old Town
nr Hebden Bridge
www.hare.and.
hounds.
connectfree.co.uk
bedrooms
Weavers Shed
01484 654284
Knowl Road
Golcar
bedrooms
R&J Lodge
01484 850571
Greens End Road
Meltham
Rhurbarb group tours
Philippa Ventom
01924 305841
pre-book only
2nd week Jan -
2nd week March

The **Keighley & Worth** Valley Railway is a marvellous line with beautifully restored and run steam trains, a vintage carriage museum at Ingrow and real ales served on the trains. You can get off the station at Haworth and it is a 15-minute walk up a steep hill to the Brontes' house and the excellent Parsonage Museum. In Haworth, **Weavers** is a good, friendly restaurant, and the chef/proprietors Colin and Jane Rushworth have dishes such as Lancashire cheese fritters with grape and apple chutney and Pennine meat-and-potato pie. Down the hill, **The Fleece** is an unspoiled plain pub with well-priced Timothy Taylor's beers. **The Hare and Hound**s, at Old Town, about a mile from Hebden Bridge, is a friendly local with gutsy food and well-kept Taylor's beers.

West of Huddersfield in Golcar, **Weavers Shed** is a restaurant with rooms in the Colne Valley where chef/proprietor Stephen Jackson uses vegetables and fruit from his own garden, alongside other good ingredients, to give the dishes a freshness and flavour that you only get with home-grown, just-picked produce.

South of here, in Meltham, **R&J Lodge** has its own dry-cured bacon sizzling on a griddle for lunchtime sarnies, and they also sell moist parkin and good pork pies. Near Wakefield, there are excellent group tours of the forced **rhubarb sheds**. The season is from January to mid-March, with a festival held at the end of January or beginning of February, depending on the weather. (*See also chapter six.*)

All over the north, and now in the south, look out for the superior Seabrooks crisps, which are made in Bradford, and small brewery beers, from Ossett, Kitchen and Springhead, to name just three.

north york moors

STARTING TO THE SOUTH OF THE MOORS, Ampleforth Abbey has an orchard, perched up high, overlooking the Vale of Pickering. In a low-key, unadvertised way, the Abbey's 50 varieties of apple are sold, as each one reaches its peak, from an informal shed-shop open during daylight hours, between September and Christmas. (*See also chapter one.*) The monks also sell their apples to the thatch-roofed **Star at Harome**, a short drive away. This is one of the best gastro-pubs in the country for its atmosphere and the way the owner/proprietor, Andrew Pern, uses local English ingredients – rhubarb, black pudding, fish, game and so on – in gutsy and well-executed modern cooking. He also sells local produce. (*See also chapter nine.*)

Helmsley is a market town with a quality-marked 'Q-Guild' butcher, **Nicholson & Son**, with beef and lamb from a traditionally run local farm. Nicholson & Son makes pies, sausages and ready-meals such as shepherd's pie. On another side of the market square is a well-stocked deli, **Hunter's**.

West of Helmsley is Rievaulx Abbey and, beyond that, Scawton with another good gastro-pub, **The Hare**. Dishes include knuckle of pork with cider gravy and apple sauce, Whitby haddock, potted shrimps, and sausages, as well as more Italian and French-influenced food. The pub itself is warm, friendly and popular.

From here you can drive up through Bilsdale on the B1257 and, in the middle of nowhere, about nine miles from Helmsley, come across The Sun Inn, known as the Spout House, an authentic, simple country pub, run by the farmer, William Ainsley. Next door to the pub is the original Spout House, first licensed as an inn in 1714 and run by the first William Ainsley (the eldest son in each generation is called William) in 1823. The 16th-century cruck-framed cottage has been left as it was when they moved to the new building and, with

The Star at Harome
01439 770397
Harome
bedrooms

Nicholson & Son
01439 770249
18 Market Place
Helmsley

Hunter's
01439 771307
13 Market Place
Helmsley

The Hare
01845 597289
Scawton

McCoy's Bistro
01609 882671
Cleveland Tontine
Staddlebridge
at junction of A19
and A172
bedrooms
D Petch
01642 722246
Great Ayton
The Horse Shoe
01947 895245
Egton Bridge
bedrooms

the help of a leaflet by the National Park Authority, you can imagine the past life inside, from the fireside oven to the bedrooms under the thatch. A Yorkshire touch: the sloping field next to the pub doubles as a cricket pitch, with the square cut into the incline.

McCoy's Bistro at Staddlebridge is well worth a visit. With its dark interior, wood, candles, mirrors, big fire and buzzing energy, it has the atmosphere of a good French brasserie and enjoyable food. *(See also chapter nine.)* Heading north to Great Ayton, where Captain Cook lived as a child, you can join the brisk queue for a **Petch's** pie from the butcher. The window is full of proud pies, their pastry glossy with lard.

The drives across the moors are particularly beautiful, not least when the big spread of heather is out, from early August to early September. It blooms in a 40-mile expanse to the sea and gives rise to the heather honey you see in local shops. Harry Mead, the father of Jill, this book's photographer, in his classic book of essays, *Inside the North York Moors*, recommends driving along the road between Kildale and Westerdale to view a microcosm of the Moors' scenery, with both the vastness of the uplands and the interlocking dales. Two other classic drives are the wild route from Osmotherly to Hawnby, in the west, and Egton Bridge to Rosedale Abbey, in the centre. The Esk Valley branch line, from Middlesborough to Whitby, goes through wonderful scenery and stops at the villages on the way.

Driving (or travelling by train) along the Esk Valley, you reach Egton Bridge, with its river and stepping stones. They hold a famous annual Gooseberry Show in the schoolhouse, on the first Tuesday in August. The champion weight for a single gooseberry is 2oz; the berries tend to be the size of golf balls. **The Horse Shoe** is a good pub where you can sit outside near the river, or inside near a fire.

A special pub in the area is **Birch Hall Inn** at Beckhole. One room is a shop selling sweets, ice-cream and so forth, the other room is a classic old-style pub with real ales. For 54 years it was run by Mrs Schofield. It has not been changed physically by the brother and sister, Colin and Glenys, who took it over, although, like all good pubs, it has evolved to suit its regulars, who come from all over North Yorkshire. The food consists of butties, and pies from the local butcher, **Radford's**.

Heading towards the coast, Radford's, the Q-Guild butcher at Sleights has made York hams for 200 years. Hams are hung from the shop's ceiling to mature: a fine sight. You can also buy slices from the counter. Among their high-quality meat, they do specialities such as rack-and-black (lamb and black pudding). (*See also chapter seven.*)

Whitby has two old-fashioned kipper makers. **Nobles'** shop is near the 199 church steps, and the better-known **Fortunes** sells from a characterful smokehouse in Henrietta Street. If you sit on a bench in the churchyard above the sheds, looking out to sea and catching your breath after climbing all those steps, you can smell the kipper smoke drifting up. The church has a three-tier pew from 1778, which has 19th-century leather ear trumpets, so that the rector's deaf wife could hear the sermon. Down on the quayside, the **Magpie Café** has good fish and chips, cooked in beef dripping, and other fish dishes including the likes of home-cooked-ham salads.

Birch Hall Inn
01947 896245
Beckhole
Radford's
01947 810229
81 Coach Road (A169)
Sleights
Nobles
01947 820413
113 Church Street,
Whitby
Fortunes
01947 601659
22 Henrietta Street
Whitby
Magpie Café
01947 602058
14 Pier Road
Whitby

northumbria

The Rose and Crown
01833 650213
Romaldkirk
www.rose-and-
crown.co.uk
bedrooms

Bowes Museum
01833 690606
Newgate
Barnard Castle
www.bowesmuseum.
org.uk

Eggleston Hall
Gardens
01833 650115
Egglestone

Joan Cross
01833 650351
Marwood

YOU CAN FIND LOCAL WILD SALMON and sea trout in the summer in Northumbria, and, in the autumn and winter, game from heather moors and other parts of the area's beautiful countryside. Stotty cakes, round, flour-dusted breads, are commonly found in pubs and bakeries. Northumbrian cheeses include Coquetdale, Cotherstone and Doddington. There are excellent beers to be found, made by small breweries such as Durham Brewery and Mordue (its Workie Ticket was Camra's Champion Beer of Britain in 1997).

Starting in the south, in County Durham, **The Rose and Crown** is an 18th-century coaching inn in the village of Romaldkirk, and makes a good, warm base for a gastro-break in the hills beyond Barnard Castle. Sea trout in the summer might be served with a samphire hollandaise; another speciality is grouse. The owners, Christopher and Alison Davy, have written an exemplary guide to the area for their guests, which includes the walking country in upper Teesdale, High Force waterfall and Barnard Castle's mad gem, the **Bowes Museum**, which rears up suddenly on the outskirts of the town. It is stuffed with treasures, both mainstream and curious (I found myself absorbed by the corset display). The Davys get fruit in season from the attractive walled organic garden at **Eggleston Hall** which is open to the public. The owners, Malcolm and Gordon, specialise in rare and unusual hardy perennials and also sell fruit and vegetables. A stream runs through the garden and there are still the two stone troughs in the water where, in the old days, they used to wash all the vegetables before they went to the cook in the hall.

Cotherstone, near Romaldkirk, is the village that gives its name to the Teesdale cow's milk cheese. It comes from the same farmhouse tradition as Wensleydale and Swaledale in Yorkshire, and has likewise dwindled, in this case to just one maker, **Joan Cross**, based in

Marwood. She learned from her mother, who started making Cotherstone again when she was snowed in for six weeks during the terrible winter of 1947 and had to use up the milk from their dairy herd. You can find Joan's cheese in village shops in Cotherstone, Egglestone, Middleton in Teesdale and Staindrop, as well as in delis and other food shops.

Just south of Barnard Castle, **The Morritt Arms** is an old coaching inn at Greta Bridge. The back bar is covered in a mural of Dickensian characters by J V Gilroy, who was famous for creating, among other images, the classic advertising symbol of the Guinness Toucan. The inn has an imposing entrance; you can imagine coaches sweeping up to it, as they did in Dickens' day when he came to the area to investigate boarding schools for Nicholas Nickelby.

Further north in County Durham, **The Manor House Inn** at Carterway Heads is a friendly pub with well-priced food, including 15 north-country cheeses and puddings such as sticky toffee pudding and a simple, creamy rice pudding. The pub has views onto the moor and is close to walking country and the pretty village of Blanchland.

Terence Laybourne is an exceptional restaurateur with four places in the northeast. His place in Durham, **Bistro 21**, is in an old farmhouse near the hospital. The main dining room is in the former farmhouse kitchen, and has plump, whitewashed walls. In the city centre, is a cheery, down-to-earth local with a good beer selection, and has a back snug with service bells. The pub has comfortable bedrooms for B&B. The city's covered market has a butcher near the entrance with well-priced game in season. The Cathedral (so severe on the outside, so beautiful within) has a well-designed café with unrepentant cakes; the nearby Almshouses café and restaurant provide another good place to eat and drink.

The Morritt Arms
01833 627232
Greta Bridge
signposted off A66 west of Scotch Corner
bedrooms

The Manor House Inn
01207 255268
Carterway Heads
on A68
bedrooms

Bistro 21
0191 384 4354
Aykley Heads
Durham

The Victoria
0191 386 5269
86 Hallgarth Street
Durham
bedrooms

Almshouses
0191 3861054
Palace Green
Durham

The North of England
Open Air Museum
01207 231811
Beamish
www.beamish.
org.uk
Newcastle Farmers'
Market
0191 211 5533
Café 21
0191 222 0755
19-21 Queen Street
Princes Wharf
Quayside
Newcastle-upon-Tyne
The Crown Posada
0191 232 1269
31 The Side
Newcastle-upon-Tyne
Out of This World
0191 213 0421
Gosforth Shopping
Centre
Gosforth High Street
Corbridge Larder
01434 632948
Hill Street
Corbridge
Cragside
01669 620333
1 mile from Rothbury
on the B6341

The North of England Open Air Muesum at Beamish is a superb day out. Set in 300 acres, it includes a town, colliery village, railway station, farm and other areas. Buildings under threat of demolition have been moved here in their entirety and filled with people and objects to recreate a vivid impression of day-to-day life at the start of the 20th century. In the 1913 sweet shop, you can watch the sweets being made and there is an early co-op where you can ask the shop-keeper to take down groceries like beef tea from the shelves.

I loved the covered Grainger Market in Newcastle-upon-Tyne, as a scene to wander through. It is close to the Grey's monument in the city centre. (*See also chapter eight.*) There is also a monthly farmers' market on the first Friday of the month near here. Close to the quayside, under the Tyne Bridge, Terence Laybourne's **Café 21** looks like a glam version of an Edward Hopper painting: big windows, plain paint and retro lights. My pot-roasted pheasant with brandied grapes, cabbage and bacon was excellent. The couple at the next door table also recommended the other two Laybourne restaurants, in Sunderland and Ponteland. A minute's walk from Café 21, is a long, narrow, classic Victorian pub, **The Crown Posada**, with pre-Raphaelite stained glass and local beers. A stottie sarnie and a packet of crisps cost £1 here.

North of Newcastle, in Gosforth, **Out of This World** is a one-stop ethical shop that has eschewed the hair-shirt approach to wholefoods and is fitted out in light, bright, recycled chic. West of Newcastle, heading towards Hadrian's Wall, Corbridge has a big deli, the **Corbridge Larder**, with plenty of regional produce.

Cragside, near Rothbury, is one of those National Trust houses where you can get absorbed by the details of Victorian domestic life, including the innovative Victorian hydro-electric system which turned the spits in the kitchen. The landscaped grounds are good for walks, and further west, Coquetdale has great countryside.

The spare **Star Inn** at Netherton, up above Rothbury, is run by Vera Willson-Morton, the third generation of the family to run the pub. She brings in Castle Eden beer from a back room: it is one of the few remaining classic country pubs which feels like a farmhouse with a simple room at the front for locals and visitors.

Going back towards the coast, **Robertson's Prime** sells game in a shop on an industrial estate in Alnwick. The coast of this northern part of Northumberland is famous for kippers. **L Robson & Sons** in Craster makes very good kippers, which they also sell by mail order. Here, you can have them glistening from the smokehouse. They also run a summer time restaurant. **The Jolly Fisherman** is a pub with crabmeat, whisky and cream soup, crab sandwiches and kipper pâté. It is worth going into the shop at **Swallow Fish** in Seahouses, both to buy their kippers and other products and to look at the black-and-white photographs of the herring lassies and the old fishing boats. *(See also chapter seven.)* **The Olde Ship** nearby has real ales.

Going on up the coast, past Holy Island, Berwick-on-Tweed is a border town where you find yourself trying to hear which way the accents are swinging. **RG Foreman & Son's** butcher has its own smoked salmon, and is in the proud tradition of butchers who make everything themselves. The main shop is in Norham. Cowie's, at the end of the Old Bridge, is a time warp with an on-off production of the traditional Berwick sweets made in the shape of cockles.

Brown roadsigns from Berwick-on-Tweed take you towards the **Chain Bridge Honey Farm** in Horncliffe, which has an excellent exhibition on bees and honey, as well as other local foods.

The Star Inn
01669 630238
Netherton

Robertson's Prime
01665 604386
Unit 1B
Willowtree Industrial Estate
Alnwick

L Robson & Sons
01665 576223
Haven Hill
Craster

The Jolly Fisherman
01665 576218
Craster

Swallow Fish
01665 721052
2 South Street
Seahouses

The Olde Ship
01665 720200
Seahouses
bedrooms

R G Foreman & Son
Berwick-on-Tweed -
01289 304442
Norham -
01289 382260
www.borderbutcher.co.uk

Chain Bridge Honey Farm
01289 386362
Horncliffe
near Berwick-on-Tweed

selected bibliography

Belsey, James *Heritage Pubs of Great Britain* (1998) CAMRA Books

Blythman, Joanna *The Food We Eat* (1996) Michael Joseph

Boxer, Arabella *Book of English Food* (1991) Penguin

Brandon, Peter *The South Downs* (1998) Phillimore & Co

Bruning, Ted *Historic Pubs of London* (1998) Prion

Bunyard, Edward *The Anatomy of Dessert* (1933) Chatto & Windus

Burnett, John *Plenty and Want* (1989) Routledge

Common Ground Book of Orchards (2000) Common Ground

Chapman, Kit *Great British Chefs* (1989) Mitchell Beazley

Chapman, Kit *Great British Chefs 2* (1995) Mitchell Beazley

Coates, Dorothy *Tuppeny Rice and Treacle* (1975) David & Charles

Cutting, C.L. *Fish Saving, A History of Fish Processing from Ancient to Modern Times* (1955) Hill

David, Elizabeth *English Bread and Yeast Cookery* (1977) Allen Lane

Davidson, Alan *On Fasting and Feasting* (anthology), particularly the extract on Christmas Pudding by Maggie Black

Davidson, Alan *The Oxford Companion to Food* (1999) Oxford University Press

Day, Ivan *Further Musings on Syllabub* (August 1996) Petits Propos Culinaires 53

Driver, Christopher *The British at Table 1940-1980* (1983) Chatto & Windus

Driver, Christopher and Berriedale-Johnson, Michelle *Peyps at Table* (1984) Book Club Associates

Drummond, J.C and Wilbraham, Anne *The Englishman's Food* (1991) Pimlico

Fearnley-Whittingstall, Hugh *The River Cottage Cookbook* (2001) HarperCollins

Freeman, Sarah *The Real Cheese Companion* (1998) Little, Brown

Girouard, Mark *Victorian Pubs* (1975) Studio Vista

Grigson, Jane *English Food* (1977) Penguin

Grigson, Jane *Fruit Book* (1982) Michael Joseph

Grigson, Jane *Vegetable Book* (1980) Penguin

Hartley, Dorothy *Food in England* (1996) Little, Brown

Hardyment, Christina *Slice of Life* (1995) BBC Books

Harvey, Graham *The Killing of the Countryside* (1997) Jonathan Cape

Orchards (1989) Common Ground

Hoskins N W.G *The Making of the English Landscape* (1985) Penguin Books

Hudson, Kenneth *Food, Clothes and Shelter* (1978) John Baker

Jackson Michael *Beer Companion* (1994) Mitchell Beazley

Johnston, James *A Hundred Years of Eating* (1977) Gill and Macmillan

Mabey, David in association with Mabey, Richard *In Search of Food* (1978) Macdonald and Jane's

Mabey, Richard (ed) *Flora Britannica* (1997) Chatto & Windus

Mabey, Richard *The Common Ground* (1993) J.M. Dent

Mason, Laura with Brown, Catherine *Traditional Foods of Britain* (1999) Prospect Books

Mason, Laura *Sugar-plums and Sherbet* (1998) Prospect Books

McGee, Harold *On Food and Cooking* (1991) HarperCollins

McGee, Harold *The Curious Cook* (1990) HarperCollins

McKenzie J.C. and Yudkin, J (eds) *Changing Fare, Two Hundred Years of British Food Habits* (1966) Macgibbon & Kee

Mennell, Stephen *All Manners of Food; Eating and Taste in England and France from the Middle Ages to the Present* (1985) Basil Blackwell

Morgan, Joan and Richards, Alison *The Book of Apples* (1993) Ebury Press

Murcott, Anne **(ed)** *The Nation's Diet* (1998) Longman

Oddy, Derek J and Miller, Derek **(ed)** *The Making of the Modern British Diet* (1976) Croom Helm

Protz, Roger *The Great British Beer Book* (1992) Impact Books

Rackham, Oliver *The History of the Countryside* (1995) Weidenfeld & Nicholson

Rance, Patrick *The Great British Cheese Book* (1992) Papermac

Seymour, John *The Countryside Explained* (1977) Faber and Faber

Smith, Drew *Modern Cooking* (1990) Sidgwick & Jackson

Turner, R.C. and R.G Scaife *Bog Bodies, new discoveries and new perspectives* (1995) Britsh Museum Press

Walton, John *Fish & Chips and the British Working Class 1870-1940* (2000) Leicester University Press

Wilson, Anne *The Book of Marmalade* (1985) Constable

Wilson, Anne **(ed)** *Traditional Food East and West of the Pennines* (1991) Alan Sutton Publishing

Wood, Eric *Historical Britain* (1997) Harvill

Guides

Lynda Brown *The Shopper's Guide to Organic Food* (1998) Fourth Estate

Charles Campion *London Restaurants, the Rough Guide* Rough Guides

Diana Crighton *English Excursions, Home Counties and London* (1996) Excursion Publishing

Diana Crighton *English Excursions, Northern Journey* (1998) Excursion Publishing

Henrietta Green *Food Lovers' Guide to Britain* (1995) BBC Books

Alastair Sawday *Special Places to Stay in Britain* Alastair Sawday Publishing

Eric Treuille *The Guide to Cookery Courses* (2000) Metro Publications

Jill Turton *Good Food in Yorkshire and Humberside* (1995) Fig Tree Press

The Essential Guide to London's Best Food Shops (2000) New Holland Publishers

Good Beer Guide (annual) CAMRA Books

The Good Food Guide (annual) Which? Books

The Good Guide to Britain (annual) Ebury Press

The Good Pub Guide (annual) Ebury Press

Top UK Restaurants (annual) Harden's Guides

A few useful contacts

The Campaign for Real Ale
01727 867201 www.camra.org.uk

Common Ground
020 7267 2144 www.commonground.org.uk

Farm Retail Association
02380 362150 www.farmshopping.com

Focus on Food
(a campaign for food education in schools)
01422 383191 www.waitrose.com/focusonfood

Henrietta Green's Food Lovers' Fairs
www.foodloversfairs.com

Kids' Cookery School
0208 992 8882 www.kidscookery.org

The National Association of Farmers' Markets
01225 460840 www.farmersmarkets.net

Rare Breeds Survival Trust
02476 696551 www.rare-breeds.com

The Soil Association
0117 929 0661 www.soilassociation.org

W.I Markets
0118 939 4646 www.wimarkets.co.uk

index